POCKET
GUIDES

ITALIAN PHRASES

FOR BEGINNERS

T0015831

GABRIELLE EUVINO

Publisher Mike Sanders
Editor Christopher Stolle
Designer William Thomas
Compositor Ayanna Lacey
Technical Editor Linda Ruggeri
Proofreader Linda Ruggeri
Indexer Celia McCoy

First American Edition, 2021
Published in the United States by DK Publishing
1745 Broadway, 20th Floor, New York, NY 10019

ISBN: 978-1-6156-4984-6
Library of Congress Catalog Number: 2020941350

DK books are available at special discounts when purchased in bulk for sales
promotions, premiums, fund-raising, or educational use. For details, contact
SpecialSales@dk.com.

Printed and bound in China

All images © Dorling Kindersley Limited
For further information see: www.dkimages.com

For the curious
www.dk.com

MIX
Paper | Supporting
responsible forestry
FSC™ C018179

This book was made with Forest
Stewardship Council ™ certified
paper – one small step in DK's
commitment to a sustainable future.
For more information go to
www.dk.com/our-green-pledge

Contents

1   Pronunciation Guide 1

2   Essentials 19

3   Friends & Family 45

4   Transportation...69

5   Driving in Italy 83

6   Home Away From Home 101

7   Food & Eating 125

8   Shopping..151

9   Friendship & Romance..............................171

10 Staying Healthy..183

11 Business & Communications 199

A   Verbs at a Glance.....................................219

B   Commonly Used Expressions
    in Everyday Conversation 237

C   English–Italian Dictionary 241

D   Italian–English Dictionary 263

    Index 287

Dedication

This book is dedicated to all of you whose dream to speak Italian is only a few pages away. Life passes by so quickly. Enjoy every moment. Don't worry if you can't get it all done perfectly. Do the best you can in the time you've got. And keep smiling. *Tanti baci*.

A special *grazie* to the Italian American Foundation of Ulster County (UCIAF). Love you guys.

Of course, to my beautiful child: Sabine, you make the world a better and brighter place. *Ti amo!*

Introduction

Learning Italian is no more difficult than rolling out your own pasta dough and making handmade tortellini. After you know how to do it, it's easy and a lot of fun. You likely learned how to speak English long before you were taught how to identify parts of speech. If you allow the intuitive process to guide you, you'll be speaking Italian in no time.

Here are a few suggestions to enhance your study:

- Download an Italian–English dictionary to your phone or computer. You'll find many versions out there.

- Invest in a good bilingual dictionary (*dizionario*), preferably one that offers the Italian pronunciation. These will likely be printed by English publishers. Foreign dictionaries, such as the Garzanti or Zanichelli Italian–English dictionaries, along with Langenscheidt, are also excellent products.

- Call your local university (*università*) and discover whether it has an Italian department. Find out if it has a mailing list for events and make a point of meeting other "Italo-philes."

- Join an Italian-speaking language or cultural group. If you can't find one, why not create it?

- Rent an Italian movie every week. Listen to the actors and read the subtitles while you try to decipher the Italian words within each sentence. Isolate words that are repeated. There are many selections now available on YouTube, Amazon Prime, HBO, Netflix, and free from Kanopy (through your local library). Visit Kanopy.com to find out more.

- Pick up a box of Italian language flash cards at any bookstore or make your own using that unused box of business cards from your old job.

- Listen to the Italian news station RAI while you clean your house. If you spend a lot of time in the car, invest in language apps, mp3s, or CDs. Check out the Slow Italian podcasts: everything new about Italy but slowed down. Visit www.newsinslowitalian.com.

- Why not change your social media sites over to Italian? Facebook, Google, WhatsApp, WeChat, Instagram, Twitter, Snapchat, and LinkedIn are among many that offer their services in many languages.

About This Book

This book lists helpful vocabulary and phrases and tells you exactly what you need to say (and how to say it) in myriad situations: at the train station, at your hotel, in a restaurant, at the pharmacy, and so on. It also summarizes grammar, vocabulary, and verbs in the most concise manner possible, explaining how it all works and what you can do to start speaking the language immediately. I've also improved the pronunciation guide by adding all caps to the stressed syllables.

Acknowledgments

Special thanks to the Alpha team that made the original version of this book happen: Paul Dinas, Megan Douglass, Jennifer Moore, and Keith Cline. *Mille grazie!*

Gratitude goes to Matteo and Dante Lagnese, two great kids, and Kimbo the dog.

A big *grazie* to Christopher Stolle for his patience and guidance while this book was being revised. In addition, thank you to Linda Ruggeri for her excellent technical editing and proofreading.

Chapter 1

Pronunciation Guide

This chapter is all about Italian pronunciation—from accents and the alphabet to cognates and grammar. Trying to learn a new language takes courage. Don't be afraid to make mistakes. Italians are incredibly accommodating and will appreciate your efforts to communicate any way you can.

A Note on Dialects (*Dialetti*)

What you read in this book might vary considerably from what you might hear on the streets, especially once you're outside the main cities. Dialects are to the Italian language what spices are to Italian food: They add variety and depth. Some of the dialects include Apulian, Calabrese, Catalan, Friulian, Ligurian, Roman, Neapolitan, Sardinian, Sicilian, and Venetian. In fact, Sicilian and Sardinian are considered their own languages.

The diversity and richness of Italian culture are exemplified through this smorgasbord of linguistic delicacies. When family and friends are bantering and teasing one another, no doubt it's probably in some form of dialect. If you're an Italian American studying the language of your ancestors, you'll often find the official Italian language to be quite different from what you're used to hearing.

While most locals will appreciate your attempts to speak Italian, avoid speaking in dialect. They might interpret this as making fun of Italian.

Pronunciation and Enunciation (*Pronuncia e Accento*)

Italian sounds so beautiful because the words connect to each other like in an opera. *Per fortuna*, Italian is super easy to pronounce and read. Pretty much what you see is what you say: It's all about the vowels (*vocali*; like "vocals"). The letters *a*, *e*, *i*, *o*, and *u* are all vowels. If you can say them correctly, you can "fake your way" to fluency in no time.

Because Latin is the mother tongue for Italian and one of the two root systems (German being the other) used predominantly in English, you'll see how many cousins the two languages share. For example, in Italian, the word *cinema* is written exactly the same as in English; however, in Italian, it's pronounced *CHEE-neh-mah*. The same *ci* sound is used in the popular greeting *ciao*. Conversely, *ch* in Italian is pronounced as a *k*, as in the popular wine Chianti. Throughout this book, stressed syllables will appear in all caps. In words of two syllables, you'll find most are equally stressed.

The fun part is rolling your Rs. If you see one *r,* like with the city *Roma*, gently tickle the back of your upper front teeth with your tongue. If you can't quite get the *r* at first, just keep practicing!

Words with double consonants, such as *anno* (AHN-noh) (year), *gatto* (GAHT-toh) (cat) and *palla* (PAHL-lah) (ball), are emphasized and held but always pronounced as one sound.

Getting the Accent (*Accento*)

Italian uses two accents to indicate words where the stress falls on the final syllable and they're always used over a vowel:

- The grave accent ('), pronounced *grav*

caffè	*città*
kah-FAY	chee-TAH
coffee	city

- The acute accent (´), pronounced *acuto*, used especially in older text and phrasebooks

benché	*perché*
ben-KAY	per-KAY
although	because/why

The accent is also used to distinguish several Italian words from others that have the same spelling but a different meaning. These basic examples are all useful vocabulary words to include in your Italian lexicon. Where you see an accent, gently offer a slightly stronger emphasis on that letter.

Accented		Unaccented	
dà (DAH)	gives	*da* (dah)	from
è (AY)	is	*e* (ay)	and
là (LAH)	there	*la* (lah)	the
né (NEY)	nor	*ne* (ney)	some
sé (SEY)	himself	*se* (sey)	if
sì (SEE)	yes	*si* (see)	oneself

A few Italian words change meaning simply by changing where the word is stressed. Examples include the words *ancora* (ahn-KOH-rah) (again) and *ancora* (AHN-koh-rah) (anchor).

Apostrophes are used to indicate the dropping of a final vowel. Remember: Nouns are often preceded by an article, such as *l'* or *la*, which will affect how you hear a particular word. Examples include:

l'animale	*d'Italia*
l'ah-nee-MAH-leh	d'ee-TAL-yah
the animal	of Italy

Don't Stress—Enunciate!

Minus an accent telling you where the emphasis should go, assume that most Italian words are emphasized on the next-to-last syllable. Examples include:

lo studente	*il viaggio*
loh stoo-DEN-teh	eel vee-AHJ-joh
student	trip

An exception is *la macchina* (la MAH-kee-nah) (car).

Words with two syllables are generally given equal emphasis, although the first syllable might be gently emphasized. Examples include:

la pizza	*la casa*
lah PEEZ-zah	lah KAH-zah
pizza	house

You'll also learn that some words are accented on the third-, fourth-, or fifth-to-last syllable. Your Italian–English dictionary should indicate these irregularities, usually with an accent over the stressed syllable or a dot placed below it. Common exceptions include:

la camera	*il numero*
la KAH-meh-rah	eel NOO-meh-roh
room	number

difficile	*sùbito*
dee-FEE-chee-leh	SOO-bee-toh
difficult	immediately

Refer to an online video for audio examples, such as www.wordreference.com. Choose Italian–English as your language combination and start to explore. You'll find ample opportunities to hear and practice your newly developing Italian vocabulary along with a terrific verb conjugator.

Italian ABCs

The alphabet contains only 21 letters, borrowing *j*, *k*, *w*, *x*, and *y* for words of foreign origin.

a	*a* ah	*Ancona* ahn-KOH-nah	
b	*bi* bee	*Bologna* boh-LOH-nyah	
c	*ci* chee	*Cagliari* KAHL-yah-ree	
d	*di* dee	*Domodossola* doh-moh-DOH-soh-lah	
e	*e* eh	*Empoli* EM-poh-lee	
f	*effe* EHF-feh	*Firenze* fee-REN-zeh	
g	*gi* jee	*Genova* JEH-noh-vah	
h	*acca* AHK-kah	*hotel* oh-tel	
i	*i* ee	*Imola* EE-moh-lah	
j	*i lunga* ee LOON-gah	*jolly* joh-lee	
k	*cappa* kahp-pah	*kiwi* kee-wee	
l	*elle* EHL-leh	*Livorno* lee-VOR-noh	
m	*emme* EHM-meh	*Milano* mee-LAH-noh	
n	*enne* EHN-neh	*Napoli* NAH-poh-lee	

o	*o* oh	*Otranto* oh-TRAHN-toh
p	*pi* pee	*Palermo* pah-LER-moh
q	*cu* koo	*quaderno* kwah-DER-noh
r	*erre* EHR-reh	*Roma* roh-mah
s	*esse* EHS-seh	*Sassari* SAHS-sah-ree
t	*ti* tee	*Torino* toh-REE-noh
u	*u* oo	*Udine* OO-dee-neh
v	*vu* voo	*Venezia* veh-NEH-zee-ah
w	*doppia vu* DOHP-pee'-yah voo	*Washington* WASH-eeng-ton
x	*ics* eeks	*raggi-x* raj-jee eeks [x-ray]
y	*ipsilon* EEP-see-lohn	*Yogurt* yoh-goorl
z	*zeta* ZEH-tah	*Zebra* ZEH-brah

Vowels

Vowel	Example
a ah	*artista* ar-TEE-stah
e eh	*elefante* eh-leh-FAHN-teh
i ee	*isola* EE-zoh-lah
o oh	*opera* OH-peh-rah
u oo	*uno* oo-noh

Consonants

The following examples demonstrate most of the different letter *combinazioni* you'll encounter. Assume that any letters not included follow the English pattern of pronunciation. For example, the letter *b* will always be pronounced the same regardless of the letters that follow.

Letter Combo	Italian Example	English Meaning
c + a, o, u hard c (as in *cat*)	*candela, corso, cubo* kahn-DEH-lah, kor-soh, koo-boh	candle, course, cube
c + e, i *ch* (as in *chest*)	*centro, cinema* CHEN-troh, CHEE-neh-mah	center, cinema
ch hard c (as in *cat*)	*Chianti* kee-AHN-tee	Chianti
g + a, o, u *hard g* (as in *go*)	*Gabriella, lago, gufo* gah-bree-EHL-lah, LAH-goh, goo-foh	Gabriella, lake, owl
g + e, i *jay* (as in *jet*)	*gelato, Giorgio* jeh-LAH-toh, JOR-joh	ice cream, Giorgio
gli *ylee* (as in *million*)	*figlio* FEEL-yoh	son
gn *nyah* (as in *onion*)	*gnocchi* NYOH-kee	potato dumplings
h (called *acca*) silent	*hotel* oh-TEL	hotel

s (begins words) *ess* (as in *see*)	*sasso* SAHS-soh	stone
s (after a vowel) *zee* (as in *busy*)	*casa*, *peso* KAH-zah, PEH-zoh	home, weight
sc + *a*, *o* *sk*	*scala*, *scopa* SKAH-lah, SKOH-pah	stair, broom
sc + *e*, *i* *sh*	*scena*, *scienza* SHEH-nah, she-EN-zah	scene, science

Grammar 101

A few basic facts about *la grammatica* will give you a better sense of what you'll hear when you travel. After you understand the essentials, you'll be able to form Italian *frasi* with relative ease.

Nouns (*Sostantivi*)

In Italian, the word *nome* means "name" as well as "noun." Every *nome* (noun) is masculine or feminine and singular or plural. Usually, you can tell a noun's gender and its number by looking at the ending. Some nouns are masculine and feminine, such as *artista* (artist), *parente* (relative), and *turista* (tourist).

Gender (*Genere*)

A noun's gender affects its relationship with other words in a sentence, including adjectives. Similar to other Romance languages, in Italian, nouns and adjectives must always agree in number and gender. If the noun is masculine, it usually ends in *-o*.

If a noun is feminine, it usually ends in -*a*. The adjective follows suit. For example, *il gatto nero* literally translates to "the cat black." Likewise, with feminine nouns, the adjective reflects the gender, as in *la casa bianca* ("the house white").

Some singular nouns and adjectives end in -*e*, such as *l'animale* (m.) ("the animal") and *la stazione* (f.) ("the station"). You can often infer a word's gender from the noun markers and surrounding adjectives.

Plurals (*Plurali*)

In Italian, the ending of a word must always reflect the number and gender of the noun. The following illustrates how regular endings change in the plural. Keep in mind that if a noun ends in -*o*, it's generally masculine. If a noun ends in -*a*, it's generally feminine. Nouns ending in -*e* can be either gender.

Singular Ending	Singular Noun Example	Plural Ending	Plural Noun Example
-*o*	*ragazzo* (boy)	-*i*	*ragazzi* (boys)
-*a*	*donna* (woman)	-*e*	*donne* (women)
-*ca*	*amica* (f.) (friend)	-*che*	*amiche* (f.) (friends)
-*e*	*cane* (dog)	-*i*	*cani* (dogs)

Noun Markers (*Articoli*)

Just about every Italian noun is preceded by a noun marker to note whether a noun is masculine (m.), feminine (f.), singular (s.), or plural (p.). Indefinite and definite articles are examples of noun markers.

Indefinite Articles (*Articoli Indefiniti*)

In Italian, an *indeterminativo* article ("a," "an," or "one") is only used before singular nouns. Here are some rules for using indefinite articles in Italian.

Masculine (*Maschile*)

- *Un* is used before all singular masculine nouns beginning with either a consonant or a vowel, such as *un palazzo* (a building) and *un animale* (animal), except for nouns beginning with a *z* or an *s* followed by a consonant.

- *Uno* is used before singular masculine nouns beginning with a *z* or an *s* followed by a consonant, such as *uno zio* (an uncle) and *uno stadio* (a stadium).

Feminine (*Feminile*)

- *Una* is used before any feminine noun that begins with a consonant, such as *una farfalla* (a butterfly), *una storia* (a story), and *una strada* (a street).

- *Un'* is the equivalent of *an* in English and is used before all feminine nouns that begin with a vowel, such as *un'italiana* (an Italian woman), *un'amica* (a friend), and *un'opera* (an opera).

"The" Definite Article (*Articoli Determinativo*)

In Italian, the *determinativo* article "the" denotes a specific example of a person, place, or thing. Here are some rules for using the definitive article.

- *Il* is used in front of most singular masculine nouns that begin with a consonant, such as *il ragazzo* (the boy), *il vino* (the wine), and *il sole* (the sun), except for nouns beginning with a *z* or an *s* followed by a consonant.

- *I* is used in front of most plural masculine nouns that begin with a consonant, such as *i ragazzi* (the boys), *i libri* (the books), and *i gatti* (the cats), except for nouns beginning with a *z* or an *s* followed by a consonant.

- *Lo* is used in front of all singular masculine nouns that begin with a *z* or an *s* followed by a consonant, such as *lo zio* (the uncle) and *lo studente* (the student), as well as masculine nouns starting with *gn*, *ps*, *x*, and *y*.

- *Gli* (pronounced ylee as in million) is used in front of all masculine plural nouns that use either *lo* or *l'* in the singular, such as *gli zii* (the uncles), *gli studenti* (the students), *gli alberi* (the trees), and *gli animali* (the animals).

- *L'* is used in front of all singular nouns— whether masculine or feminine—that begin with a vowel, such as *l'albero* (m.) (the tree), *l'animale* (m.) (the animal), and *l'opera* (f.) (the opera, the work).

- *La* is used in front of all other singular feminine nouns, such as *la ragazza* (the girl), *la macchina* (the car), and *la casa* (house).

- *Le* is used in front of all plural feminine nouns, such as *le ragazze* (the girls), *le macchine* (the cars), and *le case* (the houses).

Adjectives (*Aggettivi*)

Italian adjectives follow the same general rules as nouns and they must agree in gender and number with the nouns they describe. Similar to Italian nouns, some singular adjectives end in *-e*.

Singular Ending	Singular Noun Example	Plural Ending	Plural Noun Example
-o	*famoso* (famous)	*-i*	*famosi* (famous)
-a	*curiosa* (curious)	*-e*	*curiose* (curious)
-ca	*magnifica* (magnificent)	*-che*	*magnifiche* (magnificent)
-e	*intelligente* (intelligent)	*-i*	*intelligenti* (intelligent)

Prepositions (*Preposizioni*)

Prepositions show the relationship between a noun and another word. Prepositions are highly idiomatic (meaning they follow their own set of rules) and they should be remembered within a context rather than memorized. The following are the most important prepositions.

Preposition	English Meaning	Italian Example	English Meaning
a ah	to/at/in	*Andiamo a Roma.*	We're going to Rome.
con kohn	with	*Vado con Roberto.*	I'm going with Roberto.

continues

da dah	from/by	*Leonardo da Vinci*	Leonardo from Vinci
di dee	of/from	*Sono di New York.*	I'm from New York.
in een	in/to/by	*Viaggiamo in Italia.*	We're traveling to Italy.
per per	for	*Questo regalo è per te.*	This present is for you.
su soo	on	*Il libro sta sulla* scrivania.*	The book is on the desk.

* *su + la = sulla (a contraction)*

Possession (*Possessivi*)

In Italian, a possessive adjective must always be followed by a noun, which is generally preceded by an article. For example, *la mia casa* literally translates to "the my house." The possessor and what's possessed must agree in gender and number.

Posses- sive Adjective	Singular Mascu- line	Singular Feminine	Plural Mascu- line	Plural Feminine
my	*il mio*	*la mia*	*i miei*	*le mie*
your	*il tuo*	*la tua*	*i tuoi*	*le tue*
his/her/ its*	*il suo*	*la sua*	*i suoi*	*le sue*
Your (polite)	*il Suo*	*la Sua*	*i Suoi*	*le Sue*
our	*il nostro*	*la nostra*	*i nostri*	*le nostre*
your	*il vostro*	*la vostra*	*i vostri*	*le vostre*
their	*il loro*	*la loro*	*i loro*	*le loro*

*The third person singular possessive adjectives il suo *and* la sua *can mean his or her. For example,* la sua casa *can mean his or her house.*

Keep in mind that by the time you're using a possessive pronoun, the subject has already been determined.

Subject Pronouns (*Pronomi Personali*)

Italian subject pronouns are often omitted because the endings indicate the subject. For example, *Viaggiamo in Italia* literally translates to "We're traveling to Italy." The *-iamo* ending on the verb tells us that the subject is *noi* (we).

Italian	English
io (ee-yoh)	I
tu (too)	you (informal)
*lui/lei/Lei** (louie/lay/lay)	he/she/you (polite)
noi (noy)	we
voi (voy)	you (plural)
loro (loh-roh)	they

* *The uppercased pronoun* Lei *(with a capital L) signifies "you" (polite or formal), while the lowercased pronoun* lei *signifies "she."*

You and You and You and You

Yes, Italian has four forms of "you." Here are some rules for knowing when to use them.

- *Tu* is used in informal settings with friends and relatives or when adults address children.

- *Lei* is the polite form of you and is used with strangers and persons in authority and to show respect or maintain a more formal relationship with someone. It's always capitalized to distinguish it from *lei*, meaning "she."

- *Voi* is primarily used to address a group of people, although it can still be used as a formal address for an individual, especially in the south.

• *Loro* is used in rare cases when an extreme form of politeness is required—either when addressing a group of people or someone in a high position, such as a president or the Pope. It was once used more commonly and can still be heard in old films.

Verbs (*Verbi*)

Italian verbs are a bit more complicated because of the many different conjugations that affect their endings. Because you won't find most conjugated verbs in the dictionary, it's *importante* to listen for the root of the word.

Verb Families

Italian has three kinds of verb families: *-are*, *-ere*, and *-ire*. Each family has its own particular way of doing things. All three families of verbs are called regular verbs because they prescribe to a given set of consistent rules. In addition, each conjugation is also called a "person" in grammatical terms. There are three persons: first, second, and third. They can be either singular or plural.

	Singular	Plural
First person	I (io)	We (noi)
Second person	You (tu)	You All (voi)
Third person	He, She, You (formal) (lui/lei/Lei)	They (loro)

Irregular verbs follow their own rules. For an overview of some of these verbs, see Appendix A (pages 219–236).

Conjugating Regular Verbs

To conjugate (*coniugare*) verbs, drop the infinitive ending from the stem and then add the conjugated endings (in bold). Study the verbs *celebrare* (to celebrate), *scrivere* (to write), *dormire* (to sleep), and *capire* (to understand) to see how the ending changes. Note that all the regular verbs end in -*o* for the first person (I). Also, -*ire* verbs have two forms of conjugation. The most commonly used verbs tend to be irregular and often don't conform to the regular rules outlined here.

Subject Pronoun	Celebrare	Scrivere	Dormire	Capire
io	celebr**o**	scriv**o**	dorm**o**	cap**isco**
tu	celebr**i**	scriv**i**	dorm**i**	cap**isci**
lui, lei, Lei	celebr**a**	scriv**e**	dorm**e**	cap**isce**
noi	celebr**iamo**	scriv**iamo**	dorm**iamo**	cap**iamo**
voi	celebr**ate**	scriv**ete**	dorm**ite**	cap**ite**
loro*	celebr**ano**	scriv**ono**	dorm**ono**	cap**iscono**

* Verbs using loro *tend to be emphasized on the third-to-last syllable.*

Cognates (*Parole Simili*)

Cognates are words that are similar to or look the same as other words in a foreign language. The endings and pronunciation of certain Italian/English cognates might be slightly different, but the words are essentially the same. You'll see an astounding number of similarities between English and Italian, especially when you begin looking at the roots of both language systems.

The following table shows some English and Italian cognates. (Note that there are always exceptions to every rule.) By simply changing an ending, you'll learn some Italian rather quickly.

English Ending	Italian Ending	English Example	Italian Example
-ble	-ibile	terrible	terribile
-ence	-enza	patience	pazienza
-ent	-ente	present	presente
-ion	-ione	vision	visione
-ism	-ismo	realism	realismo
-ous	-oso	famous	famoso
-ty	-tà	identity	identità

Beware of False Friends

A false cognate is a word in Italian that sounds like an English word but means something different.

Italian Word	English Meaning
ape	bee
assumere	to hire
caldo	hot
camera	room
cane	dog
caro	expensive
coincidenza	connection
come	how
con	with
fabbrica	factory
fattoria	farm
firma	signature
libreria	bookstore
parente	relative

Chapter 2

Essentials

Grammar basics will help you apply everything
in this book to real-world situations in Italy.
At its most fundamental, language is about
communicating your needs. This chapter features
the words and phrases you need to do this and more.

Being Polite (*Comportamento*)

Excuse me.	*Mi scusi.* mee SKOO-zee
Please.	*Per favore.* per fah-VOH-reh *Per piacere.* per pee-ah-CHEH-reh
Thank you.	*Grazie.* GRAH-zee-yay
You're welcome.	*Prego.* PRAY-goh
I'm sorry.	*Mi dispiace.* mee dee-spee-AH-cheh
May I? Can I?	*Posso?* POHS-soh
I'd like …	*Vorrei …* vohr-RAY
I want …	*Desidero …* deh-ZEE-deh-roh
I need …	*Ho bisogno di …* oh bee-ZOHN-yoh dee
I beg you! (informal)	*Ti prego!* tee PRAY-goh
Come on! (informal)	*Dai!* dye
Good job!	*Bravo/a!* (m./f.) BRAH-voh/vah
Ready! Hello!*	*Pronto!* PROHN-toh
Let's go./We're going.	*Andiamo.* ahn-dee-YAH-moh

* Pronto (ready) is used to answer the telephone and goes back to the days when the operator first gathered everyone on the line before connecting the callers.

The informal terms *salve* and *ciao* are used to say "Hello" and, more often, "Goodbye" almost everywhere in Italy. Also commonly used among friends are the expressions *Ci vediamo* and *A presto!*, which are equivalent to saying "See you later." *Arrivederci* literally means "to re-see one another." *ArrivederLa* means the same thing but is used under more formal circumstances.

Days of the Week (*I Giorni della Settimana*)

Almost every day corresponds with a planet or celestial body. For example, *lunedì* corresponds with *la luna*, as in "moon day." Italians have adopted the English way of expressing the end of the week by using the English word "weekend," but you'll also hear *il fine settimana* expressed.

Monday	*lunedì* loo-neh-DEE
Tuesday	*martedì* mar-teh-DEE
Wednesday	*mercoledì* mer-koh-leh-DEE
Thursday	*giovedì* joh-veh-DEE
Friday	*venerdì* veh-nor-DEE
Saturday	*sabato* SAH-bah-toh
Sunday	*domenica* doh-MEH-nee-kah
the weekend	*il fine settimana* eel fee-neh set-tee-MAH-nah
	il weekend eel weekend

Months (*I Mesi*)

January	*gennaio* jen-NY-yoh
February	*febbraio* feb-BRY-yoh
March	*marzo* MAR-zoh
April	*aprile* ah-PREE-leh
May	*maggio* MAH-joh
June	*giugno* JOON-nyoh
July	*luglio* LOOL-lyoh
August	*agosto* ah-GOH-stoh
September	*settembre* seht-TEM-breh
October	*ottobre* oht-TOH-breh
November	*novembre* noh-VEM-breh
December	*dicembre* dee-CHEM-breh

Months aren't capitalized in Italian.

Seasons (*Le Stagioni*)

autumn	*autunno* ow-TOON-noh
spring	*primavera* pree-mah-VEH-rah
summer	*estate* ess-TAH-teh
winter	*inverno* een-VER-noh

Dates (*Le Date*)

Like the days of the week, the months aren't capitalized in Italian. The month always comes after the day and you must always put the definite article in front of the day. Ditto for abbreviations. Keep this in mind when reading Italian documents. For example:

> December 25, 2020
>
> *25 dicembre 2020*
>
> 25/12/2020

The ordinal number is used for the first day of any month. For example:

> April 1st
>
> *Il primo aprile.*

> April 1, 2020
>
> *Il primo aprile, 2020*
>
> 1.4.2020

When pronouncing days, remember to emphasize the last syllable, as indicated by the grave accent (').

Holidays (*I Giorni Festivi*)

Most businesses, banks, and many stores close on holidays. Four-day weekends are not uncommon if a holiday falls on a *giovedì* (Thursday) or *lunedì* (Monday). When this happens, it's referred to as *fare il ponte* (making the bridge). Keep this in mind when planning your trip.

Weather (*Il Tempo*)

The term *il tempo* can be used to talk about weather and time. Think of the word *la temperatura* (the temperature). For example:

> *Che tempo fa?*
> kay tem-poh fah
> What's the weather?

> *Non ho tempo.*
> nohn oh tem-poh
> I don't have time.

Weather will determine whether you spend the day *fuori* (outdoors) or *dentro* (inside). Italian uses two verbs to talk about the weather: *essere* (to be) and *fare* (to do/make).

What's the weather?	*Che tempo fa?* kay tem-poh fah
It's beautiful.	*Fa bel tempo.* fah bel tem-poh
It's hot.	*Fa caldo.* fah KAHL-doh
It's cold.	*Fa freddo.* fah FRED-doh
It's bad.	*Fa brutto tempo.* fah BROOT-toh tem-poh
It's cool.	*Fa fresco.* fah FREH-skoh
It's sunny.	*C'è sole.* ch'AY SOH-leh
It's windy.	*C'è vento.* ch'AY VEN-toh
It's cloudy.	*È nuvoloso.* AY noo-voh-LOH-zoh

It's humid.	*È umido.* AY OO-mee-doh
It's raining.	*Piove.* pee-OH-veh
It's snowing.	*Nevica.* NEH-vee-kah
There's a storm.	*C'è un temporale.* ch'AY oon tem-poh-RA-leh
What's the temperature today?	*Quanto fa oggi?* KWAHN-toh fah OHJ-jee
It's ... degrees.*	*Fa ... gradi.* fah GRAH-dee

* *Italian uses the metric system (Celsius) for the temperature.*

Climate (*Il Clima*)

air	*l'aria* l'AH-ree-yah
avalanche	*la valanga* lah vah-LAHN-gah
calm	*sereno* seh-REH-noh
centigrade (Celsius)	*il grado centigrado* eel GRAH-doh chen-tee-GRAH-doh
climate	*il clima* eel KLEE-mah
cloud	*la nuvola* lah NOO-voh-lah
cloudy	*nuvoloso* noo-voh-LOH-zoh
degree	*grado* grah-doh
dry	*secco* SEK-koh
earth	*la terra* lah TER-rah

continues

environment	*l'ambiente*
	l'ahm-bee-YEHN-teh
flood	*l'alluvione*
	l'ahl-loo-vee-OH-neh
frost	*la brina*
	lah BREE-nah
humid	*umido*
	OO-mee-doh
ice	*il ghiaccio*
	eel ghee-YAH-choh
lightning	*il fulmine*
	eel FOOL-mee-neh
mud	*il fango*
	eel FAHN-goh
ozone	*l'ozono*
	l'oh-ZOH-noh
pollution	*l'inquinamento*
	l'een-kwee-nah-MEN-toh
rain	*la pioggia*
	lah pee-YOH-jah
rainbow	*l'arcobaleno*
	l'ar-koh-bah-LEH-noh
rainy	*piovoso*
	pee-yoh-VOH-zoh
smog	*lo smog*
	loh smog
snow	*la neve*
	lah NEH-veh
snowflake	*il fiocco di neve*
	eel FYOH-koh dee NEH-veh
sunrise	*l'alba*
	l'AHL-bah
sunset	*il tramonto*
	eel trah-MON-toh
tropical	*tropicale*
	troh-pee-KAH-leh

Colors (*I Colori*)

Colors, like most Italian adjectives, come after the noun.
To indicate "dark," simply add the word *scuro* (SKOO-
roh) after the color. Likewise, to indicate "light," add
the word *chiaro* (kee-AH-roh) after the color.

beige	*beige* behj
black	*nero* NEH-roh
blue	*blu* bloo
brown	*marrone** mar-ROH-neh
gold	*oro* OH-roh
gray	*grigio* GREE-joh
green	*verde* VER-deh
orange	*arancione* ah-rahn-CHOH-neh
pink	*rosa* ROH-zah
purple	*viola* vee-YOH-lah
red	*rosso* ROHS-soh
silver	*argento* ar-JEN-toh
sky blue	*azzurro* ah-ZOOR-roh
white	*bianco* bee-AHN-koh
yellow	*giallo* JAHL-loh

* *Marrone is a false cognate and means "brown," not maroon.*

Temperature Conversion (*Temperatura*)

In Italy, as in all of Europe, the metric system is used to determine the temperature:

- To convert Celsius to Fahrenheit, multiply the Celsius temperature by 1.8 and add 32.

- To convert Fahrenheit to Celsius, subtract 32 from the Fahrenheit temperature and divide that number by 1.8.

Here are some basic temperature reference points:

- **Freezing:** 32°F = 0°C

- **Room temperature:** 68°F = 20°C

- **Body temperature:** 98.6°F = 37°C

- **Boiling:** 212°F = 100°C

Numbers (*I Numeri*)

0	*zero* ZEH-roh
1	*uno* OO-noh
2	*due* DOO-eh
3	*tre* treh
4	*quattro* KWAHT-troh
5	*cinque* CHEEN-kweh
6	*sei* say

7	*sette*	SEHT-teh
8	*otto*	OHT-toh
9	*nove*	NOH-veh
10	*dieci*	dee-YAY-chee
11	*undici*	OON-dee-chee
12	*dodici*	DOH-dee-chee
13	*tredici*	TREH-dee-chee
14	*quattordici*	kwaht-TOR-dee-chee
15	*quindici*	KWEEN-dee-chee
16	*sedici*	SAY-dee-chee
17	*diciassette*	dee-chah-SEHT-teh
18	*diciotto*	dee-CHOHT-toh
19	*diciannove*	dee-chahn-NOH-veh
20	*venti*	VEN-tee
21	*ventuno*	ven-TOO-noh
22	*ventidue*	ven-tee-DOO-weh
23	*ventitré*	ven-tee-TREH
24	*ventiquattro*	ven-tee-KWAHT-troh
25	*venticinque*	ven-tee-CHEEN-kweh
26	*ventisei*	ven-tee-SAY

continues

27	*ventisette* ven-tee-SET-teh	
28	*ventotto* ven-TOH-toh	
29	*ventinove* ven-tee-NOH-veh	
30	*trenta* TREN-tah	
40	*quaranta* kwah-RAHN-tah	
50	*cinquanta* cheen-KWAHN-tah	
60	*sessanta* sehs-SAHN-tah	
70	*settanta* seht-TAHN-tah	
80	*ottanta* oht-TAHN-tah	
90	*novanta* noh-VAHN-tah	
100	*cento* CHEN-toh	
101	*centouno* chen-TOO-noh	
200	*duecento* doo-way-CHEN-toh	
300	*trecento* treh-CHEN-toh	
400	*quattrocento* kwaht-troh-CHEN-toh	
500	*cinquecento* cheen-kway-CHEN-toh	
1.000	*mille* MEEL-leh	
1.001	*milleuno* meel-leh-OO-noh	
1.200	*milleduecento* meel-leh-doo-eh-CHEN-toh	
2.000	*duemila* doo-weh-MEE-lah	

3.000	*tremila*	treh-MEE-lah
10.000	*diecimila*	dee-ay-chee-MEE-lah
20.000	*ventimila*	ven-tee-MEE-lah
100.000	*centomila*	chen-toh-MEE-lah
200.000	*duecentomila*	doo-weh-chen-toh-MEE-lah
1.000.000	*un milione*	oon meel-YOH-neh
1.000.000.000	*un miliardo*	oon meel-YAR-doh

Keep in mind these brief notes on writing numbers:

- Use a period to indicate units of thousands.

  English   2,000

  Italian   2.000

- Use a comma for a decimal number. (It's read as *e* [and].)

  English   1.25

  Italian   1,25

Numbers under 100 that end in a vowel, such as *venti* (20), drop the vowel when connected to secondary numbers. For example:

  ventuno   21

  trentotto   38

  quarantuno   41

After the number *mille* (1,000), *mila* is used in the plural. For example:

  due mila   2,000

What Time Is It? (*Che Ora è?*)

Italian trains, buses, and planes all use military time for schedules (the 24-hour clock).

What time is it?	*Che ora è?* kay oh-rah AY *Che ore sono?* kay oh-reh SOH-noh
It's noon.	*È mezzogiorno.* AY mez-zoh-JOR-noh
It's midnight.	*È mezzanotte.* AY mez-zah-NOHT-teh
It's bedtime.	*È l'ora di dormire.* AY l'oh-rah dee dor-MEE-reh
It's 1:00.	*È l'una.* AY L'OO-nah
It's 2:00.	*Sono le due.* soh-noh leh DOO-weh
It's 2:05.	*Sono le due e cinque.* soh-noh leh DOO-weh eh CHEEN-kweh
It's 3:10.	*Sono le tre e dieci.* soh-noh leh tray eh dee-YEH-chee
It's 4:15.	*Sono le quattro e un quarto.* soh-noh leh KWAH-troh eh oon KWAR-toh
It's 5:20.	*Sono le cinque e venti.* soh-noh leh CHEEN-kweh eh VEN-tee
It's 6:25.	*Sono le sei e venticinque.* soh-noh leh say eh VEN-tee-CHEEN-kweh
It's 6:30.	*Sono le sei e trenta.* soh-noh leh say eh TREN-tah
It's 8:40. (20 minutes to 9:00)	*Sono le nove meno venti.* soh-noh leh NOH-veh MEH-noh VEN-tee

It's 9:45. (quarter to 10:00)	*Sono le dieci meno un quarto.* soh-noh leh dee-YEH-chee MEH-noh oon KWAR-toh
It's 10:50. (10 minutes to 11:00)	*Sono le undici meno dieci.* soh-noh leh OON-dee-chee meh-noh dee-YEH-chee
It's 11:55. (5 minutes to noon)	*È mezzogiorno meno cinque.* AY mez-zoh-JOR-noh meh-noh CHEEN-kweh
It's 14:00. (2 p.m.)	*Sono le quattordici.* soh-noh leh kwah-TOR-dee-chee
It's 17:30. (5.30 p.m.)	*Sono le diciassette e trenta.* soh-noh le dee-chah-SEHT-teh eh TREN-tah
	Sono le cinque e mezzo. soh-noh le cheen-kweh eh mez-zoh

Asking Questions (*Domande*)

It's super simple to ask a question in Italian. Make a sentence and then raise your voice at the end—just like you'd do in English. There's no need to change the word order. To indicate your confusion, say *Non capisco.* (I don't understand.) Use *non* in front of any verb in any sentence to express its opposite. For example, *Non è difficile parlare la lingua italiana.* (It's not hard to speak the Italian language.)

Do you speak English?	*Parla inglese?* par-lah een-GLEH-zeh
I don't understand.	*Non capisco.* nohn kah-PEE-skoh
Can you repeat that again?	*Può ripetere di nuovo?* p'WOH ree-PEH-teh-reh dee NWOH-voh

continues

What does it mean?	*Che significa?* kay seeg-NEE-fee-kah
How do you say … ?	*Come si dice … ?* koh-meh see DEE-chay
How much does it cost?	*Quanto costa?* KWAHN-toh KOHS-tah
How … ?	*Come … ?** koh-meh
What … ?	*Che cosa … ?* kay KOH-zah
When … ?	*Quando … ?* KWAHN-doh
Where … ?	*Dove … ?* doh-veh
Where is … ?	*Dov'è … ?* doh-VAY
Who is he/she?	*Chi è?* kee AY
Why … ?	*Perché … ?* per-KAY

* *Come?* is used to say *"how,"* but it's also used to express *"Huh?"* as well as disbelief, depending on the circumstances.

Animals (*Gli Animali*)

Italians *love* their pets and more than 55% of Italian families have one. All dogs must be registered with the *Anagrafe Canina* and should have a microchip identification. Stray cats, called *randagi* as well as *gatti liberi* (free cats), can often be found living in feline communities. Now protected by law, they're guaranteed the right to live freely while roaming parks, streets, and wooded areas.

ant	*la formica* lah for-MEE-kah
bear	*l'orso* l'or-soh

bird	*l'uccello* l'oo-CHEL-loh
bull	*il toro* eel TOH-roh
butterfly	*la farfalla* lah far-FAHL-lah
canary	*il canarino* eel kah-nah-REE-noh
cat	*il gatto* eel gat-toh
chicken	*il pollo* eel pol-loh
cow	*la mucca, la vacca* lah MOO-kah, lah VAH-kah
crocodile	*il coccodrillo* eel koh-koh-DREEL-loh
elephant	*l'elefante* l'eh-leh-FAHN-teh
fish	*il pesce* eel PEH-sheh
fly	*la mosca* lah MOHS-kah
fox	*la volpe* lah VOHL-peh
frog	*la rana* lah rah-nah
giraffe	*la giraffa* lah jee-RAHF-fah
hen	*la gallina* lah gahl LEE-nah
kitten	*il gattino* eel gaht-TEE-noh
lion	*il leone* eel leh-OH-neh
monkey	*la scimmia* lah SHEEM-m'yah
mosquito	*la zanzara* lah zan-ZAH-rah
mouse	*il topo* eel toh-poh

continues

ostrich	*lo struzzo* loh stroo-zoh
parrot	*il pappagallo* eel pap-pah-GAHL-loh
pet	*l'animale domestico* l'ah-nee-MAH-leh doh-MES-tee-koh
pig	*il maiale* eel my-AH-leh
rabbit	*il coniglio* eel koh-NEEL-yoh
rhino	*il rinoceronte* eel ree-noh-cher-OHN-teh
shark	*lo squalo* loh swah-loh
sheep	*la pècora* lah PEH-koh-rah
snake	*il serpente* eel ser-PEN-teh
squirrel	*lo scoiattolo* loh skoy-AT-toh-loh
swan	*il cigno* eel CHEEN-yoh
tiger	*la tigre* lah tee-greh
toad	*il rospo* eel ROS-poh
turtle	*la tartaruga* lah tar-tah-ROO-gah
wolf	*il lupo* eel LOO-poh
zebra	*la zebra* lah zeh-brah

Customs and Manners

Your *esperienza* in Italy will be greatly enhanced if you know about Italian customs and manners. To understand these traditions and modalities, it helps to have a basic understanding of Italian history.

Once Upon a Time
(*C'era una Volta*)

Italians value their history, which is long and varied. But most travelers don't realize it wasn't until 1871 that Italy officially became a nation with Rome as its capital. It made geographical sense too: You've got the Alps to the north and a wonderful seaside border to the south. Prior to the infamous *Risorgimento* (Resurgence)—the term used to describe the Italian unification—the boot was dominated by city-states and monarchies, often at odds with one another. The diversity of Italian culture that makes it so rich and textured is because of the thousands of years of intermingling from all directions.

Because of its location smack-dab in the "middle" of Earth, giving the word *meddittereano* (mediterranean) additional meaning, Italy has always been a strategic hub for business. Italy is a perfect example of a melting pot, reflected by the dozens, if not hundreds, of dialects that are spoken. From the Greeks, Gauls, and Goths to the Moors, Saracens, and Normans to the countless invaders, marauders, and traders, just about everyone had to have a piece of her! And who could blame them? A temperate climate, ample sun, endless fishing, easy access to the many natural ports, hot springs, cool rivers, beautiful vistas, and gorgeous sunsets certainly helped. Did everyone agree and get along well? Hardly. They didn't speak the same language, they held different belief systems, and they often had completely different lineages. But somehow, Italy—a country no bigger than Arizona—has helped shape the world in myriad ways.

This in part explains why Italians identify first and foremost with their parental lineage (*la famiglia*), then with their hometown (*il paese*), and finally with the greater country (*paese*) of Italy. For the Italians, family comes first. Even late at night, you'll find entire families out in restaurants while the kids run around the tables. Multiple generations often live close to one another. College students usually study close to home and there are very few live-on campuses in Italy. If you live near Rome, you'll probably go to school in Rome. If you're outside Naples, again, you'll still live at home while you're taking classes.

Here are some things every traveler to Italy should know:

- Italy's population is about 60 million. The average Italian lifespan is 84, ranking one of the highest in the world. The official religion is Catholic and includes 85% of the population.

- The *capitale* (capital) is Rome, also called *la città eterna* (the eternal city). Rome has more than 280 fountains and 900 churches. The monies thrown into Rome's *Fontana di Trevi* (Trevi Fountain), roughly 700,000 Euro annually, are collected and donated to various charities to help the needy. The expression "All roads lead to Rome" stems from the fact that of the 53,000 miles of roads already in place by the 4th century, every Roman mile was marked with a milestone. Rome's mascot is *il lupo* (the wolf). To wish someone good luck, Italians say *In bocca al lupo!* (In the mouth of the wolf!). In response, people often say *Crepi il lupo!* (May the wolf die!)

- The Vatican, an independent city-state, is located in the capital of Rome and is encircled by a two-mile border within Vatican City. It's one of the smallest countries in the world and prints its own Euro and stamps. It's governed as an absolute monarchy, with the Pope at its helm. The Swiss Guard (recognized by its colorful striped uniforms) was originally hired as a mercenary force exclusively dedicated to protecting the Pope and has been protecting the Vatican since 1506.

- Although many dialects are spoken, the official language of Italy is Italian. This is thanks to Italy's most cherished poet, Dante Alighieri (1265–1321), who wrote the epic poem *La Divina Commedia* (*The Divine Comedy*). Don't be surprised if you get to Italy and try to use the terms you remember hearing as a kid, only to discover no one understands a word of what you're saying. It's wise to save slang until you have a pretty good command of the language.

- If you're doing business or meeting someone for the first time, err on the side of caution and address people by their last name with *Signore* or *Signora*. Shake hands with a strong, confident grip. Use the appropriate greeting for the time of the day. If you're dealing with people of authority, use their title. (See pages 58–60 for more on honorifics.) More than likely, you'll be invited to use the "tu" form of the verb (the informal "you"). They'll say something like *Mi dai del tu.* ("Give me the *tu*"—"Call me by my first name.")

- Once you're on familiar territory with someone, it's considered appropriate to offer kisses. This is for women and men. Start on the left cheek and give another peck on the right.

- Italians look like they just walked off the runway, even if they're wearing jeans. They enjoy looking their best and aren't shy about showing off their assets. While shorts, sleeveless shirts, and sweatshirts are perfect for the *palestra* (gym), they wouldn't be appropriate for churches, even if you're just sightseeing. Nowadays, everyone wears jeans. Also, it's okay to wear the same items day in and day out as long as they're clean. Better to have a nice jacket you wear every day than having a wardrobe filled with cheap imitations. *Complimenti* (compliments) are a nice way to show your appreciation. Italians also love their shoes—and for good reason. They'll often "scan" a person from the feet up. Paying attention to shoes offers a lot of insights: profession, status, and position in life. Rich or poor, young or old, if you're out people-watching, check out their shoes!

- Never show up empty-handed to someone's house. This is a given. *Una bottiglia di vino* (a bottle of wine), a box of *cioccolatini* (chocolates), or *un mazzo di fiori* (a bunch of flowers) are good ideas.

- *Benvenuti tutti!* Everyone is invited. It's true! Italians are notoriously generous about ensuring inclusion. If you're doing the inviting, make sure to include *soci* (associates), family members, and partners of the invitees.

- Business is for business hours. If you're out in a *ristorante* with a potential business *cliente*, wait until you're in the office or field before discussing business details. Your lunch or dinner is an opportunity to forge trust and relax. It's a lot easier to do business when you know you're with someone who shares your values. Once on-site, it's perfectly acceptable to ask about how the company you're interested in conducts its business. Find out who the key players are.

- *Agosto* (August) is vacation month. *Ferragosto* describes the period in which most Italians go *in vacanza* (on vacation). If you're planning to do business, this is probably not your month. Holidays and festivities are inseparable from daily life and most holidays have a religious nature. Because stores, schools, and businesses often close, plan your visit accordingly. Unless you're in a major city, most establishments (outside restaurants) close on Sundays.

- Italians never order a latte unless they want actual milk. Cappuccino (which comes from the word *cappuccio*, meaning "hood") is consumed in the *mattina* (morning) or maybe as an afternoon pick-me-up, never after a meal. *L'insalata* (salad) always comes *dopo* (after) the main course. Italians rarely drink tap water. They'll order *una bottiglia d'acqua*, either *con gas* or *naturale*. Contrary to movies and TV, Italians don't eat a four-course meal every day.

- Italians celebrate their "name day" (*Onomàstico*). Also known as their "Saint's day," they celebrate this day like their birthdays. For example, if it's

October 4 and your name is Franco, you'd celebrate St. Francis day. This is often more celebrated than even one's own birthday, especially in southern Italy. Cakes are baked and presents exchanged.

- Italians rarely chew gum.

- Italians love *conversazione* (conversation) and just "being" with each other. It's *maleducato* (rude) to be on your phone unnecessarily, especially if you're in company. Social media is used to facilitate face-to-face interactions, not substitute for them.

- Italy boasts more sites on the World Heritage Site list than any other country in the world. Why not make a point to visit some of them? Check out whc.unesco.org to learn more. Although the following list is hardly comprehensive, the most commonly visited sites include:

  - *Agrigento (Sicily):* archeological ruins
  - *Alberobello:* the Triulli
  - *Assisi:* the Basilicata of San Francesco
  - *Milan: The Last Supper* by da Vinci
  - *Pompeii:* archeological ruins
  - *Rome:* the Forum, the Pantheon, the Colosseum
  - *Tarquinia:* the Etruscan Necropolises
  - *Tivoli:* Villa d'Este, Villa Adriana
  - *Tuscany:* Medici villas and gardens

- Italians take their time to eat. The Slow Food movement was begun by Carlo Petrini in 1986 in response to the fast-food chains that were starting to move into the major cities. Their symbol is the snail, called the *chiocciola* (kee-OH-choh-lah), and it's this same word that's used to describe the "at" (@) symbol used in email addresses. This has become an international movement. According to their website: "Slow Food envisions a world in which all people can access and enjoy food that is good for them, good for those who grow it and good for the planet. Our approach is based on a concept of food that is defined by three interconnected principles: good, clean and fair." For more information, visit their website at www.slowfood.com.

- Giuseppe Garibaldi (1807–1882) is given credit for uniting Italy. This is why you see a Via Garibaldi in every town, village, and city.

- The Republic of San Marino, in central Italy, is officially considered independent from Italy.

- Venice, known as the City of Canals and the Floating City, goes by the moniker *Serenissima*. Because of the city's celebration of Carnevale, masks became part of its artistic heritage. Venice is sinking about 1 to 2 millimeters per year. As a result, a public works project aptly called *Il MOSE* (Moses) was engineered to help by using a series of mobile locks and gates to protect Venice and the lagoon from the *acqua alta* (high tide). Begun in 2003, it wasn't until October 2020 that *Il MOSE* was finally put into operation.

- Florence, located in Tuscany, is considered the "Jewel of the Renaissance" and was and remains today a major force. Bartolomeo Cristofori built the first piano of the 18th century in Florence. The Tuscan dialect, Fiorentino, was chosen as the official language of Italy. The mascot for Florence is *il leone* (the lion). Florence's history is inseparable from the Medici Family, who ruled for more than three centuries and became leaders in the fields of commerce, banking, and art. Florence is also home to *L'Ospedale di Santa Maria Nuova*, one of the oldest hospitals in Italy. Founded in 1288, it also possesses some of the most beautiful art collections.

- Although flatbreads have been around for centuries, pizza was invented in Italy—no surprise here. The first pizza is attributed to Naples in 1860. Called "Pizza Margherita," it was named in honor of Queen Margherita and showcased the three colors of the *bandiera italiana* (Italian flag): *verde*, *rosso*, and *bianco*.

- All three of Europe's active volcanoes are found in Italy: Mt. Vesuvius, located just outside Naples; Mt. Etna on the island of Sicily; and Mt. Stromboli, which is located just off the Sicilian coast.

- Italians put a lot of emphasis on the subtle art of being elegant. *La bella figura* literally translates to "the beautiful figure" and is a decidedly Italian notion that means making a "good first impression." Conversely, *la brutta figura* refers to a "bad impression."

Friends & Family

This chapter gives you the *vocabolario* to describe you and your *famiglia*, who you are, and what you do. It also offers you three essential verbs—*essere*, *stare*, and *avere*—that will help you express yourself in countless ways. You'll also learn more about titles and how to properly address the people you meet along the way.

Basic Italian Greetings and Other Common Exchanges (*Espressioni Utili*)

Hello./Good day.	*Buon giorno.* bwon JOR-noh
Good evening.	*Buona sera.* bwoh-nah seh-rah
Good night.	*Buona notte.* bwoh-nah NOHT-teh
Goodbye.	*Arrivederci/ArrivederLa* [formal]. ah-ree-veh-DER-chee/ah-ree-veh-DER-lah
Mr./Sir	*Signore* see-NYOH-reh
Mrs./Ms.	*Signora* see-NYOH-rah
Miss	*Signorina* see-nyoh-REE-nah
How are you?	*Come sta?** koh-meh stah
Very well.	*Molto bene.* mohl-toh beh-neh
Not bad.	*Non c'è male.* nohn ch'AY MAH-leh
Pretty well.	*Abbastanza bene.* ah-bah-STAHN-zah beh-neh
What's your name?	*Come si chiama?** (How do you call yourself?) koh-meh see kee-AH-mah
My name is …	*Mi chiamo …* (I call myself …) mee kee-AH-moh
See you soon.	*A presto.* ah preh-stoh
Excuse me.	*Mi scusi.** mee skoo-zee

Please.	*Per favore.* per fah-VOH-reh
Please.	*Per piacere.* per pee-ah-CHEH-reh
Thank you.	*Grazie.* GRAH-tsee-yay
You're welcome.	*Prego.*** pray-goh
You're welcome. (It's nothing.)	*Non c'è di che.* nohn ch'AY dee kay
You're very kind.	*Lei è molto gentile.* leh AY mohl-toh jen-TEE-leh

* *These are all being used in the formal "you" (Lei) form of the verb.*

** Prego *is also used as a catchall phrase to mean "Make yourself at home," "After you," and "Welcome" depending on the context.*

Informal Expressions (*Espressioni Informali*)

Hi!/Bye-bye!	*Ciao!* chow
Greetings!	*Saluti!* sah-LOO-tee
How are you?	*Come stai?* koh-meh sty
Hey there!	*Salve!* SAL-veh
How's it going?	*Come va?* koh-meh vah
Things are good/great.	*Va bene/benissimo.* vah beh-neh/ beh-NEES-see-moh
Not so good.	*Va male.* vah mah-leh
Not bad.	*Non c'è male.* nohn ch'AY mah-leh

continues

So-so.	*Così così.* koh-ZEE koh-ZEE
See you later.	*Arrivederci.* ah-ree-veh-DER-chee
	Ci vediamo. chee veh-dee-YAH-moh
Until later.	*A più tardi.* ah p'YOO tar-dee
Until tomorrow.	*A domani.* ah doh-MAH-nee

Your Family (*Famiglia*)

In Italy, one of the first things people will want to know about is your *famiglia* (fah-MEE-lyah).

In the following, substitute the word in parentheses with the appropriate term. Notice that the possessive adjective changes depending on the gender of the thing or person being possessed.

Feminine:

Questa è mia (moglie).

kwes-tah AY mee-yah (MOHL-yeh)

This is my (wife).

Masculine:

Questo è mio (marito).

kwes-toh AY mee-yoh (mah-REE-toh)

This is my (husband).

When discussing one's children of both sexes, Italian reverts to the masculine plural: *figli* (feel-yee). The same goes for friends: *amici* (ah-MEE-chee). One's parents—*genitori* (jeh-nee-TOH-ree)—can be simply referred to as *i miei*.

Feminine	
aunt	*zia* zee-yah
cousin	*cugina* koo-JEE-nah
daughter	*figlia* feel-yah
daughter-in-law	*nuora* nwoh-rah
fiancée	*fidanzata* fee-dahn-ZAH-tah
friend	*amica* ah-MEE-kah
girlfriend	*ragazza* rah-GAH-tsah
godmother	*madrina* mah-DREE-nah
granddaughter	*nipote* nee-POH-teh
grandmother	*nonna* NOHN-nah
infant	*bambina* bam-BEE-nah
mother	*madre* mah-dreh
mother-in-law	*suocera* SWOH-cheh-rah
niece	*nipote* nee-POH-teh
sister	*sorella* soh-REL-lah
sister-in-law	*cognata* kohn-YAH-tah

continues

stepsister	*sorellastra*
	soh-rel-LAHS-trah
wife	*moglie*
	MOHL-yeh
widow	*vedova*
	VEH-doh-vah

Masculine

boyfriend	*ragazzo*
	rah-GAH-tsoh
brother	*fratello*
	frah-TEL-loh
brother-in-law	*cognato*
	koh-NYAH-toh
cousin	*cugino*
	kooh-JEE-noh
father	*padre*
	pah-dreh
father-in-law	*suocero*
	SWOH-cheh-roh
fiancé	*fidanzato*
	fee-dahn-ZAH-toh
friend	*amico*
	ah-MEE-koh
godfather	*padrino*
	pah-DREE-noh
grandfather	*nonno*
	NOHN-noh
grandson	*nipote*
	nee-POH-teh
husband	*marito*
	mah-REE-toh
infant	*bambino*
	bahm-BEE-noh
nephew	*nipote*
	nee-POH-teh
son	*figlio*
	feel-yoh
son-in-law	*gènero*
	GEH-neh-roh

stepbrother	*fratellastro*
	frah-tel-LAHS-troh
uncle	*zio*
	zee-yoh
widower	*vedovo*
	VEH-doh-voh

Anytime you see a vowel, remember to use the Italian pronunciation. The sound for *gli* is like the *ll* in the word "million." Also, always remember to emphasize double consonants while sliding them together to form a single sound. For example: *mamma* (mahm-mah).

Occupations and Professions (*Occupazioni e Professioni*)

What do you profess to be? If you're retired, simply say *Sono pensionato* if you're a man and *Sono pensionata* if you're a woman. For people who work freelance, Italian uses the English term "freelance." Self-starters can also say *Lavoro in proprio.* (I work for myself.) Independent contractors can also use the term *autonomo/a* (as in autonomous). A family-run business calls itself *una azienda a gestione familiare.* The term *abbracciatutto* (ah-BRAH-chah-TOO-toh) literally means "hugs everything" and describes people who adapt to the circumstances.

What's your profession?	*Che professione fa?*
	kay proh-fes-see-OH-neh fah
What kind of work do you do?	*Che lavoro fa?*
	kay lah-VOH-roh fah

continues

I'm a (an) …	*Sono un (una) …* soh-noh oon/oo-nah
accountant.	*contabile.* kohn-TAH-bee-leh
actor.	*attore.* aht-TOH-reh
administrator.	*amminstratore/* *amministratrice.* ahm-mee-nee-strah-TOH-reh/ahm-mee-nee-strah-TREE-cheh
agent.	*agente.* ah-JEN-teh
analyst.	*analista.* ah-nah-LEES-tah
architect.	*architetto.* ar-kee-TET-toh
artist.	*artista.* ar-TEES-tah
assistant.	*assistente.* ahs-sees-TEN-teh
athlete.	*atleta.* at-LEH-tah
author.	*autore.* ow-TOH-reh
baker.	*fornaio, panettiere.* for-NYE-yoh, pah-net-tee-YEH-reh
banker.	*bancario/a.* bahn-KAH-ryoh/ah
barber.	*barbiere.* bar-bee-YEH-reh
boss.	*capo.* kah-poh
builder.	*costruttore.* koh-stroo-TOH-reh
businessman.	*uomo d'affari.* woh-moh dah-FAH-ree
businesswoman.	*donna d'affari.* dohn-nah dah-FAH-ree

butcher.	*macellaio.* mah-chel-LY-yoh
carpenter.	*falegname.* fah-leh-NYAH-meh
cashier.	*cassiere.* kas-see-YEH-reh
chef.	*cuoco.* KWOH-koh
chiropractor.	*chiropratico.* kee-roh-PRAH-tee-koh
coach.	*allenatore.* al-leh-nah-TOH-reh
confectioner.	*pasticciere.* pas-tee-cheh-REE-yeh
consultant.	*consulente.* kohn-soo-LEN-teh
dean.	*preside.* PREH-see-deh
dentist.	*dentista.* den-TEE-stah
designer.	*designer.* designer
director (film).	*regista.* reh-JEES-tah
director (management).	*direttore/direttrice.* dee-ret-TOH-reh/dee-ret-TREE-cheh
doctor.	*dottore/dottoressa.* doh-TOH-reh/doh-toh-REHS-sah
driver.	*autista.* ow-TEES-tah
editor.	*editore/editrice.* eh-dee-TOH-reh/eh-dee-TREE-cheh
electrician.	*elettricista.* eh-let-tree-CHEES-tah
employee.	*impiegato/a.* eem-pyeh-GAH-toh/ah
employer.	*responsabile.* res-pohn-SAH-bee-leh

continues

engineer.	*ingegnere.* een-jen-YEH-reh
entrepreneur.	*imprenditore.* eem-pren-dee-TOH-reh
executive.	*dirigente.* dee-ree-JEN-teh
farmer.	*agricoltore.* ahg-ree-kol-TOH-reh
firefighter.	*pompiere.* pom-pee-YEH-reh
florist.	*fioraio.* fyoh-RY-yoh
guard.	*guardia.* GWAR-d'yah
hairdresser.	*parrucchiere.* pah-rooh-kee-YEH-reh
headmaster.	*caposcuola.* kah-poh-SKWO-lah
herbalist.	*erbalista.* er-bah-LEES-tah
historian.	*storico/a.* STOH-ree-koh/ah
housewife.	*casalinga.* kah-zah-LEEN-gah
instructor.	*istruttore/istruttrice.* ees-troot-TOH-reh/ees-troot-TREE-cheh
interpreter.	*interprete.* een-TER-preh-teh
investigator.	*investigatore.* een-ves-tee-gah-TOH-reh
landlord.	*padrone/padrona.* pah-DROH-neh/pah-DROH-nah
landscaper.	*giardiniera.* gwar-deen-YEH-rah
lawyer.	*avvocato, giurista.* av-voh-KAH-toh, joo-REES-tah
leader.	*dirigente.* dee-ree-JEN-teh

librarian.	*bibliotecario/a.* bee-blee-yoh-teh-KAH-ryoh/ah
manager.	*amministratore.* am-mee-nee-strah-TOH-reh
manufacturer.	*produttore.* proh-doot-TOH-reh
mechanic.	*meccanico.* meh-KAH-nee-koh
merchant.	*commerciante.* kohm-mer-CHAHN-teh
midwife.	*levatrice.* leh-vah-TREE-cheh
minister.	*ministro/parroco.* mee-NEES-troh/par-ROH-koh
musician.	*musicista.* moo-zee-CHEES-tah
negotiator.	*negoziatore.* neh-goh-zyah-TOH-reh
notary.	*notaio.* noh-TYE-yoh
nun.	*suora/monaca.* swoh-rah/MOH-nah-kah
nurse.	*infermiera.* een-fer-mee-YEH-rah
official.	*funzionario.* foon-zee-oh-NAH-ryoh
painter.	*pittore/pittrice.* peet-TOH-reh/peet-TREE-cheh
partner.	*socio.* SOH-choh
pediatrician.	*pediatra.* peh-dee-AH-trah
pharmacist.	*farmacista.* far-mah-CHEES-tah
photographer.	*fotografo.* foh-TOH-grah-foh
plumber.	*idraulico.* ee-DRAU-lee-koh

continues

police officer.	*vigile.* VEE-jee-leh
postal carrier.	*portalettera, postino.* por-tah-LET-teh-rah, pos-TEE-noh
priest.	*prete.* preh-teh
producer.	*produttore/produttrice.* pro-doot-TOH-reh/pro-doot-TREE-cheh
professor.	*professore/professoressa.* pro-fes-SOH-reh/pro-fes-soh-RES-sah
proprietor.	*proprietario/a.* proh-pre-yeh-TAH-r'yoh/ah
psychologist.	*psicologo/a.* psee-KOH-loh-goh/ah
real estate broker.	*agente immobiliare.* ah-JEN-teh eem-moh-beel-YAH-reh
representative.	*rappresentante.* rahp-preh-zen-TAHN-teh
scientist.	*scienziato/a.* shee-yehn-zee-AH-toh/ah
sculptor.	*scultore/scultrice.* skool-TOH-reh/skool-TREE-cheh
secretary.	*segretaria.* seh-greh-TAH-r'yah
social worker.	*assistente sociale.* ahs-sees-TEN-teh soh-CHAH-leh
stockbroker.	*agente di cambio.* ah-JEN-teh dee kahm-byoh
student.	*studente/studentessa.* stoo-DEN-teh/stoo-den-TES-sah
supervisor.	*supervisore.* soo-per-vee-ZOH-reh
tailor.	*sarto/a.* sar-toh/ah

teacher.	*insegnante.* een-sen-YAHN-teh
trader.	*negoziante.* neh-goh-tsee-AHN-teh
vendor.	*venditore.* ven-dee-TOH-reh
veterinarian.	*veterinario/a.* veh-teh-ree-NAH-r'yoh/ah
vintner.	*vignaiolo.* VEEN-y'eye-OH-loh
volunteer.	*volontario/a.* voh-lon-TAH-r'yoh/ah
waiter.	*cameriere.* kah-meh-ree-YEH-reh
wholesaler.	*grossista.* groh-SEES-tah
winemaker.	*enologo.* eh-NOH-loh-goh
workman.	*operaio.* oh-per-EYE-yoh
writer.	*scrittore/scrittrice.* skree-TOH-reh/skree-TREE-cheh

When referring to a feminine subject, unless otherwise indicated, change the ending (which is by default masculine) to an *-a*. For example, *scienziato* signifies a male scientist, whereas *scienziata* would refer to a female scientist. (Of course, a scientist is a scientist regardless of the gender.)

Some words work for either gender, such as *artista* (artist), *musicista* (musician), and *poeta* (poet). Others descriptives follow similar patterns. For example, *dottore/dottoressa* (doctor) and *professore/professoressa* (professor).

Religious descriptives include *pastore* (pastor), *rabbino* (rabbi), and *imam* (imam).

Italian Honorifics and Titles (*Onorifici e Titoli Italiani*)

A lot of *comunicazione* (communication) happens just by understanding the subtle art of getting others to help you. Italians are no strangers to protocol and demonstrating the appropriate manners is essential. Whether you're a *studente* (student), *turista* (tourist), an ex-Pat, or serving abroad in Italy, a simple way of ingratiating yourself with officials and people working in the tangled, often frustrating Italian bureaucracy is to know their titles. When it comes to Italian monikers, they can be long and complicated. (A word of *consiglio* (advice): Be super nice to the people you encounter at the desk, front door, or lobby. These are the gatekeepers to the people who can make or break your day.)

I'd like to speak with …	*Vorrei parlare con …* vohr-RAY par-LAH-reh kohn
I'd like to make an appointment with …	*Vorrei fare un appuntamento con …* vohr-RAY fah-reh oon ahp-poon-tah-MEN-toh kohn
Can you tell me with whom I should speak …	*Mi può dire con chi dovrei parlare?* mee p'WOH dee-reh kohn kee doh-VREI par-LAH-reh
Thank you for your time.	*Grazie per il suo tempo.* GRAH-zee-yeh per eel soo-oh tem-poh
I'm grateful.	*Sono grato/a.* soh-noh grah-toh/ah
Is (Thomas) here?	*È … qui?* AY (…) kwee

General Titles (*Titoli Generali*)

Assistant	*Assistente* ahs-see-TEN-teh
Associate	*Socio* soh-choh
Consul	*Console* KOHN-soh-leh
Customs agent	*Agente della dogana* ah-JEN-teh del-lah doh-GAH-nah
Doctor	*Dottore/Dottoressa** doh-TOH-reh/doh-toh-RES-sah
Emeritus president	*Presidente emerito* preh-zee-DEN-teh eh-meh-REE-toh
Honorable	*Onorevole* oh-noh-REH-voh-leh
Judge	*Giudice* JOO-dee-cheh
Lawyer	*Avvocato* ah-voh-KAH-toh
Manager	*Dirigente* dee-ree-JEN-teh
Master	*Maestro/Maestra* my-EHS-troh/my-EHS-trah
Mayor	*Sindaco* SEEN-dah-koh
Minister	*Ministro* mee-NEE-stroh
Officer	*Agente, Funzionario* ah-JEN-teh, foon-zee-oh-NAH-ryoh
Official (used in the military)	*Ufficiale* oof-fee-CHAH-leh
President	*Presidente* preh-zee-DEN-teh

continues

Prime Minister	*Primo Ministro* pree-moh mee-NEES-troh
Professor	*Professore/Professoressa* proh-fes-SOH-reh/proh-fes- soh-RES-sah
Secretary	*Segretario/a* seh-greh-TAH-r'yoh/ah
Senator	*Senatore* seh-nah-TOH-reh
Teacher	*Maestro/Maestra* my-ESS-troh/my-ESS-trah

* *This term can also be used to describe anyone with an advanced university degree.*

Military Terms

Aeronautics	*L'Aeronautica* l'au-roh-NOW-tee-kah
Air Force	*l'Aeronautica Militare* l'au-roh-NOW-tee-kah mee- lee-TAH-reh
Army	*l'Esercito* l'eh-ZEH-chee-toh
Civil Service	*il Servizio Civile* eel ser-VEE-zee-yoh chee-VEE- leh
Corrections	*La Polizia Penitenziaria* lah poh-lee-ZEE-yah peh-nee- ten-zee-AH-ree-yah
Finance Police	*La Guardia di Finanza* lah-GWAR-dee-yah dee fee- NAHN-zah
Forestry	*Il Corpo Forestrale dello Stato* eel kor-poh foh-res-TRAH-leh del-loh stah-toh
Government	*Il Governo* eel goh-VER-noh
Gendarmerie	*I Carabinieri* ee kah-rah-bee-NYEH-ree
Marines	*Marina Militare* lah mah-REE-nah mee-lee-TAH- reh

Military Police	*Polizia Militare* poh-lee-ZEE-yah mee-lee-TAH-reh
National Fire Brigade	*Il Corpo Nazionale dei Vigili del Fuoco* eel kor-poh nah-zee-oh-NAH-leh day VEE-jee-leh del fwoh-koh
Navy	*la Marina Militare* lah nah-REE-nah
Police	*La Polizia* lah poh-lee-ZEE-yah

Useful Verbs: *Essere* and *Stare* (To Be)

The verbs *essere* (to be) and *stare* (to be, to stay) can help you enormously in your communications. You'll hear these used often and you're strongly encouraged to memorize these verbs. Italian subject pronouns are provided but are rather redundant, given the conjugation already indicates the subject. Therefore, Italian uses subject pronouns for emphatic purposes only and they don't need to be included most of the time.

Essere	
Italian	**English**
io sono ee-yoh soh-noh	I am
tu sei too say	you are (familiar)
lui/lei/Lei è louie/lay/lay AY	he is/she is/You are
noi siamo noy see-AH-moh	we are

continues

voi siete voy see-YEH-teh	you are
loro sono loh-roh soh-noh	they are

Stare

Italian	English
io sto ee-yoh stoh	I am
tu stai too sty	you are (familiar)
lui/lei/Lei sta louie/lay/lay stah	he is/she is/You are
noi stiamo noy stee-YAH-moh	we are
voi state voy stah-teh	you are
loro stanno loh-roh STAHN-noh	they are

When to Use *Essere*

This verb is used in compound tenses like the present perfect, called *il passato prossimo* in Italian. In addition, you'll see it used in the following ways.

- To describe nationalities, origins, and inherent unchanging qualities

Maurizio è di Verona. mao-REE-zee-oh AY dee veh-ROH-nah	Maurizio's from Verona.
Siamo Italiani. see-YAH-moh ee-tah-lee-YAH-nee	We're Italians.
La banana è gialla. lah bah-NAH-nah AY jahl-lah	The banana's yellow.

- To identify the subject or describe the subject's character traits

Voi siete gentili. voy see-YEH-teh jen-TEE-lee	You're all kind.
Michele è un musicista. mee-KEH-leh AY oon moo-zee- CHEES-tah	Michael's a musician.
Sono io. soh-noh ee-yoh	It's me.

• To talk about the time and dates

Che ora è? kay oh-rah AY	What time is it?
Sa l'ora? sah l'oh-rah	Can you tell me the time?
Che giorno è? kay jor-noh AY	What day is it?

• To indicate possession

Questo è lo zio di Anna. kweh-stoh AY loh zee-oh dee ahn-nah	This is the uncle of Anna. (This is Anna's uncle.)
Quella è la mia casa. kwel-lah AY lah myah kah-zah	That's my house.

When to Use *Stare*

Use this verb to describe a temporary state or
condition of the subject, such as in the following.

• To ask someone how they're doing

Come sta? koh-meh stah	How are you?
Sto bene grazie. stoh beh-neh grah-TSEE-yeh	I'm well thanks.

• To express location

Stiamo in città. stee-YAH-moh een chee-TAH	We're staying in the city.

Patrizia sta a casa.
pah-TREE-zee-yah stah ah kah-
zah

Patricia's at home.

- For many idiomatic expressions, especially when you're telling someone what to do

Sta' attento! stah at-TEN-toh	Pay attention!
Sta' zitto! stah ZEET-toh	Be quiet!

Forming the Progressive with *Stare*

The verb *stare* is used to formulate the progressive tense (called *il progressivo*), used to describe when something's happening in the moment. Because of the nature of Italian verbiage, the Italian present tense is sufficient to express "I eat" and "I'm eating." That said, however, if you're intimidated by all the conjugations, try using the progressive tense instead.

To form the present progressive (present continous), change your infinitive verb to a gerund and then attach the gerund to the verb *stare*.

- Infinitive verbs ending in *-are* change their ending to *-ando*:

parlare (to speak)   >   *parlando* (speaking)
par-LAH-reh   par-LAHN-doh

Sto parlando con la gestione.
stoh par-LAHN-doh kohn lah jes-tee-OH-neh

I'm speaking with management.

- Infinitive verbs ending in *-ere* and *-ire* change their ending to *-endo*.

leggere (to read)   >   *leggendo* (reading)
LEH-jeh-reh   leh-JEN-doh

Roberto sta leggendo il documento.
roh-BER-toh stah leh-JEN-doh eel doh-koo-MEN-toh

Robert's reading the document.

finire (to finish)   >   *finendo* (finishing)
fee-NEE-reh   fee-NEN-doh

La partita sta finendo.
lah par-TEE-tah stah fee-NEN-doh

The game is finishing.

Useful Verb: *Avere* (To Have)

It's highly recommended you memorize this one. Keep in mind that the *h* is always silent and there to distinguish the verb from other Italian words. Similar to *essere* and following the same rules used in Spanish and French, this verb is also used in compound tenses, such as the present perfect.

Italian	English
io ho ee-yoh oh	I have
tu hai too eye	you have (familiar)
lui/lei/Lei ha louie/lay/lay ah	he has/she has/You have
noi abbiamo noy ah-bee-YAH-moh	we have

continues

voi avete voy ah-VEH-teh	you have
loro hanno loh-roh ahn-noh	they have

Useful idiomatic expressions using *avere* include:

> *Quanti anni ha?*
> kwahn-tee AHN-nee eye

How old are you? (How many years do you have?)

> *Ho (venticinque) anni.*
> oh (ven-tee-CHEEN-kweh) AHN-nee

I'm (twenty-five) years old.

> *Ho freddo/caldo.*
> oh fred-doh/kahl-doh

I'm cold/warm.

> *Abbiamo fretta.*
> ah-bee-YAH-moh fret-tah

We're in a rush.

Using *Essere* and *Avere* in the Present Perfect

To speak in the past, such as "I have studied," Italian uses *essere* and *avere* as "helping" or auxiliary verbs plus the past participle. To form a past participle, Italian follows these rules:

-are > *-ato*

studiare (to study)   >   *studiato* (studied)
stoo-dee-YAH-reh   stoo-dee-YAH-toh

Anna ha studiato.
ahn-nah ah stoo-dee-YAH-toh

Anna has studied.

-ere > *-uto*

vendere (to sell)   >   *venduto* (sold)
VEN-deh-reh   ven-DOO-toh

Abbiamo venduto la macchina.
ah-bee-YAH-moh ven-DOO-toh lah MAH-kee-nah

We've sold the car.

-ire > *-ito*

capire (to understand) >   *capito* (understood)
kah-PEE-reh   kah-PEE-toh

Ho capito la lezione.
oh kah-PEE-toh lah loh-zee-OH-neh

I've studied the lesson.

When do you use *avere* versus *essere*? Transitive verbs (verbs that impact the object of the sentence) take *avere*. Intransitive verbs take *essere*. Commonly used verbs that take *avere* include the following. (The past participle is in parentheses.)

- *abitare (abitato)* (to live)
- *avere (avuto)* (to have)
- *ballare (ballato)* (to dance)
- *capire (capito)* (to understand)
- *comprare (comprato)* (to buy)
- *finire (finito)* (to finish)
- *leggere (letto)* (to read)*
- *mangiare (mangiato)* (to eat)
- *vedere (visto)** (to see)

Commonly used verbs that take *essere* include:

- *arrivare (arrivato)* (to arrive)
- *andare (andato)* (to go)
- *entrare (entrato)* (to enter)
- *essere (stato)** (to be)
- *partire (partito)* (to leave)
- *uscire (uscito)* (to go out)
- *salire (salito)* (to go up, get on)
- *scendere (sceso)** (to go down, get off)

These past participles are irregular and must be memorized.

Past participles that take *essere* act like adjectives and must reflect the gender and number of the subject. For example:

- *Roberto è partito.* (Robert has left.)
- *Maria è arrivata.* (Mary has arrived.)

Transportation

This chapter gives you the vocabulary you need to get around. Most likely, you'll still get lost, but if you consider it all part of the *avventura*, however, you'll enjoy the ride a whole lot more!

Italian Regions and Provinces (*Regioni e Provincie*)

Italian regions (given here by their Italian names) are similar to states or provinces and each has its own governing body and capital. Passports, driver's licenses, and other official business are addressed in the capital of a particular region. This table notes the *capitale* of each region.

Region	Capital
Basilicata	Potenza
Calabria	Catanzaro
Campania	Napoli
Emilia-Romagna	Bologna
Friuli-Venezia Giulia	Trieste
Lazio	Roma
Liguria	Genoa
Lombardia	Milano
Le Marche	Ancona
Molise	Campobasso
Piemonte	Torino
Puglia	Bari
Sardegna	Cagliari
Sicilia	Palermo
Toscana	Firenze
Trentino-Alto Adige	Trento
Umbria	Perugia
Valle d'Aosta	Aosta
Veneto	Venezia

Airport (*L'Aeroporto*)

Chances are, airline personnel will speak English at the airport. But just in case, here are terms you might need to maneuver through the airport and onto your plane.

airline	*l'aerolinea* l'ah-roh-LEE-n'yah
airplane	*aeroplano* ah-roh-PLAH-noh
airport	*aereoporto* ah-roh-POR-toh
aisle	*corridoio* kor-ree-DOY-oh
arrival	*arrivo* ah-REE-voh
arrival time	*ora d'arrivo* oh-rah d'ah-REE-voh
baggage	*bagagli* bah-GAH-ylee
baggage claim	*riconsegna, ritiro bagagli* ree-kohn-SEH-nyah, ree-TEE- roh bah-GAH-ylee
bathroom	*bagno, toilette* bah-nyoh, toy-LET
car rental	*autonoleggio* ow-toh-noh-LEH-joh
cart	*carrello* kar-REL-loh
connection	*coincidenza* koh-een-chee-DEN-zah
customs	*dogana* doh-GAH-nah
departure	*partenza* par-TEN-zah
departure time	*ora di partenza* oh-rah dee par-TEN-zah
destination	*destinazione* des-tee-NAH-zee-oh-neh

continues

elevator	*ascensore* ah-shen-SOH-reh
emergency exit	*uscita d'emergenza* OO-shee-tah d'eh-mer-GEN-zah
flight	*volo* voh-loh
flight attendant	*assistente di volo* ahs-see-TEN-teh dee voh-loh
gate	*la porta d'imbarco* lah por-tah d'eem-BAR-koh
information	*informazioni* een-for-mah-zee-OH-neh
landing	*atterraggio* aht-ter-AH-joh
life vest	*giubbotto di salvataggio* joob-BOHT-toh dee sal-vah-TAH-joh
lost and found	*ufficio oggetti smarriti* OO-fee-choh oh-JET-tee smar-REE-tee
money exchange	*cambio* KAHM-b'yoh
on board	*bordo* bor-doh
porter	*porta-bagagli* por-tah bah-GAHL-yee
reservation	*prenotazione* preh-noh-tah-zee-OH-neh
row	*fila* fee-lah
seat	*posto* pohs-toh
seatbelt	*cintura di sicurezza* cheen-TOO-rah dee see-koo-REH-tsah
takeoff	*decollo* deh-KOH-loh
ticket	*biglietto* beel-YET-toh

trip	*viaggio*
	vee-AH-joh
window	*finestrino*
	fee-neh-STREE-noh

Expressing Yourself

Helpful airport-related expressions include the following. (Keep in mind that all Italian nouns require an article in front of them. For example, *l'ora d'arrivo* [loh-rah dar-REE-voh] translates to "the hour of arrival.")

Where's customs?	*Dov'è la dogana?*
	doh-veh eh lah doh-GAH-nah
I've nothing to declare.	*Non ho niente da dichiarare.*
	nohn oh nee-YEN-teh dah dee-kee-YAH-rah-reh
I'd like a seat near the window/aisle.	*Vorrei un posto vicino al finestrino/corridoio.*
	vohr-RAY oon poh-stoh vee-CHEE-noh ahl fee-NEH-stree-noh/cor-ree-DOY-oh
I'd like to travel in first/second class.	*Vorrei viaggiare in prima/seconda classe.*
	vohr-RAY vee-ahj-JAH-reh een pree-mah/seh-KOHN-dah klahs-seh
I'd like to reserve a place.	*Vorrei prenotare un posto.*
	vohr-RAY preh-noh-TAH-reh oon poh-stoh

Asking for Directions (*Indicazioni*)

The most basic expressions you can use are *Dov'è ... ?* (Where is ... ?) and *C'è ... ?* (Is there ... ?).

Ho capito (oh kah-PEE-toh) means "I've understood." Negation is created by adding *non* in front of any verb. For example, *Non ho capito* (nohn oh kah-PEE-toh) means "I don't understood."

Asking Questions and Getting Answers

When asking for *indicazioni*, stick with simple questions that allow for simple responses.

C'è ... ? ch'AY	Is there ... ?
Ci sono ... ? chee soh-noh	Are there ... ?
Dov'è ... ? doh-VAY	Where is ... ?
Sinistra/Destra see-NEE-strah/des-trah	Left/Right
Dritto/Diritto DREET-toh/dee-REET-toh	Straight*

* Italians will often tell you Sempre dritto *(always straight), meaning* "Stay on this road."

How Do I Get to ... ? (*Come Arrivo a ... ?*)

When you're going *a piedi* (by foot), these phrases will help you get around.

At the corner	*all'angolo* ahl-L'AHN-goh-loh
At the intersection	*all'incrocio* ahl-l'een-KROH-choh

At the stop sign	*allo stop* ahl-loh stop
At the traffic light	*al semaforo* ahl seh-MAH-foh-roh
Can I get there by foot?	*Posso andarci a piedi?* pohs-soh ahn-DAR-chee ah pee-YEH-dee
Can you please repeat that?	*Me lo ripeti per favore?* me loh ree-PEH-tee per fah-VOH-reh
Can you tell me how to get to ... ?	*Mi può dire come arrivare a ... ?* me p'WOH dee-reh koh-meh ar-ree-VAH-reh ah
Can you indicate where *centro** is?	*Mi può indicare dov'è il centro?* me p'WOH een-dee-KAH-reh doh-VAY eel chen-troh
Can you tell me ... ?	*Sa dirmi ... ?* sah deer-me
Cross	*Attraversi* aht-trah-VER-see
Down at the end (of the street)	*giù in fondo* JOO een fon-doh
Further on	*più avanti* P'YOO ah-VAHN-tee
Go down./Get off.	*Scenda.* SHEN-dah
Go straight ahead.	*Vada sempre dritto.* VAH-dah SEMP-reh DRFE-toh
Go up./Get on.	*Salga.* sal-gah
Here/There	*qui, qua/lì, là* kwee, kwah/LEE, LAH
I'm lost.	*Mi sono perso/a.* me soh-noh per-soh/sah

continues

It is far/near.	*È lontano/vicino.* AY lon-TAH-noh/vee-CHEE-noh
Take this street.	*Prenda questa strada.* pren-dah kweh-stah strah-dah
Turn around.	*Torni indietro.* tor-nee een-dee-YEH-troh
Turn left/right.	*Giri a sinistra/a destra.* jee-ree ah see-NEE-strah/ah des-trah
We're looking for …	*Cerchiamo …* cher-kee-YAH-moh

* Centro is the generic term used for "downtown"—usually where you'll find most of the action in any città.

Modes of Transportation (*I Mezzi di Trasporto*)

bicycle	*bicicletta* bee-chee-KLEHT-tah
bus	*autobus* OW-toh-boos
car	*automobile, macchina* ow-toh-MOH-bee-leh, MAH-kee-nah
ferry	*traghetto* trah-GHET-toh
subway	*metropolitana* meh-troh-poh-lee-TAH-nah
taxi	*tassì* tahs-SEE
train	*treno* treh-noh
the avenue	*il viale* eel vee-AH-leh

the dirt road	*la strada non asfaltata* lah strah-dah nohn ahs-fal-TAH-tah
the highway	*l'autostrada* l'au-toh-strah-dah
the road	*la strada* lah STRAH-dah
the street	*la via* lah vee-yah
the turnpike	*l'autostrada a pedaggio* l'ao-toh-STRAH-dah ah peh-DAH-joh

Train and Bus (*Il Treno e L'Autobus*)

It's a good idea to purchase bus tickets at a *cartoleria* (stationery store), *edicola* (newsstand), or *tabacchi* (tobacco store). (City buses don't accept cash or coins.) You can also buy *biglietti* (tickets) at train stations and from automated machines. When you get on *l'autobus*, you must validate your ticket with the time and date by punching the ticket into the small metal box usually affixed to a pole near the center of the bus. Whether you're traveling by *treno* or *autobus*, you'll need to know the following.

connection	*la coincidenza* lah koh-een-chee-DEN-zah
first/second class	*di prima/seconda classe* dee pre-mah/seh-KOHN-dah KLAHS-seh
one-way	*solo andata* soh-loh ahn-DAH-tah
railway	*la ferrovia* lah fer-roh-VEE-yah
restaurant car	*il vagone ristorante* eel vah-GOH-neh rees-toh-RAHN-teh

continues

round-trip	*di andata e ritorno* dee ahn-DAH-tah eh ree-TOR-noh
schedule	*l'orario* l'oh-RAH-r'yoh
sleeping car	*il vagone letto* eel vah-GOH-neh let-toh
the last stop	*il capolinea* eel kah-poh-LEE-n'yah
the stop	*la fermata* lah fer-MAH-tah
ticket	*il biglietto* eel beel-YET-toh
ticket counter, ticket office	*la biglietteria* lah beel-yet-teh-REE-ah
track	*il binario* eel bee-NAH-r'yoh
train	*il treno* eel treh-noh
train station	*la stazione ferroviaria* lah stah-zee-OH-neh fer-roh-vee-AH-r'yah
waiting room	*la sala d'attesa* lah sah-lah d'aht-TEH-zah

Cardinal Directions

north	*nord* nord
south	*sud* sood
east	*est* est
west	*ovest* oh-vest

In Italian, *le direzioni* refer to the poles. Keep in mind that most Italians follow the highways from town to town, as you'll see when confronted with the names of 12 cities and just as many arrows pointing you in opposite directions.

Taxi (*Tassi*)

Where's the nearest taxi stand?	*Dov'è il posteggio dei tassì più vicino?* doh-VAY eel poh-STEJ-joh dee tas-SEE P'YOO vee-CHEE-noh
I need a taxi.	*Ho bisogno di un tassì.* oh bee-ZOH-nyoh dee oon tas-SEE
I'd like to go …	*Vorrei andare … .* vor-REH ahn-DAH-reh
Stop here.	*Si fermi qui.* see fer-mee kwee
Please wait for me.	*Mi aspetti per favore.* mee ah-SPET-tee per fah-VOH-reh

Making the Trip (*Il Viaggio*)

How many kilometers to (Narni) from here?	*Quanti chilometri dista (Narni) da qui?* KWAHN-tee kee-LOH-meh-tree dee-stah (nar-nee) dah kwee
How much does it cost?	*Quanto costa?* KWAHN-toh koh-stah
I'd like a round-trip ticket to (Florence).	*Vorrei un biglietto di andata e ritorno per (Firenze).* vohr-RAY oon beel-YET-toh dee ahn-DAH-tah eh ree-TOR-noh per (fee-REN-zeh)

continues

I'd like a seat next to the window.	*Vorrei un posto accanto al finestrino.* vohr-RAY oon pohs-toh ahk-KAHN-toh ahl fee-neh-STREE-noh
I'd like to reserve a seat.	*Vorrei prenotare un posto.* vohr-RAY preh-noh-TAH-reh oon pohs-toh
Is (it) on time/late?	*È in orario/ritardo?* AY een oh-RAH-r'yoh/ree-TAR-doh
Is it close?	*È vicino?* AY vee-CHEE-noh
Is it far?	*È lontano?* AY lon-TAH-noh
Is there a connection?	*C'è la coincidenza?* ch'AY lah koh-een-chee-DEN-zah
On what track does the train leave?	*Su quale binario parte il treno?* su KWAH-leh bee-NAH-ree-yoh par-teh eel treh-noh
We're going to (Rome).	*Andiamo a (Roma).* ahn-dee-YAH-moh ah (roh-mah)
We're lost.	*Ci siamo persi.* chee see-YAH-moh per-see
What time does the train/bus leave for … ?	*A che ora parte il treno/l'autobus per … ?* ah kay oh-rah par-teh eel treh-noh/L'AU-toh-boos
When does (it) leave/arrive?	*Quando parte/arriva?* KWAHN-doh par-teh/ar-REE-vah
Where's the bus stop?	*Dov'è la fermata dell'autobus?* doh-VAY lah fer-MAH-tah deh-L'AO-toh-boos
Where's the waiting room?	*Dov'è la sala d'attesa?* doh-VAY lah sah-lah d'aht-TEH-zah

More Useful Travel Verbs and Expressions

For the more adventuresome (linguistically, that is), here are some commonly used travel-related verbs that might come in handy. Refer to the verb tables on pages 219–236 for additional terminology and a review of the verb *essere* (to be).

to be early	*essere in anticipo*
to be late	*essere in ritardo*
to be on time	*essere in orario*
to board	*imbarcare*
to change	*cambiare*
to come	*venire*
to commute	*fare il pendolare*
to go	*andare*
to go down/to get off	*scendere*
to go up/to get on	*salire*
to leave	*partire*
to lose	*perdere*
to return	*ritornare/tornare*
to take	*prendere*
to turn	*girare*

Chapter 5

Driving in Italy

Italy is known for its excellent roadways, many of which go back to ancient Roman times. In fact, we say *cavallo vapore* (horsepower) in honor of those resilient *Romani* and we can thank them for the current measurements used in everything from cars, trains, and planes to the space program. This chapter will help you navigate a number of situations you might encounter while driving a car in Italy.

Going By Car (*In Macchina*)

If you're going *nord* or *sud*, you'll want to take the main motorway, elegantly named the *Autostrada del Sole* (the Sun Highway) and abbreviated to the simple A1. (Remember to pronounce your "A" as in "Ah.") At each exit (*uscita*), you'll have to pay the toll (*pedaggio*) and you can use either cash or your credit card (*carta di credito*).

Additionally, you can purchase a magnetic card (Viacard) for use at the tollbooth or a Telepass that uses recognition technology and allows drivers to circumvent the tollbooths. If you need directions or want information about weather conditions, look for the *Punto Blu* (Blue Point) information signs. For more information, visit www.telepass.com/en/Private-owners/support/sales-network/blu-point.

Renting a Car (*Noleggiare una Maccina*)

Italians use two words to describe their vehicles: *l'automobile* and *la macchina* (which literally means "the machine"). Once you've collected your bags (*bagagli*) from the luggage collection area (*ritiro bagagli*), you'll head down toward the car rental area (*l'autonoleggio*). You'll often find better rates if you reserve a car from home, but if you're renting in person, ask about specials, particularly during the offseason (called *fuori stagione*) when there's less demand. Before you drive away, check your vehicle for existing scratches, dents, or damage so you won't be charged for them when you return the car.

How much does automobile insurance cost?	*Quanto costa l'assicurazione per l'auto?* kwahn-toh koh-stah l'ahs-see-koo-rah-tsee-OH-neh per l'ao-toh
How much does it cost … ?	*Quanto costa … ?* kwahn-toh koh-stah
per day	*al giorno* ahl jor-noh
per week	*alla settimana* ah-lah set-tee-MAH-nah
per kilometer	*al chilometro* ahl kee-LOH-meh-troh
I'd like to rent a car with automatic transmission.	*Vorrei noleggiare una macchina con il cambio automatico.* vohr-RAY noh-lehj-JAH-reh oo-nah MAHK-kee-nah kohn eel KAHM-bee-oh ow-toh-MAH-tee-koh
There's some damage.	*C'è un danno.* ch'AY oon dahn-noh

Rules (*Regole*)

Wearing a seatbelt (*una cintura di sicurezza*) is mandatory in Italy. Remember to stay in the right lane unless you're passing someone. And go easy on the horn—it's illegal to use it unless there's an emergency. Contrary to popular belief, Italian *autostrade* do have speeding limits. It's advisable not to exceed 50 km/h (about 30 mph) inside towns and residential areas and no more than 110 km/h (just less than 70 mph) on the expressway (*superstrada*). You can let loose on the highway (*autostrada*), which is 130 km/h (roughly 80mph). Watch out for motorcycles and Vespas, which are much more common in Italy.

Make sure you know whether your car requires *benzina* (the European equivalent to gasoline) or diesel before you need to fill up. Some stations are open all night but require a credit card; others will do the filling for you, especially when you're in small towns.

When traveling to Italy, your valid US driver's license will do, but there are advantages to getting an international driver's license, which can include discounts on the price of a rental. Call your local AAA office or home auto insurer for more details. (Note: Almost all European rental cars are stick shift. You need to specifically ask for an automatic transmission car if you don't know how to drive a manual transmission.)

The following list provides you with all the car talk terms you might require. Many car companies will also rent a GPS for directions. Simply ask. The letters are the same but pronounced *jee-pee-esse*. When you're done traveling, don't forget to check the trunk for your belongings before you hand over the keys.

accelerator	*l'acceleratore* l'ah-cheh-leh-rah-TOH-reh
air-conditioning	*l'aria condizionata* l'ah-ree-ah kohn-dee-zee-oh-NAH-tah
auto	*l'auto* l'au-toh
automobile	*l'automobile* l'au-toh-MOH-bee-leh
battery	*la batteria* lah baht-teh-REE-yah
brakes	*i freni* ee freh-nee

car	*la macchina* lah MAHK-kee-nah
carburetor	*il carburatore* eel kar-boo-rah-TOH-reh
door handle	*la maniglia* lah mah-NEEL-yah
engine, motor	*il motore* eel moh-TOH-reh
exhaust pipe	*il tubo di scarico* eel too-boh dee SKA-ree-koh
fan belt	*la cinghia del ventilatore* lah CHEEN-ghee-yah del ven- tee-lah-TOH-reh
fender	*il parafango* eel pah-rah-FAHN-goh
flat tire	*una gomma, una ruota a terra* oo-nah gohm-mah, oo-nah rwoh-tah ah ter-rah
gas	*la benzina* lah ben-ZEE-nah
gas cap	*il tappo del serbatoio* eel tap-poh del ser-bah-TOY-yoh
gas tank	*il serbatoio* eel ser-bah-TOY-yoh
gear stick	*il cambio* eel KAHM-bee-oh
glove compartment	*il casetto portaoggetti* eel kah-SET-toh por-tah-ohj-JET-tee
handbrake	*il freno a mano* eel freh-noh ah mah-noh
headlights	*i fari* ee fah-ree
hood	*il cofano* eel KOH-fah-noh
horn	*il clacson* eel clacson
hubcap	*il coprimozzo* eel koh-pree-MOH-tsoh

continues

ignition	*l'accensione* l'ah-shen-see-OH-neh
insurance documents	*i documenti dell'assicurazione* ee doh-koo-MEN-tee del-l'ahs-see-koo-rah-zee-OH-neh
jack	*un cric* oon kreek
keys	*le chiavi* leh kee-YAH-vee
license (driver's)	*la patente* lah pah-TEN-teh
license plate	*la targa* lah tar-gah
muffler	*la marmitta* lah mar-MEET-tah
oil	*l'olio* l'ohl-yoh
radiator	*il radiatore* eel rah-dee-ah-TOH-reh
radio	*la radio* lah RAH-dee-yoh
rear-view mirror	*lo specchietto retrovisore* loh speh-kee-YET-toh reh-troh-vee-SOH-reh
sign	*il segnale* eel sen-YAH-leh
spare tire	*la ruota di scorta* lah rwoh-tah dee skor-tah
spark plug	*la candela d'accensione* lah kan-DEH-lah d'ah-shen-see-OH-neh
speed limit	*il limite di velocità* eel LEE-mee-teh dee veh-loh-chee-TAH
speedometer	*il tachimetro* eel tah-KEE-meh-troh
steering wheel	*il volante* eel voh-LAHN-teh
tail light	*la luce di posizione* lah loo-ch'AY dee poh-zeet-zee-OH-neh

tire	*la ruota, la gomma* lah rwoh-tah, lah GOHM-mah
trunk	*il bagagliaio* eel bah-gahl-YAI-yoh
turn signals	*le frecce* leh freh-cheh
vehicle	*il veicolo* eel vay-EE-koh-loh
water	*l'acqua* l'ah-kwah
window	*il finestrino* eel fee-neh-STREE-noh
windshield	*il parabrezza* eel pah-rah-BREH-zah
windshield fluid	*il liquido lavavetri* eel LEE-kwee-doh lah-vah-VEH-tree
windshield wiper	*il tergicristallo* eel ter-jee-krees-TAHL-loh

On the Road (*Per Strada*)

police	*la polizia* la poh-lee-ZEE-yah
traffic officer	*il vigile/la vigilessa* eel VEE-jeh-leh/lah vee-jee-LESS-sah
This car is a rental.	*Questa macchina è a noleggio.* kweh-stah MAHK-kee-nah ay ah noh-LEH-joh
Can you show me on the map where I am?	*Mi può indicare dove sono sulla mappa?* me pwoh een-dee-KAH-reh doh-veh soh-noh sool-lah mahp-pah
Follow me.	*Mi segua.* mee seh-gwah

continues

How do I find this address?	*Come posso arrivare a quest'indirizzo?* koh-meh pohs-soh ahr-ree-VAH-reh ah kwest-een-dee-REE-tsoh
How many kilometers to ... ?	*Quanti chilometri dista ... ?* kwahn-tee kee-LOH-meh-tree dees-tah
How do I get to ... ?	*Come arrivo a ... ?* koh-meh ahr-REE-voh ah
Is this the correct road for ... ?	*È questa la strada per ... ?* ay kweh-stah lah strah-dah per
Is there traffic?	*C'è traffico?* ch'AY TRAHF-fee-koh
In which direction is ... ?	*In quale direzione è ... ?* een kwah-leh dee-reh-tsee-OH-neh ay

Make sure you have change for the toll (*pedaggio*) when you take your exit (*uscita*). The word *direzione* refers to your "direction." When asking for directions, use the word *indicazioni* ("indications").

Parking (*Parcheggio*)

Parking in Italy takes a combination of luck and skill. On-street parking is permitted, but you'll want to look out for the blue lines. Whether on the streets, *in centro*, or in the *piazza*, wherever you end up finding a parking space (*un posto macchina*)—especially in the city (*città*)—the first thing you'll want to look for is a parking meter (*un parchimetro*). The meter will ask you to prepay based on how long you'll be parking. After you've inserted the appropriate Euro amount or used a credit card (*carta di credito*), the meter will print out a small receipt (*scontrino*). Place this on the dashboard (*cruscotto*) so it's visible from the outside.

White lines indicate free parking, whereas yellow lines allow for disabled parking (permit required). If you see a green zone, parking is prohibited during workdays from 8:00 to 9:30 a.m. and again from 2:30 to 4:00 p.m.

The letters ZTL (*Zona Traffico Limitato* [Limited Traffic Zone]) enclosed in a red circle indicate restricted parking (either for residents [*residenti*] or for the local hotel or establishment). Unless you have a permit, avoid parking where you see ZTL.

Full It Up (*Fare il Pieno*)

In Italy, about 50% of the cars use diesel, which is called (confusingly) *il gasolio*. Incidentally, while more expensive, *il gasolio* provides excellent mileage per liter. Italians refer to the service station as *la stazione di servizio* and the gas station as *il benzinaio*. Keep these tips in mind:

- Make sure to ask which fuel your particular rental uses.

- Fill up often because Italy doesn't have as many stations as you might be accustomed to finding.

- Keep cash on hand for the self-service kiosks that are open 24/7. Although they accept most Italian debit cards, they might not necessarily accept your credit card.

- When available, allow the attendant to fill up your car. Just say *Mi fa il pieno grazie*. ("Fill it up thanks.") If you're just topping things off, you can also specify the amount.

10 Euro	*dieci Euro* dee-YEH-chee YEH-roh
20 Euro	*venti Euro* ven-tee YEH-roh
30 Euro	*trenta Euro* tren-tah YEH-roh
Where can I park?	*Dove posso trovare parcheggio?* doh-veh pohs-soh troh-VAH-reh par-KEH-joh
Is here good?	*Va bene qui?* vah beh-neh kwee
Is my car safe?	*La macchina è al sicuro?* lah mahk-KEE-nah ay ahl see-KOO-roh
Is there a parking meter?	*C'è un parcheggio a pagamento?* ch'AY oon par-KEHJ-joh ah pah-gah-MEN-toh
How much per hour?	*Quanto costa all'ora?* kwahn-toh koh-stah ahl-l'oh-rah

Signage (*Segnale Stradale*)

Signs are important to understand and you'll also hear people offer directions around certain signs and/or traffic signals. *Il cartello* refers to a notice, while *il segnale stradale* refers to a traffic notice. Keep in mind it's a lot easier to express what you need than to understand the response. You can always point to your map and smile. In the event you stop and ask for directions, you'll likely hear these common expressions.

Di fianco a ... dee fee-AHN-koh ah	Adjacent to ...
Dietro all'angolo ... dee-EH-troh ahl-AHN-goh-loh	Around the corner/block ...
All'entrata ... ahl-len-TRAH-tah	At the entrance ...
All'uscita ... ahl-loo-SHEE-tah	At the exit ...
Al semaforo ... ahl seh-MAH-foh-roh	At the traffic signal ...
In dietro a ... een dee-YEH-troh ah	Behind ...
Giù/su joo/soo	Down/up
Va fino in fondo. vah fee-noh een fohn-doh	Go all the way to the end.
Scenda ... shen-dah	Go down/Get off ...
Salga ... sahl-gah	Go up/Climb ...
Qui/Qua kwee/kwah	Here
Lì/Là* LEE/LAH	There
Davanti a ... dah-VAHN-tee ah	In front of ...
È vicino/lontano. AY vee-CHEE-noh/lohn-TAH-noh	It's near/far.
È proprio qui vicino. AY PROH-pree-yoh kwee vee-CHEE-noh	It's really close by.
Va sempre diritto. vah sem-preh dee-REET-toh	Keep going straight.
Vicino a ... vee-CHEE-noh ah	Near to ...

continues

| *Accanto a ...*
ah-KAHN-toh ah | Next to ... |
| *Giri a sinistra/destra al cartello.*
JEE-ree ah see-NEE-strah/
des-trah ahl kar-TEL-loh | Turn left/right at the sign. |

Deviazione	Detour
Divieto di ingresso	No Entrance
Divieto di sorpasso	No Passing
Divieto di sosta	No Parking
Sosta autorizzata	Parking Permitted
Doppio senso	Two-Way Traffic
Senso unico	One-Way Traffic

Motorcycles and Vespas (*Moto e Vespe*)

The same rules apply to motorcycles as they do to cars, but you'll find you have to deal with pedestrians, given Italy is a walker's haven. If you're planning to rent a Vespa (which sounds like a wasp, hence its name), your driver's license will do. Anything bigger than 125cc and you'll need to have an official motorcycle license.

If you're walking across the street and see a *motocicletta* (abbreviated to *la moto*) coming your way, keep your pace. It's not so much a game of chicken as it is about how drivers guide their way through *la folla* (the crowd). They'll expect you to keep going at the same speed. If you slow down or start to run, they won't know where you're headed. That's a crash waiting to happen.

An experienced rider should know the rules of the road. Common riding sense applies everywhere. Wear your helmet (*un casco*)—this is mandatory in Italy. Park in designated areas. Wear sunglasses (*occhiali da sole*) to protect your eyes. Cover your toes, knees, and elbows. Wear practical closed-toes shoes. If you have a rider holding onto your waist, make sure they're also wearing a helmet. And watch out for pedestrians!

Breakdowns and Other Issues (*Guasti e Problemi*)

Can you tell me where the nearest mechanic is?	*Mi può indicare dov'è il meccanico più vicino?* mee pwoh een-dee-KAH-reh doh-VAY eel MEK-kah-nee-koh p'YOO vee-CHEE-noh
The car has a flat tire.	*La macchina ha una gomma a terra.* lah MAHK-kee-nah ah oo-nah gohm-mah ah ter-rah
Can you change a tire?	*Mi può cambiare la ruota?* mee p'WOH KAM-bee-ah-reh lah rwoh-tah
Can you send a tow truck please?	*Può mandare un carro attrezzi per favore?* p'WOH man-DAH-reh oon kar-roh aht-TREH-tsee per fah-VOH-reh
The car needs oil/water.	*La macchina ha bisogno di olio/acqua.* lah MAHK-kee-nah ah bee-ZOH-nyoh dee ohl-yoh/ah-kwah
Here's my license.	*Ecco la mia patente.* ek-koh lah mee-yah pah-TEN-teh

continues

Here are my documents.*	*Ecco i documenti della macchina.* ek-koh ee doh-koo-MEN-tee del-lah MAHK-kee-nah
How long will the repairs take?	*Quanto tempo ci vuole per riparare la macchina?* kwahn-toh tem-poh chee vwoh-leh per ree-pah-RAH-reh lah MAHK-kee-nah
I've lost the keys.	*Ho perso le chiavi.* oh per-soh leh kee-AH-vee
My car has broken down.	*La macchina è guasta.* lah MAHK-kee-nah ay gwah-stah
My car won't start.	*La macchina non si mette in moto.* lah MAHK-kee-nah nohn see met-teh een moh-toh
When will it be ready?	*Quando sarà pronta?* kwahn-doh sah-RAH pron-tah

* When Italians refer to i documenti (the documents), they're referring to the registration and insurance cards.

Help! (*Aiuto!*)

In the event things don't go according to your plan (*piano*), the following phrases will enable you to summon help (*aiuto*) and assistance (*assistenza*).

Help!	*Aiuto!* eye-YOO-toh
I'm (he's/she's) hurt.	*Sono (è) ferito/a.* soh-noh (AY) feh-REE-toh/tah
Call an ambulance!	*Chiami un'ambulanza!* kee-YAH-mee oon-am-boo-LAHN-zah
Call the police!	*Chiami la polizia!* kee-YAH-mee lah poh-lee-TSEE-ah

Please write down your name and address.	*Per favore scriva il suo nome e indirizzo.* per fah-VOH-reh skree-vah eel soo-oh noh-meh eh een-dee-REE-tsoh
There's been an accident.	*C'è stato un'incidente.* ch'AY stah-toh oon-een-chee-DEN-teh
What's your insurance company?	*Qual'è la sua assicurazione automobilistica?* kwahl-AY lah soo-ah ahs-see-koo-rah-tsee-OH-neh ow-toh-moh-bee-LEE-stee-kah

Useful Links and Numbers

In case of emergency, use these phone numbers:

Police	113
Fire	115
Ambulance	118

Learn more about driving rules, regulations, and advice here: Automobile Club of Italy: www.aci.it.

In the event you're traveling during a health crisis, you can download an app called Immuni, which was created by the Ministry of Health to help track and limit the spread of COVID-19. To find out more and access the FAQ pages, check out www.immuni.italia.it.

For more information about travel in Italy, visit the National Italian Tourist Agency at www.enit.it/wwwenit/en.

Useful Travel Verbiage

The following verbs and phrases are given in their unconjugated forms.

to be prohibited	*essere vietato, essere proibito*
to break down	*guastare*
to check	*controllare*
to drive	*guidare*
to get a ticket	*prendere una multa*
to get off	*scendere da*
to get on	*salire su*
to give a ride	*dare un passaggio*
to leave	*partire*
to obey traffic signs	*rispettare i segnali stradali*
to park	*parcheggiare*
to return	*ritornare, tornare*
to run out of gas	*rimanere senza benzina*
to run/function	*funzionare*
to turn around	*tornare indietro*

How to Avoid Trouble

- **Keep an eye open for cameras:** Unless you're extremely proactive, don't be surprised if you receive a ticket (*una multa*) in the mail long after your trip is over. Surveillance cameras are now installed in small black metal boxes along most roads. You might not even notice them. But if you're speeding, they'll catch you! If you're dropping off at the airport and remain in place longer than the 10-minute limit, you'll probably get a ticket. Parking in cities is often determined by odd and even numbers. Make sure you're informed before you go to avoid unnecessary headaches and expenses.

- **Don't drink and drive:** Italy has become much stricter about drinking and driving. Penalties are stiff. According to Article 186 of the road regulations (*codice della strada*), a blood alcohol level exceeding 0.05% is considered intoxicated. If you're under 21 or have had your license for less than three years, that number goes down to zero. Unless you want to see the inside of an Italian jail, you're wise to designate a driver, called an *autista sobrio* (the sober driver). Otherwise, consider purchasing a keychain breathalyzer, called an *etilometro*, to keep handy in the event you're on your own.

- **Keep your hands on the wheel (*volante*):** As in most of Europe and North America, unless you're using a hands-free system in your car, it's illegal to text and drive in Italy.

- **Read the signs:** Italian signs conform to European standards. But there can be a lot of them all at once, and between the colors and the shapes, one might end up feeling a little bit like they're taking an intelligence test back in grade school. The blue highway signs indicate non-toll roads, while green refers to the *Autostrada*. You'll know when you've entered a town by the sign and you'll see the same sign with a red slash through it indicating you've left and can speed up past the 30-kilometer speed limit for when you're in the *centro*.

  - *Circles:* These generally tell you *not* to do something.

  - *Triangles:* These give warnings.

  - *Squares:* These are informational.

  o *Stop:* Stop signs, especially in smaller
    towns, aren't often adhered to, so don't
    assume the person coming from the
    other side is going to stop.

Remember that pedestrians have the right of way.
If you see someone trying to cross the road, even
though you might have the right of way, let them
cross. If you were the pedestrian, you'd expect the
same thing.

Tools (*Gli Attrezzi*)

In your travels, you might need a tool or two. Here
are some of the more commonly used.

first aid kit	*kit di pronto soccorso* kit dee pron-toh soh-KOR-soh
hammer	*il martello* eel mar-TEL-loh
flashlight	*la pila, la torcia* lah PEE-lah, lah TOR-chah
jumper cables	*i cavi con morsetti* ee KAH-vee kohn mor-SET-tee
monkey wrench	*la chiave inglese* lah kee-YAH-veh een-GLEH-zeh
pliers	*le pinze* leh peen-zeh
screwdriver	*il cacciavite* eel kah-chah-VEE-teh

Chapter 6

Home Away From Home

Maybe you're visiting Italy for the first time and want to ensure clear communications. Perhaps you're going to invest in a second home away from home. If you're staying in a hotel, chances are the staff speak enough English to assist you. If you're in an *agriturismo* (bed and breakfast), you'll need to be flexible and communicate your requirements in Italian. This chapter will help you with all your language and communication needs.

At Home (*A Casa*)

The Italian word for house is the same as it is for home: *casa*. Wherever you'll be, these terms describe a lot of the everyday objects you use.

In the Bathroom (*In Bagno*)

bathtub	*la vasca da bagno* lah vas-kah da BAHN-yoh
bidet	*il bidet* eel bidet
clothing dryer	*l'asciugatrice* l'ah-shoo-gah-TREE-cheh
hair dryer	*l'asciugacapelli* l'ah-shoo-gah-kah-PEL-lee
hand towel	*l'asciugamano** l'ah-shoo-gah-MAH-noh
mirror	*lo specchio* loh SPEH-kyoh
plunger	*lo sturalavandini* lo stoo-rah-lah-vahn-DEE-nee
soap	*il sapone* eel sah-POH-neh
shampoo	*lo shampoo* loh shampoo
shower	*la doccia* lah DOH-chah
sink	*il lavandino* eel lah-vahn-DEE-noh
tap	*il rubinetto* eel roo-bee-NET-toh
toilet	*la toilette* lah toilette
towel*	*l'asciugamano* l'ah-shoo-gah-MAH-noh
washing machine	*la lavatrice* lah lah-vah-TREE-cheh

* *A large beach towel is* telo da spiaggia (teh-loh dah spee-AH-jah).

While not necessarily the most romantic of topics, bathroom verbiage is a necessary part of life. Use the verb *fare* (to do/make) to express when you need to "take" something—for example, a shower. Almost all the expressions in English that use the idiom "to take" substitute with this verb in Italian.

The Verb *Fare* (to do/make)

io faccio ee-yoh FAH-choh	I do/make
tu fai too fye	you do/make (informal)
lui/lei/Lei fa louie/lay/lay fah	he/she makes/You do/make (formal)
noi facciamo noy fah-CHAH-moh	we make
voi fate voy FAH-teh	you do/make (plural)
loro fanno loh-roh FAHN-noh	they do/make

I'm taking a shower.	*Faccio la doccia.* FAH-choh lah DOH-chah
Gino takes beautiful pictures.	*Gino fa delle belle foto.* jee-noh fah del-leh bel-leh foh-toh
We're taking a vacation.	*Facciamo una vacanza.* fah-CHAH-moh oo-nah vah-KAHN-zah
It's cold/hot.	*Fa freddo/caldo.* fah FRED-doh/KAHL-doh
It's nice out.	*Fa bel tempo.* fah bel tem-poh
It's bad weather.	*Fa brutto tempo.* fah BROOT-toh tem-poh

In the Living Room (*Il Salotto*)

Many Italian living rooms are used exclusively for guests, while most "living" happens in the *cucina* (kitchen). That said, wherever you put your feet up, try your tongue at the following terms. Italians have a saying for everything, including this one: *Il mondo è fatto a scale: chi le scende e chi le sale.* (The world is made of stairs: those that go down and those that go up.) In other words, life has its ups and downs.

In Italian, the word for floor is *piano* (just like the instrument). The first floor (*primo piano*) is actually the floor above the ground floor (*pianterreno*) and equal to what's considered the second floor in the United States. By the way, the number 13 is considered *buona fortuna*—just the opposite from what one might expect. But watch out for 17 … .

armchair	*la poltrona* lah pohl-TROH-nah
bookshelf	*lo scaffale* loh skah-FAH-leh
couch	*il divano* eel dee-VAH-noh
door	*la porta* lah por-tah
entrance	*l'entrata* l'ehn-TRAH-tah
furniture	*gli arredamenti* ylee ar-reh-dah-MEN-tee
lamp	*la lampada* lah LAHM-pah-dah
painting	*il quadro* eel kwah-droh
photograph	*la foto* lah FOH-toh
plant	*la pianta* lah pee-AHN-tah

remote	*il telecomando*
	eel teh-leh-koh-MAHN-doh
stairs	*le scale*
	leh skah-leh
study	*lo studio*
	loh studio
television (TV)	*la televisione (la TV)*
	lah teh-leh-vee-ZOH-neh (lah tee-voo)
window	*la finestra*
	lah fee-NESS-trah

In the Kitchen (*La Cucina*)

See Chapter 7 for more food-related vocabulary.

bowl	*la ciotola*
	lah CHOH-toh-lah
burner	*il fornelllo*
	eel for-NEL-loh
coffeepot	*la caffettiera*
	lah kaf-fet-tee-EH-RAH
corkscrew	*l'apribottiglie*
	l'ah-pree-boht-TEEL-yeh
cup, mug	*la tazza*
	lah TAH-zah
dishwasher	*la lavastoviglie*
	lah lah-vah-stoh-VEEL-yeh
fork	*la forchetta*
	lah for-KET-tah
freezer	*il congelatore*
	eel kohn-jeh-lah-TOH-reh
frying pan	*la padella*
	lah pah-DEL-lah
glass	*il bicchiere*
	eel bee-kee-YEH-reh
iron	*lo stiro*
	loh stee-roh

continues

microwave	*il forno a microonde* eel for-noh ah mee-kroh-OHN-deh
mixer	*il frullatore* eel frool-lah-TOH-reh
oven	*il forno* eel for-noh
pantry	*la dispensa* lah dees-PEN-sah
plate	*il piatto* eel pee-YAHT-toh
refrigerator (fridge)	*il frigorifero (il frigo)* eel free-goh-REE-feh-roh (eel free-goh)
sink	*il lavandino* eel lah-vahn-DEE-noh
spoon	*il cucchiaio* eel kooh-kee-EYE-oh
teapot	*la teiera* lah TEH-yeh-rah
toaster	*il tostapane* eel tos-tah-PAH-neh

In the Bedroom (*La Camera da Letto*)

Almost every Italian bedroom has curtains (*le tende*) on the interior and shutters (*le persiane*) on the exterior. These provide privacy as well as insulation.

alarm clock	*la sveglia* lah svel-yah
bed	*il letto* eel let-toh
blanket	*la coperta* lah koh-PER-tah
chair	*la sedia* lah seh-d'yah
closet	*l'armadio* l'ar-MAH-d'yoh

curtains	*le tende* leh ten-deh
laundry	*il bucato* eel boo-KAH-toh
mattress	*il materasso* eel mah-teh-RAHS-soh
nightstand	*il comodino* eel koh-moh-DEE-noh
nursery	*la camera dei bambini* lah KAH-meh-rah dey bam- BEE-nee
pillow	*il cuscino* eel koo-SHEE-noh
rug	*il tappeto* eel tap-PET-toh
sheets	*le lenzuola* leh len-ZWOH-lah
shelf	*la mensola* lah MEN-soh-lah
shutters	*le persiane* leh per-zee-YAH-neh
single bed (twin)	*letto singolo* lah let-TOH SEEN-goh-lah

Locations: The Hotel and Nearby (*L'Albergo e Vicino*)

Location is everything. Perhaps you want your hotel to be in the heart (*cuore*) of the city and close to the action. Maybe you want a place that's slightly off the beaten track. A popular destination is the *agriturismo*. Literally, "agricultural tourism," such a venue offers visitors the opportunity to stay on a working farm while enjoying the products from it. There are quite a few options for where you can stay in Italy.

Agricultural tourism	*l'agriturismo* l'ah-gree-too-REEZ-moh
Apartment	*l'appartamento* l'ahp-par-tah-MEN-toh
Bed and breakfast	*il bed and breakfast* eel bed and breakfast
Estate	*la tenuta* lah teh-NOO-tah
Farm, ranch	*la fattoria* lah fat-toh-REE-yah
Hotel	*l'albergo* l'ahl-BER-goh
Inn	*la pensione* lah pen-see-OH-neh
Lodging	*l'alloggio* l'ahl-LOH-joh
Room for rent	*l'affittacamere* l'ahf-feet-tah-KAH-meh-reh
Villa	*la villa* lah veel-lah

Around Your Hotel

bar	*il bar* eel bar
barber	*il barbiere* eel bar-bee-YEH-reh
church	*la chiesa* lah kee-YEH-zah
clinic	*la clinica* lah KLEE-neh-kah
concierge	*il portiere* eel por-tee-YEH-reh
gift shop	*il negozio di regali* eel neh-GOH-zee-oh dee reh-GAH-lee
gym	*la palestra* lah pah-LEH-strah

hairdresser	*il/la parrucchiere/a* eel/lah par-rook-kee-YEH-reh/ rah
hospital	*l'ospedale* l'os-peh-DAH-leh
hotel	*l'albergo* l'ahl-BER-goh
housekeeper	*la cameriera* lah kah-meh-ree-YEH-rah
laundry service (including dry-cleaning)	*la lavanderia* lah lah-vahn-deh-REE-yah
parking	*il parcheggio* eel par-KEH-joh
pharmacy	*la farmacia* lah far-mah-CHEE-ah
room service	*il servizio in camera* eel ser-VEE-zee-oh een KAH-meh-rah
swimming pool	*la piscina* lah pee-SHEE-nah
tailor	*la sartoria* lah sar-toh-REE-yah

Italy has few laundromats. Generally, you must give your laundry to the hotel or bring it to a *lavanderia*, where it will be cleaned and pressed. You usually pay per piece and not by weight. You can also get something dry-cleaned at a *lavanderia*. Most Italian households have washing machines but generally hang their clothes to dry. Your best bet is to wash your clothes in the sink and let them dry overnight.

See Chapter 10 for more health-related vocabulary. Italian pharmacies are generally closed at night; major cities have 24/7 pharmacies but often on a rotating schedule. If you have health issues, find out where the local hospital is and how to call them in case of emergency.

Making Your Reservation

I'd like to make a reservation ...	*Vorrei fare una prenotazione ...* vohr-RAY fah-reh oo-nah preh-noh-tah-tsee-OH-neh
for one person.	*per una persona.* per oo-nah per-SOH-nah
for two/four people.	*per due/quattro persone.* per doo-eh/KWAHN-troh per-SOH-neh
How much does it cost ... ?	*Quanto costa ... ?* KWAHN-toh koh-stah
per day	*al giorno?* ahl jor-noh
per week	*alla settimana?* ah-lah seht-tee-MAH-nah
Is there a discount for ... ?	*C'è lo sconto per ...* ch'AY loh skon-toh per
seniors	*i pensionati?* ee pen-see-oh-NAH-tee
students	*gli studenti* ylee stoo-DEN-tee
I'm paying ...	*Pago ...* pah-goh
with cash.	*in contanti.* een kohn-tan-tee
by check.	*con assegno.* kohn ahs-SEN-yoh
with a credit card.	*con la carta di credito.* kohn lah kar-tah dee KREH-dee-toh
with a debit card.*	*con la carta di debito.* kohn lah kar-tah dee DEH-bee-toh

* *Italians informally use the term* Bancomat *to describe a debit card.*

Expressing Your Needs (*Esigenze*)

I'd like …	*Vorrei …* vor-RAY
I need …	*Ho bisogno di …* oh bee-ZOH-nyoh dee
I need …	*Mi serve …* me ser-veh
a room …	*una stanza …* oo-nah stan-zah
a single room …	*una singola …* oo-nah SEEN-goh-lah
a double room …	*una doppia …* oo-nah DOHP-pee-yah
with air-conditioning.	*con l'aria condizionata.* kohn L'AH ree-yah kohn-dee-zee-oh-NAH-tah
with a terrace.	*con terrazza.* kohn ter-RAH-tsah
with a private bathroom.	*con bagno privato.* kohn eel bah-nyoh pree-VAH-toh
Can you please wake me?*	*Mi può svegliare?* mee pwoh sveh-LYAH-reh
Is breakfast included?	*La colazione è compresa?* lah koh-lah-tsee-OH-neh AY kohm-PREH-zah
At what time is check-in/checkout?**	*Qual è l'ora di arrivo/partenza?* kwahl AY l'oh-rah dee ah-REE-voh/par-TEN-zah
Is everything included?	*È tutto compreso?* AY too-toh kohm-PREH-zoh
Did I receive any messages?	*Ho ricevuto dei messaggi?* oh ree-cheh-VOO-toh dey mes-SAH-jee

continues

I'd like to leave a message.	*Vorrei lasciare un messaggio.*
	vohr-RAY lah-SHAH-reh oon
	mehs-SAH-joh

* They might ask A che ora? *(At what hour?) Consult your numbers ahead of time to be ready.*
** You can use the English terms "check-in" and "checkout" or go for the Italian.

When you check out, you'll be given an invoice (*fattura*), bill (*conto*), or receipt (*ricevuta*). Take your receipts: Italian law requires it.

Services and In-Room Amenities (*I Servizi*)

I need a (an) ...	*Mi serve un (una) ...*
	mee ser-veh oon (oo-nah)
adaptor.	*adattatore.*
	ah-daht-tah-TOH-reh
alarm clock.	*sveglia.*
	sveh-lyah
ashtray.	*portacenere.*
	por-tah-CHEH-neh-reh
bathtub.	*vasca da bagno.*
	vah-skah dah BAHN-yoh
blanket.	*coperta.*
	koh-PER-tah
blow-dryer.	*asciugacapelli.*
	ah-shoo-gah-kah-PEL-lee
CD player.	*lettore CD.*
	let-TOH-reh chee dee
charger.	*caricabatteria.*
	kah-ree-kah-baht-teh-REE-yah
DVD player.	*lettore DVD.*
	let-TOH-reh dee voo dee
earbuds.	*auricolari.*
	ow-ree-koh-LAH-ree
elevator.	*ascensore.*
	ah-shen-SOH-reh

extension cord.	*prolungo.* pro-LOON-goh
fax machine.	*fax.* fax
heat.	*riscaldamento.* ree-skahl-dah-MEN-toh
headphones.	*cuffie.* KOO-fee-yey
ice.	*ghiaccio.* ghee-AH-choh
Internet.	*internet.* IN-ter-net
key.	*chiave.* lah kee-YAH-veh
laundry detergent.	*detersivo.* deh-ter-SEE-voh
outlet (electric).	*presa.* preh-zah
pillow.	*cuscino.* koo-SHEE-noh
remote control.	*telecomando.* teh-leh-koh-MAN-doh
refrigerator.	*frigorifero.* free-goh-REE-feh-roh
safe (deposit box).	*cassaforte.* kahs-sah-FOR-teh
shower.	*doccia.* DOH-chah
soap.	*sapone.* sah-POH-neh
stairway.	*scala, la scalinata.* skah-lah, lah skah-LEE-nah-tah
telephone.	*telefono.* teh-LEH-foh-noh
television (TV).	*television.* teh-leh-vee-zee-OH-neh
toilet paper.	*carta igienica.* kar-tah ee-JEN-ee-kah
towel.	*asciugamano.* ah-shoo-gah-MAH-noh

If you're traveling in pairs, it's best to clearly indicate what kind of bed you want. You might even need *un lettino in più* (an extra cot) for children.

There are also many options for rent in Italy, including Airbnb. It's wise to plan ahead to avoid unnecessary headaches. Plus, maybe you'll find a special deal (*un'offerta speciale*). Look at reviews to ensure you're renting from a reputable source.

Problems and Solutions (*I Problemi e Le Soluzioni*)

This room is too ...	*Questa stanza è troppo ...* kwes-tah stan-zah AY trohp-poh
cold/warm.	*fredda/calda.* fred-dah/kahl-dah
dark.	*buia.* BOO-yah
dirty.	*sporca.* spor-kah
small.	*piccola.* PEE-koh-lah
noisy.	*rumorosa.* roo-moh-ROH-zah
I can't sleep.	*Non posso dormire.* nohn pos-soh dor-MEE-reh
There's no hot water.	*Non c'è l'acqua calda.* nohn ch'AY l'ahk-wah KAHL-dah
The air conditioner doesn't work.	*Non funziona l'aria dizionata.* nohn foon-zee-OH-nah L'AH-ree-yah dee-zee-oh-NAH-tah
The toilet is clogged.	*La toilette è bloccata.* lah toy-let AY blohk-KAH-tah
The bathroom is dirty.	*Il bagno è sporco.* eel BAHN-yoh AY spor-koh

The sheets are soiled.	*Le lenzuola sono sporche.* leh len-ZWOH-lah soh-noh SPOR-keh
There's a bad smell in the room.	*C'è un'odore cattivo nella camera.* ch'AY oon-OH-doh-reh kah-TEE-voh nel-lah KAH-meh-rah
There's a monster under the bed.	*C'è un mostro sotto il letto.* ch'AY oon MOH-stroh soht-toh eel let-toh

Chores and Cleaning Terms (*Compiti e Pulizia*)

bleach	*la varecchina* lah vah-ree-KEE-nah
broom	*la scopa* lah skoh-pah
chores	*servizi di casa* ser-VEE-zee dee kah-zah
dish detergent	*il detersivo per i piatti* eel deh-ter-SEE-voh per ee pee-AHT-tee
dishwasher detergent	*il detersivo per la lavastoviglie* eel deh-ter-SEE-voh per lah lah-vah-stoh-VEEL-yey
dustpan	*la paletta* lah pah-LET-tah
grease cutter	*lo sgrassatore* loh skrahs-sah-TOH-reh
iron	*il ferro da stiro* eel fer-roh dah stee-roh
mop	*lavare la terra* lah-VAH-reh lah ter-rah
paper towels	*lah carta scottex* lah kar-tah skoh-tex
rag	*il cencio, la pezza* eel chen-cho, lah peh-zah

continues

sponge	*la spugna* lah spoon-yah
towel	*il telo* eel teh-loh
vacuum	*l'aspirapolvere* l'ah-spee-rah-POL-veh-reh

The Verb *Dovere* (to have to/must)

When you have a lot of things you have to do, you'll need the irregular modal verb *dovere* (to have to). Once conjugated, you can simply attach any one of the verb expressions listed below the conjugation table. Remember that the subject pronoun, while provided here, isn't necessary because the verb is already conjugated according to the subject. The subject pronouns, however, are used for emphasis and clarity.

io devo ee-yoh deh-voh	I have to
tu devi too deh-vee	you have to (informal)
lui/lei/Lei deve louie/lay/lay deh-veh	he/she has to/You have to (formal)
noi dobbiamo noy doh-bee-AH-moh	we have to
voi dovete voy doh-VEH-teh	you have to (plural)
loro devono loh-roh DEH-voh-noh	they have to

I must ...	*Devo ...* deh-voh
change the bed.	*cambiare il letto.* kahm-bee-YAH-reh eel let-toh
clean.	*pulire.* poo-LEE-reh

clear the table.	*sparecchiare il tavolo.* spah-reh-KYAH-reh eel TAH-voh-loh
do the wash.	*fare il bucato.* fah-reh eel boo-KAH-toh
dust.	*spolverare.* spol-veh-RAH-reh
fold clothes.	*piegare i vestiti.* pee-yeh-GAH-reh ee ves-TEE-tee
garden.	*fare giardinaggio.* fah-reh jar-deen-AHJ-joh
get rid of spiderwebs.	*togliere le ragnatele.* tol-YEH-reh leh rahn-yah-TEH-leh
iron.	*ferro da stiro.* fer-roh dah stee-roh
mop the floor.	*passare lo straccio sul pavimento.* pas-SAH-reh loh strah-cho sool pah-vee-MEN-toh
polish.	*lucidare.* loo-chee-DAH-reh
set the table.	*apparecchiare il tavolo.* ahp-pah-reh-kee-YAH-reh eel TAH-voh-lo
sweep the floor.	*spazzare il pavimento.* spah-TSAH-reh eel pah-vee-MEN-toh
tidy up.	*mettere in ordine.* ("to set in order") MET-teh-reh een OR-dee-neh
vacuum.	*passare l'aspirapolvere.* ("to pass the dust inhaler") pas-SAH-reh l'ah-spee-rah-POL-veh-reh
wash.	*lavare.* lah-VAH-reh
wash the windows.	*lavare i vetri.* lah-VAH-reh ee veh-tree

At the Hardware Store (*Ferramenta*)

If you need to go to a hardware store, look for the sign that says *Ferramenta*. DIY (do it yourself) in Italian is *il bricolage* (a.k.a. *il fai da te*).

I need a/an ...	*Mi serve un/una ...* me ser-veh oon (oo-nah)
axe.	*ascia.* ah-shah
blowtorch.	*cannello da saldatore.* kahn-NEL-loh dah sal-dah-TOH-reh
bolt.	*bullone.* bool-LOH-neh
broom.	*scopa.* skoh-pah
chisel (stone).	*scalpello.* scal-PEL-loh
chisel (wood).	*cesello.* cheh-ZEL-loh
clamp.	*morsa.* mor-sah
drill.	*trapano.* TRAH-pah-noh
file.	*lima.* lee-mah
hacksaw.	*seghetto.* seh-GHET-toh
hammer.	*martello.* mar-TEL-loh
key.	*chiave.* kee-YAH-veh
level.	*livella.* lee-VEL-lah
mallet.	*mazzuola.* maz-ZWOH-lah

measuring tape.	*metro a nastro.* meh-tro ah nas-troh
nail.	*chiodo.* kee-YOH-doh
nut.	*dado.* DAH-doh
paintbrush.	*pennello (small),* *pennellessa (large).* pen-NEL-loh, pen-nel-LES- sah
Phillips head screwdriver.	*cacciavite a stella.* kah-cha-VEE-teh ah stel-lah
plane (carpenter's).	*tavolo da carpentiere.* TAH-voh-loh da kar-pen- TYEH-reh
pliers.	*pinze.* peen-zeh
repairs.	*ripari.* ree-PAH-ree
sandpaper.	*carta vetrata.* kar-tah veh-TRAH-tah
saw.	*sega.* seh-gah
scraper.	*spatula.* SPAH-too-lah
screw.	*vite.* vee-teh
socket.	*presa elettrica.* preh-zah eh-LET-tree-kah
soldering iron.	*pistola saldatrice.* pees-TOH-lah sal-dah-TREE-cheh
square.	*squadra.* skwah-drah
thingamajig.	*aggeggio.* ah-JEH-joh
toolbox.	*cassetta degli attrezzi.* kah-SET-tah deh-ylee aht-TREZ-zee

continues

tool.	*attrezzo.* aht-TREZ-zoh
wire cutters.	*tronchese.* trohn-KEH-zeh
wire (metal).	*filo metallico.* feel-loh meh-TAHL-lee-koh
wrench.	*chiave inglese.* kee-YAH-veh een-GLEH-zeh

The Verb *Potere* (to be able/can)

Again, you'll find the verb *dovere* very useful here. An additional irregular verb worth including is *potere* (to be able to). The "potential" is infinite and the "possibilities" are endless with this verb. This verb is always followed by an infinitive verb.

io posso ee-yoh POHS-soh	I'm able to
tu puoi too poy	you're able to (informal)
lui/lei/Lei può louie/lay/lay poo-OH	he's/she's able to/You're able to (formal)
noi possiamo noy pohs-see-YAH-moh	we're able to
voi potete voy poh-TEH-teh	you're able to (plural)
loro possono loh-roh POH-soh-noh	they're able to

adjust	*aggiustare* ah-joos-TAH-reh
add (quantity)	*aumentare* ow-men-TAH-reh
apply	*applicare* ahp-plee-KAH-reh
attach	*attaccare* aht-tah-KAH-reh

bend, fold	*piegare*
	pee-yeh-GAH-reh
change	*cambiare*
	kahm-bee-YAH-reh
check	*controllare*
	kohn-troh-LAH-reh
cut	*tagliare*
	tahl-YAH-reh
detach	*staccare da*
	stah-KAH-reh dah
fix	*aggiustare*
	ah-joos-TAH-reh
fix up (organize, tidy up)	*mettere in sesto*
	MET-teh-reh een ses-toh
glue	*incollare*
	een-kol-LAH-reh
hammer	*martellare*
	mar-tel-LAH-reh
hit	*colpire*
	kol-PEE-reh
move	*spostare*
	spoh-STAH-reh
paint	*dipingere*
	dee-PEEN-jeh-reh
renovate	*rinnovare*
	ree-noh-VAH-reh
repair	*riparare*
	ree-pah-RAH-reh
restore	*restaurare*
	res-tau-RAH-reh
saw	*segare*
	seh-GAH-reh
scrape	*raschiare*
	ras-kee-YAH-reh

continues

screw	*avvitare* ah-vee-TAH-reh
separate	*separare* seh-pah-RAH-reh
supply	*fornire* for-NEE-reh
turn	*girare* jee-RAH-reh
twist	*torcere* TOR-cheh-reh
unscrew	*svitare* svee-TAH-reh
varnish	*verniciare* ver-nee-CHAH-reh

The Verb *Volere* (to want)

Every time you "volunteer" for something (like helping with the dishes), you're using a linguistic cousin of the irregular verb *volere* (to want). This verb can also be followed by an infinitive verb or an object. The verb used in its conditional form becomes *Vorrei* ("I'd like").

io voglio ee-yoh VOHL-yoh	I want
tu vuoi too vwoy	you want (informal)
lui/lei/Lei vuole louie/lay/lay VWOH-leh	he/she wants/You want (formal)
noi vogliamo noy vohl-YAH-moh	we want
voi volete voy voh-LEH-teh	you want (plural)
loro vogliono loh-roh VOHL-yoh-noh	they want

I don't want to clean the house.	*Non voglio pulire la casa.* nohn VOHL-yoh poo-LEE-reh lah kah-zah
The children want to play.	*I bambini vogliono giocare.* ee bahm-BEE-neh VOHL-yoh- noh joh-KAH-reh
The dog wants a biscuit.	*Il cane vuole un biscotto.* eel kah-neh VWOH-leh oon bees-KOHT-toh

Food & Eating

We need to eat to live. Italians take it a step further and live to eat! Appreciation of the culinary sciences is innate to Italy, whose *tradizioni* and diverse cultural heritage are exemplified by the varied diet found from one end of the boot to the other. This chapter will help you with all your food needs.

Food Stores (*Negozi di Alimentari*)

bakery	*la panetteria*
	lah pah-net-teh-REE-yah
bar	*il bar*
	eel bar
bread store	*il panificio*
	eel pah-nee-FEE-choh
butcher	*la macelleria*
	lah mah-chel-leh-REE-yah
dairy store	*la latteria*
	lah lat-teh-REE-yah
fish store	*la pescheria*
	lah pes-keh-REE-yah
floral shop	*il fioraio*
	eel fee-yoh-RY-yoh
grocery store	*la salumeria*
	lah sah-loo-meh-REE-yah
health food store	*l'erboristeria*
	l'er-boh-rees-teh-REE-yah
ice cream shop	*la gelateria*
	lah jeh-lah-teh-REE-yah
market	*il mercato*
	eel mer-KAH-toh
organic food shop	*il negozio di cibi biologici*
	eel neh-GOH-tsee-oh dee
	chee-bee byoh-LOH-jee-chee
pastry shop	*la pasticceria*
	lah pas-tee-cheh-REE-yah
shop, store	*il negozio*
	eel neh-GOH-tsee-yoh
supermarket	*il supermercato*
	eel soo-per-mer-KAH-toh
wine bar/store	*l'enoteca*
	l'eh-noh-TEH-kah

Fruits and Vegetables
(*Frutta e Verdura*)

apple	*la mela*
	lah meh-lah
apricot	*l'albicocca*
	l'ahl-bee-KOH-kah
artichoke	*il carciofo*
	eel kar-CHOH-foh
asparagus	*gli asparagi*
	ylee ahs-PAR-ah-jee
banana	*la banana*
	lah bah-NAH-nah
beans	*i fagioli*
	ee fah-JOH-lee
beet	*la barbabietola*
	lah bar-bah-BYEH-toh-lah
bell pepper	*il peperone*
	eel peh-peh-ROH-neh
cabbage	*il cavolo*
	eel KAH-voh-loh
carrots	*le carote*
	leh kah-ROH-teh
cauliflower	*il cavolfiore*
	eel kah-vol-FEE-yoh-reh
cherries	*le ciliegie*
	leh cheel-YEH-jeh
corn	*il mais*
	eel myss
date	*il dattero*
	eel DAHT-teh-roh
eggplant	*lu melanzana*
	lah meh-lan-ZAH-nah
figs	*i fichi*
	ee FEE-kee
fruit	*la frutta*
	lah FROO-tah
garlic	*l'aglio*
	L'AHL-yoh

continues

ginger	*lo zenzero* loh ZEN-zeh-roh
grapefruit	*il pompelmo* eel pom-PEL-moh
grapes	*l'uva* L'OO-vah
green beans	*i fagiolini* ee fah-joh-LEE-nee
hot pepper	*il peperoncino* eel peh-per-ohn-CHEE-noh
legumes	*i legumi* ee leh-GOO-mee
lemon	*il limone* eel lee-MOH-neh
lettuce	*la lattuga* lah laht-TOO-gah
melon	*il melone* eel meh-LOH-neh
mushrooms	*i funghi* ee FOON-ghee
olive	*l'oliva* l'oh-LEE-vah
onion	*la cipolla* lah chee-POHL-lah
orange	*l'arancia* l'ah-RAHN-chah
peach	*la pesca* lah PESS-kah
pear	*la pera* lah peh-rah
peas	*i piselli* ee pee-ZEHL-lee
persimmon	*il caco* eel KAH-koh
pineapple	*l'ananas* L'AH-nah-nahs
pomegranate	*il melograno* eel meh-loh-GRAH-noh
potatoes	*le patate* leh pah-TAH-teh

raisins	*l'uva secca* l'oo-vah seh-kah
spinach	*gli spinaci* ylee spee-NAH-chee
tomatoes	*i pomodori* ee poh-moh-DOH-ree
vegetables	*la verdura* lah ver-DU-rah
zucchini	*lo zucchino* loh zoo-KEE-noh

Herbs and Spices (*Erbe e Spezie*)

anise	*l'anice* L'AH-nee-cheh
baking powder	*il lievito in polvere* eel lee-EH-vee-toh een POL-veh-reh
baking soda	*il bicarbonato di sodio* eel bee-kar-boh-NAH-toh dee SOH-dyoh
basil	*il basilico* eel bah-ZEE-lee-koh
bay leaf	*la foglia di alloro* lah FOHL-yah dee ahl-LOH-roh
black pepper	*il pepe* eel peh-peh
brewer's yeast	*il lievito di birra* eel lee-EH-vee-toh dee beer-rah
capers	*il capperi* ee KAHP-peh-ree
chives	*le cipolline* leh chee-poh-LEE-neh
dill	*l'aneto* L'AH-neh-toh
flour	*la farina* lah fah-REE-nah
herb	*l'erbe* L'AH er-bah

continues

honey	*il miele* eel mee-YEH-leh
mint	*la menta* lah men-tah
mustard	*la senape* lah SEH-nah-peh
nutmeg	*la noce moscata* lah noh-cheh mos-KAH-tah
olive oil	*l'olio d'oliva* L'OHL-yoh doh-LEE-vah
oregano	*l'origano* l'oh-REE-gah-noh
paprika	*la paprika* lah pap-REE-kah
parsley	*il prezzemolo* eel preh-TSEH-moh-loh
rosemary	*il rosmarino* eel roz-mah-REE-noh
saffron	*lo zafferano* loh zaf-feh-RAH-noh
salt	*il sale* eel sah-leh
spice	*la spezia* lah spee-zee-AH
sugar	*lo zucchero* loh TSOO-keh-roh

Nuts (*Nocciole*)

almond	*la mandorla* lah MAHN-dor-lah
cashew	*l'anacardo* l'ah-nah-KAR-doh
chestnut	*la castagna* lah kah-STAH-nyah
hazelnut	*la nocciola* lah NOH-choh-lah
peanut	*la arachidi* lah ah-RAH-kee-dee

pecan	*la noce pecan*
	lah noh-cheh pecan
pistachio	*il pistacchio*
	eel pees-TAH-kyoh
walnut	*la noce*
	lah noh-cheh

Meat and Dairy Products (*Carne e Latticini*)

The root of the word *carnevale* (carnival) is *carne* (meat). Meat and poultry are best selected by your local butcher (*macellaio*). You'll find milk (*il latte*) and cheese (*formaggio*) at the dairy store (*la latteria*).

beef	*il manzo*
	eel mahn-zoh
butter	*il burro*
	eel boor-roh
cheese	*il formaggio*
	eel for-MAH-joh
chicken	*il pollo*
	eel pohl-loh
cold cuts	*i salumi*
	ee sah-LOO-mee
cream	*la panna*
	lah pahn-nah
cutlet	*la costoletta*
	lah koh-stoh-LET-tah
duck	*l'anatra*
	L'AH-nah-tra
eggs	*le uova*
	lay WOH-vah
fillet	*il filetto*
	eel fee-LET-toh
ham	*il prosciutto*
	eel proh-SHOO-toh
lamb	*l'agnello*
	l'ah-NYEL-loh

continues

liver	*il fegato* eel FEH-gah-toh
meat	*la carne* lah kar-neh
milk	*il latte* eel laht-teh
pork	*il maiale* eel my-AH-leh
pork chop	*la cotoletta di maiale* lah koh-toh-LET-tah dee my-AH-leh
quail	*la quaglia* lah KWAHL-yah
rabbit	*il coniglio* eel koh-NEE-lyoh
salami	*il salame* eel sah-LAH-meh
sausage	*la salsiccia* lah sal-SEE-chah
steak	*la bistecca* lah bees-TEK-kah
turkey	*il tacchino* eel tak-KEE-noh
veal	*il vitello* eel vee-TEL-loh
yogurt	*lo yogurt* loh yogurt

Fish Store (*Pescheria*)

anchovies	*le acciughe* leh ah-CHOO-geh
cod	*il merluzzo* eel mer-LOO-zoh
crab	*il granchio* eel GRAN-kyoh
fish	*il pesce* eel peh-sheh
flounder	*la passera* lah PAS-seh-rah

halibut	*l'halibut* l'ha-LEE-boot
herring	*l'aringa* l'ah-REEN-gah
lobster	*l'aragosta* l'ah-rah-GOHS-tah
mussel	*la cozza* lah koh-zah
oyster	*l'ostrica* L'OHS-tree-kah
salmon	*il salmone* eel sal-MOH-neh
sardines	*le sardine* leh sar-DEE-neh
scallops	*le cappesante* leh kahp-peh-sahn-teh
shrimp	*i gamberi* ee GAHM-beh-ree
sole	*la sogliola* lah sol-YOH-lah
squid	*i calamari* ee kah-lah-MAH-ree
swordfish	*il pesce spada* eel peh-sheh spah-dah
trout	*la trota* lah troh-tah
tuna	*il tonno* eel ton-noh
whitebait	*i bianchetti* ee hee-yahn-KET-tee

Sweets (*Dolci*)

candy	*la caramella* lah kah-rah-MEL-lah
chocolate	*la cioccolata* lah choh-koh-LAH-tah
cookie	*il biscotto* eel bees-KO-toh

continues

ice cream	*il gelato* eel jeh-LAH-toh
licorice	*la liquirizia* lah lee-kwee-REE-tsee-ya
mint	*la menta* lah men-ta

Kitchen Utensils and Appliances

appliance	*l'elettrodomestico* l'et-tro-doh-MES-tee-koh
blender, mixer	*il frullatore* eel frool-lah-TOH-reh
bottle opener	*l'apribottiglia* l'ahp-ree-boht-TEEL-yah
bowl	*la ciotola* lah CHOH-toh-lah
bread maker	*la macchina del pane* lah MAH-kee-nah del pah-neh
cabinet	*l'armadio* l'ahr-MAH-dee-oh
can opener	*l'apriscatole* l'ah-pree-SKAH-toh-leh
coffee grinder	*il macinino da caffè* eel mah-chee-NEE-no da kah-FAY
coffee maker	*la caffettiera* lah kaf-fet-tee-YEH-rah
colander	*lo scolapasta* loh skoh-lah-PAHS-tah
corkscrew	*il cavatappi* eel kah-vah-TAP-pee
cupboard	*la credenza* lah kreh-DEN-zah
cutlery drawer	*il cassetto delle posate* eel kah-SET-toh deh-leh poh-SAH-teh

cutting board	*il tagliere* eel tahl-YEH-reh
decanter	*la caraffa* lah kah-RAF-fah
eggcup	*il portauovo* eel por-tah-WOH-voh
fork	*la forchetta* lah for-KET-tah
fruit bowl	*la fruttiera* lah froot-tee-YEH-rah
funnel	*l'imbuto* l'eem-BOOT-toh
glass	*il bicchiere* eel beeh-kee-YEH-reh
grater	*la grattugia* lah graht-TOO-jah
gravy boat	*la salsiera* lah sal-see-YEH-rah
ice cream maker	*la macchina del gelato* lah MAH-kee-nah del jeh-LAH-toh
jar	*il barattolo* eel bah-RAT-toh-loh
jug	*la brocca* lah broh-kah
juice extractor	*l'estrattore di succo* l'eh-STRAH-tah-toh-reh dee sook-koh
knife	*il coltello* eel kol-TEL-loh
ladle	*il mestolo* eel MES-toh-loh
lid	*il coperchio* eel koh-PER-kee-oh
mug/cup	*la tazza* lah tah-zah
nutcracker	*lo schiaccianoci* loh skee-yah-chah-NOH-chee
orange squeezer	*lo spremiagrumi* loh spreh-m'yah-GROO-mee

continues

oven mitt	*la presina* lah preh-SEE-nah
pan	*la padella* lah pah-DEL-lah
pantry	*la dispensa* lah dees-PEN-sah
platter	*il vassoio* eel vah-ZOY-oh
pot	*la pentola* lah PEN-toh-lah
pressure cooker	*la pentola a pressione* lah PEN-toh-lah ah pres-see-OH-neh
rolling pin	*il mattarello* eel mat-tah-REL-loh
salad bowl	*l'insalatiera* l'en-sah-lah-tee-EH-rah
saucepan	*la pentola* lah PEN-toh-lah
scale	*la bilancia* lah bee-LAHN-chah
scissors (kitchen)	*le forbici da cucina* leh FOR-bee-chee da koo-CHEE-nah
skillet	*la padella* lah pah-DEL-lah
slow cooker	*la pentola a cottura lenta* lah PEN-toh-lah ah koht-TOO-rah len-tah
soup tureen	*la zuppiera* lah zoop-pee-YEH-rah
spatula	*la spatula* lah SPAH-too-lah
spice jar	*il barattolo delle spezie* eel bah-RAHT-toh-loh del-leh SPEH-zee-eh
spoon/teaspoon	*il cucchiaio/il cucchiaino* eel koo-kee-EYE-oh/eel koo-kee-eye-EE-noh
strainer	*il colino* eel koh-LEE-noh

sugar bowl	*la ciotola dello zucchero* lah CHOH-toh-lah del-loh ZOOK-keh-roh
tumbler	*il bicchiere* eel bee-kee-YEH-reh
utensil	*la posata, l'utensile da cucina* lah poh-ZAH-tah, l'oo-ten-SEE-leh dah koo-CHEE-nah
vegetable peeler	*la pelatrice* lah peh-lah-TREE-cheh
whisk	*il frullino* eel froo-LEE-noh
wooden spoon	*il cucchiaio de legno* el koo-kee-EYE-oh dee len-yoh

See Chapter 6 for additional terminology related to the kitchen.

Quenching Your Thirst (*Il Bere*)

As is the Italian way, certain times befit certain beverages. *Il cappuccino* is generally consumed in the morning with a *cornetto* (similar to a croissant). *L'espresso* can be consumed any time of the day but is usually taken after meals (never cappuccino). By the way, in Italy, all you need to do is ask for *un caffè* (a coffee) to get an espresso.

beer	*la birra* lah BEER-rah
coffee	*il caffè* eel kah-FAY
decaffeinated coffee	*il caffè decaffeinato* eel kah-FAY deh-kaf-feh-NAH-toh
drink	*la bibita* lah BEE-bee-tah

continues

freshly squeezed juice*	*la spremuta* lah spreh-MOO-tah
fruit juice	*il succo di frutta* eel sook-koh dee froot-tah
glass	*il bicchiere* eel bee-kee-YEH-reh
hot chocolate	*la cioccolata calda* lah choh-koh-LAH-tah kahl-dah
iced tea	*il tè freddo* eel teh fred-doh
lemon soda	*la limonata* lah lee-moh-NAH-tah
milk	*il latte* eel LAHT-teh
mineral water	*l'acqua minerale* l'ah-kwah mee-neh-RAH-leh
non-carbonated mineral water	*l'acqua minerale naturale* l'ah-kwah mee-neh-RAH-leh nah-too-RAH-leh
orange soda	*l'aranciata* l'ah-rahn-CHAH-tah
sparkling mineral water	*l'acqua minerale gassata/ frizzante* l'ah-kwah mee-neh-RAH-leh gas-SAH-tah/free-TSAN-teh
sparkling wine	*lo spumante* loh spoo-MAHN-teh
tea	*il tè* eel tay
wine	*il vino* eel vee-noh

* *If you want a freshly squeezed juice, ask for* una spremuta. *If you want a bottle of juice, ask for* un succo di frutta.

Fine Wine (*Vino*)

Italian wines fulfill one-fifth of the total world production. Finer wines are classified on the wine label as *denominazione di origine controllata* (DOC), which roughly translates to "denomination of origins checked," or *denominazione di origine controllata e garantita* (DOCG), "denomination of origins checked and guaranteed."

I'd like a glass/bottle of ...	*Vorrei un bicchiere/una bottiglia di ...* vohr-RAY oon bee-kee-YEH-reh/oo-nah boht-TEE-lyah dee
dry wine.	*vino secco.* vee-no sek-koh
house wine.	*vino della casa.* vee-no del-lah kah-zah
red wine.	*vino rosso.* vee-no rohs-soh
rosè wine.	*rosè.* roh-ZEH
sparkling wine.	*spumante.* spoo-MAHN-teh
sweet wine.	*vino dolce.* vee-no dohl-cheh
white wine.	*vino bianco.* vee-no bee-AHN-koh

A Bag, a Box, or a Can

Here are some useful requests for when you're food shopping. And while you might be used to fondling the fruit to find just the right one, in Italy, *non si tocca la frutta* (one doesn't touch the fruit).

I'd like ...	*Vorrei ...* vohr-RAY
Please give me	*Per favore mi dia ... .* per fah-VOH-reh mee dee-ah
Can you give me ... ?	*Mi può dare ... ?* mee pwoh dah-reh
I'll take	*Prendo ... .* pren-doh

continues

a bag of	*un sacchetto di* oon sahk-KEHT-toh dee
a bottle of	*una bottiglia di* oo-nah boht-TEE-lyah dee
a box of	*una scatola di* oo-nah SKAH-toh-lah dee
a can of	*una lattina di* oo-nah laht-TEE-nah dee
a dozen of	*una dozzina di* oo-nah doh-ZEE-nah dee
a kilo of	*un chilo di* oon kee-loh dee
a little of	*un po' di* oon poh dee
a pack of	*un pacchetto di* oon pahk-KEHT-toh dee
a piece of	*un pezzo di* oon peh-tsoh dee
a portion of	*una porzione di* oo-nah por-zee-OH-neh dee
a quarter pound of	*un etto di* oon eht-toh dee
a slice of	*una fetta di* oo-nah feht-tah dee
this	*questo* kweh-stoh
that	*quello* kwehl-loh

Restaurants (*Ristoranti*)

Food seems to be *una lingua internazionale* that everyone speaks. However, Italians understand that nourishment is only one aspect of food. In addition to eating, the table is a place to connect with friends (*gli amici*) and family (*la famiglia*) and to realign and relax. There are many wonderful kinds of eateries in

Italy. This brief guide will help you find your way to the right place.

- **Bar/Caffè:** The bar is a place for everyone to spend time and isn't limited to alcohol. You'll find panini, snacks, and light fare here.

- **Birreria:** A bar that specializes in *birra* (beer). Italian beers are wonderful and a nice alternative to wine.

- **Bruschetteria:** This is an establishment that specializes in bruschetta, essentially Italian toast with various toppings.

- **Enoteca:** Essentially a wine bar. Food is also served along with the wine samples available.

- **Gelateria:** This is an ice cream shop.

- **Locanda:** This is often a wine bar with nibbles.

- **Osteria:** This is usually a rustic local place with seasonal and regional delights.

- **Paninoteca/Panineria:** Like the name implies, bread and panini are offered here.

- **Pasticceria:** There are so many pastries and baked goods here, they could make you cry!

- **Pescheria:** As suggested by the name, *il pesce* (fish) is the specialty.

- **Pizzeria:** Pizza like you've never had before. Italians order their own personal pizza and get lots of toppings.

- **Ristorante:** Restaurant. This tends toward more formal dining.

- **Rosticceria:** You'll find lots of freshly prepared take-home items here.

- **Spaghetteria:** Spaghetti house. Pastas and additional main courses are offered here.

- **Taverna:** This is more like a pub. You'll find plenty of beer and lots of tapas.

- **Tavola Calda:** "Hot Table." This offers delicious takeout, usually ordered by the *porzione* (portion) or weight.

- **Trattoria:** This is less formal than a restaurant and often family-run.

At the Restaurant (*al Ristorante*)

Italian hospitality, especially in smaller establishments, is designed to make you feel at home. You won't be given a check until you ask for it. The Italian word for waiter is *cameriere*, but when calling out for someone, it's more polite to simply use *Signore* (sir) or *Signora/Signorina* (madam).

I'd like ...	*Vorrei ...* vohr-RAY
I'd like to make ...	*Vorrei fare una ...* vohr-RAY fah-reh oo-nah
a reservation ...	*prenotazione ...* preh-noh-tah-tsee-OH-neh
for (8:00) ...	*alle (otto) ...* ahl-leh (oht-toh)
for this evening.	*per stasera.* per stah-SEH-rah
for tomorrow.	*per domani sera.* per doh-MAH-nee seh-rah
for (two) people.	*per (due) persone.* per (doo-weh) per-SOH-neh

May we sit …	*Possiamo sederci …* pohs-see-YAH-moh seh-DER-chee
near the window?	*vicino alla finestra?* vee-CHEE-noh ahl-lah fee-NEH-strah
on the terrace?	*sul terrazzo?* sool ter-RAH-zoh
How long is the wait?	*Quanto tempo si deve aspettare?* kwahn-toh tem-poh see deh-veh ah-spet-TAH-reh
Make yourselves comfortable.	*AccomodateVi.* ah-koh-moh-DAH-teh vee
What do you recommend?	*Che cosa consiglia?* kay koh-zah kohn-SEE-lyah
What's the house special?	*Qual'è la specialità della casa?* kwahl-AY lah speh-chah-lee-TAH dehl-lah kah-zah
Waiter!	*Cameriere!* kah-meh-ree-YEH-reh
The check please.	*Il conto per favore.* eel kon-toh per fah-VOH-reh
We ate very well.	*Abbiamo mangiato molto bene.* ahb-bee-YAH-moh mahn-JAH-toh mol-toh BEN-neh

The Order of a Meal

L'insalata (the salad) is served after the main course.

l'antipasto l'ahn-tee-PAHS-toh	appetizer
il primo piatto eel pree-moh pee-YAHT-toh	first course
il contorno eel kohn-TOR-noh	side dish
il secondo piatto eel seh-KOHN-doh pee-YAHT-toh	second course

continues

il dolce eel dol-cheh	dessert

Special Needs (*Esigenze Speciali*)

I'm on a diet.	*Sono in dieta.* soh-noh een dee-YEH-tah
I'm a vegan/gluten-free.	*Sono vegano/a/ /senza glutine.* soh-noh VEH-gah-noh/ah/sen-zah GLOO-tee-neh
I'm a vegetarian.	*Sono vegetariano/a.* soh-noh veh-jeh-tah-ree-YAH-noh/ah
I'm allergic.	*Sono allergico/a.* soh-noh ahl-LER-jee-koh/ah
Do you serve kosher food?	*Servite del cibo kosher?* ser-VEE-teh del chee-boh koh-sher
I can't consume dairy/shellfish.	*Non posso consumare i latticini/i frutti di mare.* nohn pohs-soh kohn-soo-MAH-reh ee laht-tee-CHEE-nee/ee froot-tee dee mah-reh
That's enough.	*Basta così.* bah-stah koh-ZEE
That's just right.	*Va bene così.* vah beh-neh koh-ZEE
That's too much.	*È troppo.* ay trohp-poh

Baked, Broiled, Grilled ... (*Preparazioni*)

baked	*al forno* ahl for-noh
boiled	*bollito* bohl-LEE-toh
breaded	*impanato* eem-pah-NAH-toh
broiled	*alla fiamma* ahl-lah fee-YAH-mah

fried	*fritto*
	freet-toh
grilled	*alla griglia*
	ahl-lah greel-yah
marinated	*marinato*
	mah-ree-NAH-toh
medium	*normale*
	nor-MAH-leh
poached	*in camicia*
	een kah-MEE-chah
rare	*al sangue*
	ahl sahn-gweh
steamed	*al vapore*
	ahl vah-POH-reh
well-done	*ben cotto*
	ben koht-toh

Complaints (*Le Lamentele*)

Excuse me. We have a problem.	*Mi scusi, abbiamo un problema.*
	mee skoo-zee, ahb-bee-YAH-moh oon prob-LEH-mah
I can't eat this.	*Non posso mangiare questo.*
	nohn pohs-soh man-JAH-reh kwes-toh
This is ...	*Questo è ...*
	kwes-toh ay
burned.	*bruciato.*
	broo-CHA-toh
dirty.	*sporco.*
	spor-koh
overcooked.	*troppo cotto.*
	trohp-poh koht-toh
spoiled/not right.	*andato male.*
	ahn-DAH-toh mah-leh
too cold.	*troppo freddo.*
	trohp-poh fred-doh
too rare.	*troppo crudo.*
	trohp-poh kroo-doh

continues

too salty.	*troppo salato.* trohp-poh sah-LAH-toh
too spicy.	*troppo piccante.* trohp-poh pee-KAHN-teh
too sweet.	*troppo dolce.* trohp-poh dohl-cheh
unacceptable.	*inaccettabile.* een-ah-chet-AH-bee-leh
It's good, but my mother makes it better.	*È buono, ma mia madre lo fa meglio.* ay bwoh-noh mah mee-ah MAH-dreh loh fah MEH-lyoh

A Mini-Menu Reader

Italian food is as varied as the landscape. The following is a short glossary of dishes you might find on the menu (*la lista*).

First Course (*I Primi*)

The first course is usually a pasta, risotto, or soup. Most Italian restaurants will honor your request for *una mezza porzione* (half a portion), even if it's not listed as an option on the menu.

broth	*il brodo* eel broh-doh
ear-shaped pasta	*le orecchiette* leh oh-reh-kee-YEH-teh
egg drop soup	*la stracciatella* lah strah-chah-TEL-lah
lasagna	*la lasagna* lah lah-ZAN-yah
pasta with beans	*la pasta e fagioli* lah pas-tah eh fah-JOH-lee
potato dumpling pasta with tomato sauce	*gli gnocchi al sugo di pomodoro* ylee nyoh-kee ahl soo-goh dee poh-moh-DOH-roh

pumpkin ravioli with ricotta cheese	*i ravioli di zucca e ricotta* ee rah-vee-OH-lee dee zoo-kah eh ree-KOHT-tah
seafood risotto	*il risotto di mare* eel ree-SOHT-toh dee mah-reh
spaghetti in clam sauce	*le linguine alle vongole* leh leen-GWEE-neh ahl-leh VON-goh-leh
spaghetti in meat sauce	*gli spaghetti alla Bolognese* ylee spah-GHET-tee ahl-lah boh-loh-NYEH-zeh
tortellini with prosciutto and peas	*i tortellini con prosciutto e piselli* ee tor-tehl-LEE-nee kohn proh-SHOOT-toh eh pee-ZEL-lee
Tuscan country soup	*la zuppa di verdura Toscana* lah zoop-pah dee ver-DOO-rah tohs-KAH-nah
vegetable soup	*la minestrone* lah mee-neh-STROH-neh

Second Course (*I Secondi*)

The second course generally contains the protein of the meal. You'll have to choose whether you want meat (*la carne*), chicken (*il pollo*), or fish (*il pesce*).

breaded cutlet	*la cotoletta alla milanese* lah koh-toh-LET-tah ahl-lah mee-lah-NEH-zeh
duck with sherry	*l'anatra con vin santo* L'AH-nah-trah kohn veen san-toh
grilled chicken	*il pollo alla griglia* eel pohl-loh ahl-lah GREEL-yah
meatballs in tomato sauce	*le polpette al ragù* leh pol-PET-teh ahl rah-GU
monkfish with artichokes	*la coda di rospo con carciofi* lah koh-dah dee ros-poh kohn car-CHOH-fee
oxtail or veal shanks	*l'ossobuco* l'ohs-soh-BOO-koh

continues

roast lamb spiced with rosemary	*l'agnello arrosto al rosmarino* l'ah-NYEHL-loh ar-ROHS-toh ahl roz-mah-REE-noh
smoked sausage	*la salsiccia affumicata* lah sahl-SEE-chah ahf-foo-mee-KAH-tah
squid in tomato sauce	*i calamari alla marinara* ee kah-lah-MAH-ree ahl-lah mah-ree-NAH-rah
steak	*la bistecca* lah bees-TEK-kah
veal rolls cooked in wine	*gli involtini di vitello* ylee een-vol-TEE-nee dee vee-TEL-loh

Side Dishes and Appetizers (*I Contorni e Gli Antipasti*)

Italian *ristoranti* offer more side dishes (*contorni*) and appetizers (*antipasti*; literally, "before the meal") than could possibly be listed. Feel free to order a *contorno* as an appetizer.

baked fennel	*i finocchi al cartoccio* ee fee-NOH-kee ahl kar-TOH-choh
beans, anchovies, and garlic	*i fagioli alla veneziana* ee fah-JOH-lee ah-lah veh-neh-ZEE-ah-nah
boiled potatoes	*le patate bollite* leh pah-TAH-teh bohl-LEE-teh
fried calamari	*i calamari fritti* ee kah-lah-MAH-ree FREET-tee
fried zucchini	*gli zucchini fritti* ylee zoo-KEE-nee FREET-tee
green salad	*l'insalata verde* l'een-sah-LAH-tah ver-deh
grilled eggplant	*le melanzane alla griglia* leh meh-lan-ZAH-neh ahl-lah greel-yah

marinated artichoke hearts	*i cuori di carciofi marinati* ee kwoh-ree dee kar-choh-fee mah-ree-NAH-tee
prosciutto and melon	*il prosciutto e melone* eel proh-SHOOT-toh eh meh-LOH-neh
sautéed mushrooms	*i funghi trifolati* ee foon-ghee tree-foh-LAH-tee
skewered grilled shrimp	*gli spiedini di gamberi alla griglia* ylee spee-yeh-DEE-nee dee GAHM-beh-ree ahl-lah GREEL-yah
spinach tossed with garlic	*gli spinaci saltati con aglio* ylee spee-NAH-chee sal-TAH-tee kohn AHL-yoh
tomato salad	*l'insalata di Ppomodoro* l'een-sah-LAH-tah dee poh-moh-DOH-roh
various cheeses	*i formaggi* ee for-MAH-jee

Eating Etiquette

Eating is serious business in Italy and there are a few "rules" you should be aware of when traveling there. Just because you've eaten at Olive Garden doesn't make you an expert on Italian food. Here are a few tips to be aware of when eating in Italy.

• Avoid tourist traps and fixed menus. While it might be tempting to get a fixed price (*prezzo fisso*), your food will probably also be fixed— quickly and without a whole lot of love.

• Don't expect restaurants to serve dinner before 7:30 p.m. Italians tend to eat later than most North Americans.

- Italians never ask for cheese to put on pasta if it contains fish. This is a big no-no in Italian cuisine. This is because the flavor of the cheese will overpower the delicate flavor of the fish.

- Italians never drink a cappuccino after a meal.

- Italians always get more than one flavor when ordering ice cream (*gelato*).

- Italians order their own personal pizza and eat it with a knife and fork.

- Italians often indulge in an after-dinner liquor (*digestivo*) after their meal. Grappa, limoncello, Amaro, Cynar (made from artichokes), and Fernet Branca are popular.

- Italians don't overtip—they know *il conto* (the bill) includes a cover charge.

- Italians habitually don't ask for a doggy bag to take home their leftovers.

- Italians rarely use a spoon to eat spaghetti.

- Grandmothers will often kiss a piece of bread before throwing it away as a way to ask for forgiveness for any wasted food.

- Fish is often served deboned and with the head to show freshness. Shrimp aren't usually peeled.

- Meat sauce is either referred to as *ragù* or *bolognese*.

- Most special occasions are celebrated with prosecco, a dry sparkling white wine often consumed with desserts.

Shopping

Lo shopping is as much a part of your experience in Italy as anything else. This chapter will help you navigate many of the shopping encounters you might have while traveling. Just try not to spend all your money at once!

Exchanging Money (*Il Cambio*)

It helps to find an exchange that charges you a flat fee regardless of the amount you're changing. In addition, check the exchange rates to make sure you're not being shortchanged.

What's today's exchange rate?	*Qual è il cambio d'oggi?* kwahl AY eel KAHM-bee-oh dohj-jee
Can you give me small change?	*Mi può dare degli spiccioli per piacere?* mee pwoh dah-reh deh-ylee SPEE-choh-lee per pee-YAH-cheh-reh
I'd like to cash a traveler's check.	*Vorrei cambiare un traveler's check.* vohr-RAY kahm-bee-AH-reh oon traveler's check
Can you tell where I can find an ATM?	*Mi può dire dove posso trovare un Bancomat?* mee pwoh dee-reh doh-veh POHS-soh troh-VAH-reh oon BAHN-koh-mat

Types of Stores (*I Negrozi*)

bookstore	*la libreria* lah lee-breh-REE-yah
boutique	*la bottega* lah boht-TEH-gah
clothing store	*il negozio d'abbigliamento* eel neh-GOH-zee-oh dab-beel-yah-MEN-toh
cosmetics shop	*la profumeria* lah proh-foo-meh-REE-yah

department store	*il grande magazzino* eel gran-deh mah-gah-TSEE-noh
florist	*il fioraio* eel fyoh-RAI-yoh
furniture store	*il negozio d'arredamento* eel neh-GOH-zee-oh dar-reh-dah-MEN-toh
leather store	*la pelletteria* lah pel-let-teh-REE-yah
market	*il mercato* eel mer-KAH-toh
newspaper stand	*il giornalaio* eel jor-nah-L'YOH
pharmacy	*la farmacia* lah far-mah-CHEE-yah
shoe store	*il negozio di scarpe* eel neh-GOH-zee-oh
stationery store	*la cartoleria* lah kar-toh-leh-REE-yah
tobacco shop	*la tabaccheria* lah tah-bah-keh-REE-yah

Some Shopping Tips

Il centro commerciale (mall) is a common place to shop. Some purchases you make with a credit card might cover loss or damage. The I.V.A. (value-added tax) is a sales tax attached to all major purchases. Save your receipts—non-European travelers can apply for I.V.A. refunds when they leave the country. Ask your travel agency for details. Here's how to ask for a receipt:

May I have a receipt please?

Posso avere la ricevuta per favore?
pohs-soh ah-VEH-reh lah ree-cheh-VOO-tah per fah-VOH-reh

Shoe and Clothes Shopping

What size do you wear?	*Che taglia porta?* kay TAHL-yah por-tah
What size shoe?	*Che numero di scarpe ha?* kay NOO-meh-roh dee skar-peh ah
I wear size … .	*Porto la misura … .* por-toh lah mee-ZOO-rah
I wear shoe size … .	*Porto il numero … .* por-toh eel NOO-meh-roh
I'm just looking.	*Sto solo guardando.* stoh soh-loh gwar-DAHN-doh
Where's the fitting room?	*Dov'è il camerino?* doh-VAY eel kah-meh-REE-noh
This is too expensive.	*Questo è troppo caro.* kweh-stoh AY trohp-poh KAH-roh
price	*il prezzo* eel preh-tsoh
sale	*la svendita/gli sconti* lah SVEN-dee-tah/ylee skohn-tee
salesclerk	*il commesso/la commessa* eel kohm-MES-soh/lah kohm-MES-sah
shoe size	*il numero di scarpe* eel NOO-meh-roh dee skar-peh
shop window	*la vetrina* lah veh-TREE-nah
size	*la misura/la taglia* lah mee-ZOO-rah/lah TAHL-yah
small	*piccola* PEEK-koh-lah
medium	*media* MEH-dee-ah
large	*grande* GRAHN-deh

Fashion (*La Moda*)

There's a fun saying that says: Speak English, kiss French, drive German, and dress Italian. Italians have been paving the way in fashion, like the Romans and their roads, since ancient times. Fashions change—and the Italian word to describe fashion (*la moda*) literally translates to "the way." "Made in Italy" holds prestige and is synonymous with exclusivity. Standing out from the crowd is and always has been a reflection of the Italian spirit.

I'm looking for (a) (an) …	*Cerco* …
	cher-koh
article.	*l'articolo.*
	l'ar-TEE-koh-loh
bathing suit.	*il costume da bagno.*
	eel kos-TOO-meh dah BAHN-yoh
bra.	*il reggiseno.*
	eel reh-jee-SEH-noh
clothing.	*l'abbigliamento.*
	l'ah-beel-yah-MEN-toh
coat.	*il cappotto/il giubbotto.*
	eel kap-POHT-toh/eel joo-BOHT-toh
dress.	*l'abito.*
	L'AH-bee-toh
evening dress.	*l'abito da sera.*
	L'AH-bee-toh dah seh-rah
jacket.	*la giacca.*
	lah JAH-kah
jeans (a pair of).	*i jeans.*
	ee jeans
lining.	*la fodera.*
	lah FOH-deh-rah
pajamas.	*il pigiama.*
	eel pee-JAH-mah

continues

pants.	*i pantaloni.* ee pahn-tah-LOH-nee
pullover.	*il golf/il maglione.* eel golf/eel mahl-YOH-neh
raincoat.	*l'impermeabile.* l'eem-per-meh-AH-bee-leh
robe.	*l'accappatoio.* l'ah-kahp-pah-TOY'oh
skirt.	*la gonna* lah GOHN-nah
suit.	*il complete.* eel complete
sweat suit.	*la tuta da ginnastica.* lah too-tah dah jee-NAH-stee-kah
sweater.	*la maglia.* lah mahl-yah
T-shirt.	*la maglietta.* lah mahl-YET-tah
undershirt.	*la canottiera.* lah kah-noht-tee-YEH-rah
underwear.	*gli slip.* ylee sleep
briefs	*le mutande* leh moo-TAHN-deh
panties	*le mutandine* leh moo-tahn-DEE-neh

Tailor and Dry-Cleaner (*La Sartorial e La Lavendaria a Secco*)

There is ...	*C'è ...* ch'AY
a stain.	*una macchia.* oo-nah MAH-kee-yah

a missing button.	*un bottone che manca.* oon boht-TOH-neh kay mahn-kah
a tear.	*uno strappo.* oo-noh strahp-poh
Can you dry-clean this for me?	*Mi potete lavare questo a secco?* Mi poh-TEH-teh lah-VAH-reh kweh-stoh ah seh-koh
Can you mend/iron/starch this for me?	*Mi potete rammendare/ stirare/inamidare questo?* Mi poh-TEH-teh rahm-men-DAH-reh/stee-RAH-reh/ee-nah-mee-DAH-reh
When will it be ready?	*Quando sarà pronto?* kwahn-doh sah-RAH prohn-toh

Wardrobe Accessories (*Gli Accessori*)

accessories	*gli accessori* ylee ah-CHESS-oh-ree
belt	*la cintura* lah cheen-TOO-rah
boots	*gli stivali* ylee stee-VAH-lee
cosmetics	*i cosmetici* ee koz-MEH-tee-chee
gloves	*i guanti* ee GWAHN-tee
handkerchief	*il fazzoletto* eel fah-tsoh-LET-toh
hat	*il cappello* eel kah-PEL-loh
lingerie	*la biancheria intima* lah bee-yahn-keh-REE-yah EEN-tee-mah
pantyhose	*i collant* ee koh-LAHNT

continues

purse	*la borsa* lah BOR-sah
sandals	*i sandali* ee SAHN-dah-lee
scarf	*la sciarpa* lah SHAR-pah
shoes	*le scarpe* leh SKAR-peh
slippers	*le pantofole* leh pahn-TOH-foh-leh
sneakers	*le scarpe da tennis/ginnastica* leh SKAR-peh dah tennis/jee-NAH-stee-kah
socks	*il calzini* ee kal-ZEE-nee
stockings	*le calze* leh kal-zeh
umbrella	*l'ombrello* l'ohm-BREL-loh

Most smaller stores will offer a discount if you ask, especially if you're buying more than one item.

> Would you be able to give me a little discount by chance?
>
> *Mi può fare un piccolo sconto per caso?*
> mee pwoh fah-reh oon PEE-koh-loh skohn-toh per kah-zoh

Fabrics (*I Tessuti*)

Rather than spend a fortune on designer clothing, you might consider buying the fabrics and having a tailor (*sarto*) sew something custom-made to your style and fit.

| acetate | *l'acetato* l'ah-cheh-TAH-toh |
| cashmere | *il cachemire* eel cash-meer |

chiffon	*lo chiffon* loh sheef-FOHN
cotton	*il cotone* eel koh-TOH-neh
fabric/textile	*il tessuto* eel tes-SOO-toh
flannel	*la flanella* lah flah-NEL-lah
gabardine	*la gabardina* lah gah-bar-DEE-nah
knit	*la maglia* lah MAHL-yah
lace	*il merletto* eel mer-LET-toh
	il pizzo eel pcoz-zoh
leather	*il cuoio* eel KWOI-yoh
	la pelle lah pel-leh
linen	*il lino* eel LEE-noh
nylon	*il nylon* eel nylon
rayon	*il rayon* eel rayon
silk	*la seta* lah seh-tah
taffeta	*il taffetà* eel taf-feh-TAH
velvet	*il velluto* eel vel-LOO-toh
wool	*la lana* lah lah-nah

Jewelry (*I Gioielli*)

amethyst	*l'ametista* l'ah-meh-TEE-stah
aquamarine	*l'acquamarina* l'ah-qwah-mah-REE-nah
bracelet	*il braccialetto* eel brah-chah-LET-toh
cameo	*il cammeo* eel kah-MEH-oh
chain	*la catena* lah kah-TEH-nah
cufflinks	*i gemelli* ee jeh-MEL-lee
diamond	*il diamante* eel dee-ah-MAHN-teh
earrings	*gli orecchini* ylee oh-rek-KEE-nee
enamel	*lo smalto* loh SMAHL-toh
engagement ring	*l'anello di fidanzamento* l'ah-NEL-loh dee fee-dahn- zah-MEN-toh
gold	*l'oro* l'oh-roh
jade	*la giada* lah jah-dah
jewelry	*i gioielli* ee joy-EL-lee
mother-of-pearl	*la madreperla* lah mah-dreh-PER-lah
onyx	*l'onice* L'OH-nee-cheh
pearls	*le perle* leh per-leh
pendant	*il ciondolo* eel CHON-doh-loh
pewter	*il peltro* eel pel-troh

platinum	*il platino*
	eel PLAH-tee-noh
precious stone	*la pietra preziosa*
	lah pee-EH-trah preh-tsee-OH-zah
ring	*l'anello*
	l'ah-NEL-loh
ruby	*il rubino*
	eel roo-BEE-noh
sapphire	*lo zaffiro*
	loh ZAHF-fee-roh
silver	*l'argento*
	l'ah-ar-JEN-toh
topaz	*il topazio*
	eel toh-PAH-zee-oh
turquoise	*il turchese*
	oel toor-KEH-zeh
wedding ring	*la fede*
	lah feh-deh

Make sure you go to a reputable *gioielleria* (jewelry store) when making expensive purchases.

Cosmetics (*I Cosmetici*)

acne	*l'acne*
	l'ahk-neh
balm	*il balsamo*
	il BAHL-sa-moh
bangs	*la frangia*
	lah FRAHN-jah
barber	*il barbiere*
	eel bar-bee-YEH-reh
beauty salon	*il salone di bellezza*
	eel sah-LOH-neh dee bel-LEH-tsah
blush	*il fard*
	eel fard

continues

body	*il corpo* eel kor-poh
braid	*la treccia* lah TREH-chah
bronzer	*la terra abbronzante* lah ter-rah ahb-brohn-ZAHN-teh
clip	*il fermaglio* eel fer-MAH-lyoh
curler	*il bigodino* eel bee-goh-DEE-noh
esthetic	*l'estetista* l'eh-STEH-tee-stah
eyebrows	*le sopracciglia* leh soh-prah-CHEE-lyah
eyelashes	*le ciglia* lah chee-lyah
eyeliner	*la matita per gli occhi* lah mah-TEE-tah per ylee ohk-kee
eyes	*gli occhi* ylee ohk-kee
eyeshadow	*l'ombretto* l'ohm-BRET-toh
face mask	*la maschera per il viso* lah MAHS-keh-rah per eel vee-zoh
face	*il viso* eel vee-zoh
fake lashes	*le ciglia finte* leh chee-lyah feen-teh
foundation	*il fondotinta* eel fon-doh-TEEN-tah
freckle	*la lentiggine* lah len-TEE-jeh-neh
gel	*il gel* eel jel
gown	*la mantellina* lah man-tehl-LEE-nah

hair band	*il cerchietto* eel cher-KYEHT-toh
haircut	*un taglio di capelli* oon TAHL-yoh dee kah-PEL-lee
hair dye	*la tinta per capelli* lah teen-tah per kah-PEL-lee
hair removal	*la depilazione* lah deh-pee-lah-zee-OH-neh
hair tie	*l'elastico* l'eh-LAHS-tee-koh
hairdresser	*il parrucchiere* eel pah-rook-kee-YEH-reh
hairspray	*la lacca per capelli* lah lahk-kah per kah-PEL-lee
highlighter	*l'illuminante* l'ee-loo-mee-NAHN-teh
lip gloss	*il lucidalabbra* eel LOO-chee-dah-lahb-brah
liposuction	*la liposuzione* lah lee-poh-soo-tsee-OH-neh
lips	*le labbra* leh lahb-brah
lipstick	*il rossetto* eel roh-ZET-toh
liquid lipstick	*il rossetto liquido* eel roh-ZET-toh lee-kwee-doh
makeup	*il trucco* eel troo-koh
makeup remover	*lo struccante* loh stroo-KAHN-teh
manicure	*la manicure* lah mah-nee-KOO-reh
mascara	*il mascara* eel mahs-KAH-rah
massage	*il massaggio* eel mas-SAH-joh
nail care	*la cura delle unghie* lah koo-rah del-leh oon-ghee-ay
nail polish remover	*il solvent* eel solvent

continues

nail polish	*lo smalto* loh smahl-toh
nails	*le unghie* leh OON-ghee-ay
new style (haircut)	*un taglio nuovo* oon tahl-yoh nwoh-voh
pedicure	*la pedicure* lah peh-dee-KOO-reh
permanent	*la permanente* lah per-mah-NEN-teh
plastic surgery	*la chirurgia plastica* lah kee-yor-JEE-ah PLAH-stee-kah
plumper	*il rimpolpante* eel reem-pol-PAHN-teh
ponytail	*la coda* lah koh-dah
powder (face)	*la cipria* lah CHEE-pree-yah
razor	*il rasoio* eel rah-ZOY-yoh
scissors	*le forbici* leh FOR-bee-chee
sharpeners	*il temperamatite* eel tem-peh-RAH-mah-TEE-teh
shave	*una rasatura* oo-nah rah-zah-TOO-rah
shower gel	*il gel doccia* eel jel doh-chah
skin care	*la cura della pelle* lah koo-rah del-lah pel-leh
stylist	*lo stilista* loh stee-LEES-tah
same style (haircut)	*lo stesso taglio* loh stes-soh TAHL-yoh
tooth whitening	*lo sbiancamento dei denti* loh sbee-ahn-kah-MEN-toh dey den-tee
trim	*un'accorciatina, una spuntatina* oon-ah-kor-chah-TEE-nah, oo-nah spoon-tah-TEE-nah

wax	*la ceretta* ah ceh-RET-tah
wig	*la parrucca* lah pah-ROO-kah
wrinkle	*la ruga* lah roo-gah
I'd like …	*Vorrei …* vohr-RAY
I'm looking for …	*Cerco …* cher-koh
How much does it cost?	*Quanto costa?* kwahn-toh kohs-tah
I'd like to make an appointment.	*Vorrei fare un appuntamento.* vohr-RAY fah-reh oon ahp-pun-tah-MEN-toh
I'd like a cut.	*Vorrei un taglio.* vohr-RAY oon tahl-yoh
I'd just like a trim.	*Vorrei solo un'accorciatina.* vohr-RAY soh-loh oon-ah-kor-chah-TEE-nah
to blow dry	*asciugare con il phon* ah-shoo-GAH-reh kohn eel fohn
to cut hair	*tagliare i capelli* tahl-YAH-reh ee kah-PEL-lee
to dye hair	*tingere i capelli* TEEN-jeh-reh ee kah-PEL-lee
to iron hair	*stirare i capelli* stee-RAH-reh ee kah-PEL-lee
to make an appointment	*fare un appuntamento* fah-reh oon ahp-poon-tah-MEN-toh
to shave	*rasare, fare la barba (to shave your beard)* rah-ZAH-reh, fah-reh lah bar-bah
to straighten hair	*lisciare i capelli* lee-SHAH-reh ee kah-PEL-lee
to wash hair	*lavare i capelli* lah-VAH-reh ee kah-PEL-lee

continues

| to wax my legs | *fare la ceretta alle gambe*
fah-reh lah cheh-RET-tah ahl-
leh gahm-beh |

Electronics (*L'Elettronica*)

adapter	*l'adattatore* l'ah-daht-TAH-toh-reh
antivirus scan	*la scansione antivirus* lah skan-see-OH-neh ahn-tee- VEE-roos
battery	*la batteria, la pila* lah baht-teh-REE-yah, lah pee- lah
camera	*la macchina fotografica* lah MAH-kee-nah foh-toh- GRAH-fee-kah
clasp	*il gancio* eel GAHN-choh
computer	*il computer* eel computer
computer science	*l'informatica* l'een-for-MAH-tee-kah
desktop computer	*il computer da tavolo* ("the computer for the table") eel computer dah TAH-voh-loh
display (monitor)	*lo schermo* loh sker-moh
exposure	*l'esposizione* l'es-poh-zee-tsee-OH-neh
film	*la pellicola, il film* lah pel-LEE-koh-lah, eel film
filter	*il filtro* eel feel-troh
flash	*il flash* eel flash
hard drive	*l' hard drive* eel hard drive
headphones	*le cuffie* leh KOO-fee-yeh

keyboard	*la tastiera* lah tahs-tee-YEH-rah
laptop	*il computer portatile, il laptop* il computer por-TAH-tee-leh, eel laptop
lens	*l'obiettivo* l'oh-bee-yet-TEE-voh
memory	*la memoria* lah meh-MOH-ree-ah
memory card	*la scheda di memoria* lah skeh-dah dee mem-MOH- ree-ah
microphone	*il microfono* eel mee-KROH-foh-noh
monitor	*lo schermo* loh sker-moh
mouse	*il mouse* eel mouse
mouse pad	*il tappetino per il mouse* ("the little rug for the mouse") eel tahp-peh-TEE-noh per eel mouse
operating system	*il sistema operativo* eel sees-TEH-mah oh-per-ah- TEE-voh
printer	*la stampante* lah stam-PAHN-teh
program	*il programma* eel proh-GRAHM-mah
RAM	*la RAM* lah RAM
scanner	*lo scanner* loh scanner
software	*il software* eel software
speakers	*la casse* leh KAHS-seh
technology	*la tecnologia* lah tek-noh-loh-JEE-yah

continues

user	*l'utente* l'oo-TEN-teh
virus	*il virus del computer* eel virus del computer
watch	*l'orologio* l'oh-roh-LOH-joh
watchband	*il cinturino* eel cheen-too-REE-noh
webcam	*la webcam* lah webcam

to boot up	*inizializzare* ee-nee-zee-ah-lee-ZAH-reh
to compute	*calcolare* kahl-koh-LAH-reh
to copy	*copiare* koh-pee-YAH-reh
to cut	*tagliare* tahl-YAH-reh
to delete	*cancellare* kahn-chel-LAH-reh
to double click	*fare doppio clic* fah-reh DOH-pyoh clic
to download	*scaricare* scah-ree-KAH-reh
to drag and drop	*trascinare e lasciare* trah-shee-NAH-reh eh lah-SHAH-reh
to edit	*rivedere, aggiornare* ree-veh-DEH-reh, ah-johr-NAH-reh
to format	*formattare* for-maht-TAH-reh
to google	*googolare* goo-goh-LAH-reh
to highlight	*evidenziare* eh-vee-den-tsee-AH-reh
to load	*caricare* kah-ree-KAH-reh

to open	*aprire* ah-PREE-reh
to paste	*incollare* een-kohl-LAH-reh
to quit	*uscire* (to exit) oo-SHEE-reh
to save	*salvare* sahl-VAH-reh
to search	*cercare* cher-KAH-reh
to type	*digitare, battere* dee-jee-TAH-reh, BAHT-teh-reh
to word process	*elaborare i testi, gestire* eh-lah-boh-RAH-reh ee tes-tee, jes-TEE-reh

The monitor/computer doesn't work.	*Lo schermo/il computer è rotto.* loh sker-moh/eel com-PYOO-ter AY roht-toh
Can you fix this?	*Mi può aggiustare/riparare questo?* mee pwoh ahj-joo-STAH-reh/ree-pah-RAH-reh kweh-stoh
When will it be ready?	*Quando sarà pronto?* KWAHN-doh sah-RAH prohn-toh
My watch needs a new battery.	*Il mio orologio ha bisogno di una batteria nuova.* eel mee-oh oh-roh-LOH-joh ah bee-ZOHN-nyoh dee oo-nah baht-teh-REE-ah NWOH-vah
My camera isn't working.	*La mia macchina fotografica non funziona.* lah mee-ah MAHK-kee-nah foh-toh-GRAH-fee-kah nohn foon-zee-OH-nah
Do you have batteries?	*Avete delle batterie?* ah-veh-teh dehl-leh baht-teh-REE-yeh

Stationery Store (*La Cartoleria*)

In addition to office supplies, stationery, and candy, a stationery store (*la cartoleria*) often sells stamps and sometimes bus and subway tickets. It's also a good place to find inexpensive gift items.

candy	*le caramelle* leh kah-rah-MEL-leh
gift	*il regalo* eel reh-GAH-loh
guidebook	*una guida* oo-nah GWEE-dah
map	*la pianta, la cartina, la mappa* lah pee-YAHN-tah, lah kar-TEE-nah, lah map-pah
notebook	*il quaderno* eel kwah-DER-noh
paper	*la carta* lah kar-tah
pen	*la penna* lah PEN-nah
pencil	*la matita* lah mah-TEE-tah
postcard	*la cartolina* lah kar-tah-LEE-nah
stamp	*il francobollo* eel fran-koh-BOHL-loh
toys	*i giocattoli* ee joh-KAHT-toh-lee

In addition to typical stationery items, you can also ask for *un cavo USB* (a USB cable) and a SIM card for your phone, called *una scheda SIM*. If you're looking for printer paper, ask for *la carta per la stampante*. An ink cartridge is *una caruccia d'inchiostro*. Bluetooth is easy in Italian—it's the English word.

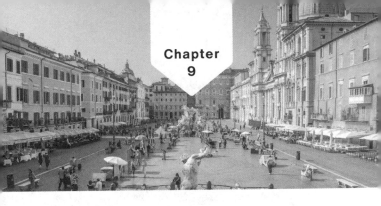

Chapter 9

Friendship & Romance

If there's one thing Italians know, it's love (*l'amore*). This chapter deals with relationships and offers the language you need to make a date or a new friend.

Love and Friendship
(*Amore e Amicizia*)

Do you want to go out this evening?	*Ti va di uscire insieme stasera?* tee vah dee oo-SHE-reh een-see-YEH-meh stah-SEH-rah
Today is our anniversary.	*Oggi è il nostro anniversario.* oh-jee AY eel nos-troh ahn-nee-ver-SAH-ree-oh
anniversary	*l'anniversario* l'ah-ahn-nee-ver-SAH-ree-oh
boyfriend	*il fidanzato*, il ragazzo* eel fee-dan-ZAH-toh, eel rah-GAH-zoh
celebration	*la celebrazione* lah cheh-leh-brah-tsee-OH-neh
date	*un appuntamento* oon ap-poon-tah-MEN-toh
engagement	*il fidanzamento* eel fee-dan-zah-MEN-toh
flowers	*i fiori* ee fee-OH-ree
friend	*l'amico/a* l'ah-mee-koh/ah
friendship	*l'amicizia* l'ah-mee-CHEE-zee-ah
girlfriend	*la fidanzata*, la ragazza* lah fee-dan-ZAH-tah, lah rah-GAH-zah
hug	*l'abbraccio* l'ah-BRAH-choh
honeymoon	*la luna di miele* lah loo-nah dee mee-YEH-leh
husband	*il marito/lo sposo* eel mah-REE-toh/loh spoh-zoh
kiss	*il bacio* eel bah-choh
love	*l'amore* l'ah-MOH-reh

lover	*l'amante* l'ah-MAN-teh
marriage	*il matrimonio* eel mah-tree-MOH-nee-yoh
nuptials	*le nozze* leh noh-tseh
relationship	*un rapporto, una relazione, una storia* oon rap-POR-toh, oo-nah reh- lah-zee-OH-neh, oo-nah STOH- ree-ah
romance	*il romanzo* eel roh-MAN-zoh
sex	*il sesso* eel sehs-soh
Valentine's Day	*il giorno di San Valentino* eel jor-noh dee san vah-len- TEE-noh
wife	*la moglie/la sposa* lah mohl-yeh/lah spoh-zah

* Fidanzato *and* fidanzata *are used interchangeably as boyfriend/*
girlfriend and fiancé/fiancée.

Love's Verbs
(*I Verbi D'amore*)

I'd like ...	*Vorrei ...* vohr-RAY
to caress you.	*accarezzarti.* ah-kah-reh-TSAR-tee
to court you.	*corteggiarti.* kor-teh-JAR-tee
to hug you.	*abbracciarti.* ah-brah-CHAR-tee
to (just) be friends.	*essere (solo) amici.* eh-SEH-reh (soh-loh) ah- MEE-chee
to kiss you.	*baciarti.* bah-CHAR-tee

continues

to make love with you.	*fare l'amore con te.* fah-reh l'ah-MOH-reh kohn teh
spend the rest of my life with you.	*passare tutta la mia vita con te.* pahs-SAH-reh too-tah lah mee-ah vee-tah kohn teh
to stay in touch.	*rimanere in contatto.* ree-mah-NEH-reh een kohn-TAH-toh

Getting Closer (*Avvicinarsi*)

Are you married?	*Sei sposato/a?* say spoh-ZAH-toh/ah
Can I have your phone number?	*Posso avere il tuo numero di telefono?* pohs-soh ah-VEH-reh eel too-oh NOO-meh-roh dee teh-leh-FOH-noh
Can I kiss you?	*Posso baciarti?* poh-soh bah-CHAR-tee
Can we meet again?	*Possiamo vederci ancora?* poh-SEE-yah-moh veh-DER-chee ahn-KOH-rah
Do you have condoms?	*Hai dei preservativi?** eye day pre-ser-vah-TEE-vee
Do you want to come home with me?	*Vorresti venire a casa mia?* vor-RES-tee veh-NEE-reh ah kah-zah mee-yah
Will you marry me?	*Mi sposi?* mee spoh-zee
Haven't we met before?	*Non ci siamo già conosciuti?* nohn chee see-YAH-moh jah koh-noh-SHOO-tee
How about dinner tonight?	*Ceniamo stasera?* cheh-nee-AH-moh stah-SEH-rah
What are you doing later/tomorrow/the day after tomorrow/forever?	*Cosa fai più tardi/domani/dopo domani/per sempre?* koh-zah fy p'YOO tar-dee/doh-MAH-nee/doh-poh doh-MAH-nee/per sem-preh

What did you say?	*Cosa hai detto?* koh-zah ay det-toh
What should we do?	*Che cosa facciamo?* kay koh-zah fah-CHAH-moh
What's a nice girl/guy doing in a place like this?	*Cosa ci fa un/a ragazzo/a come te in questo locale?* koh-zah chee fah oon/ah rah-GAH-zoh/ah koh-meh teh een kweh-stoh loh-KAH-leh
What's your name?	*Come ti chiami?* koh-meh tee kee-YAH-mee
What's your sign?	*Di che segno sei?* dee kay sen-yoh say
When?	*Quando?* KWAHN-doh
Why don't we meet?	*Perché non ci incontriamo?* per-KAY nohn chee een-kohn-tree-AH-moh
Would you like to go out?	*Vorresti uscire?* vor-RES-tee oo-SHE-reh
Your place or mine?	*Casa tua o casa mia?* kah-zah too-ah oh kah-zah mee-yah

* A false cognate—it doesn't translate to mean "preservatives." Another word for condoms is i profilattici.

Sweet Talk (*Le Parole Dolci*)

Che bello! is one of those *espressioni* you can use just about anywhere you go in Italy. It literally means "What beauty!" If the object of your praise is feminine, you would say *Che bella!*

Hey gorgeous!	*Ciao bellissimo/a!* chow bel-LEES-see-moh/ah
I care about you.	*Ti voglio bene.* tee vol-yoh beh-neh

continues

I don't have anyone.	*Non ho nessuno.* nohn oh nes-SOO-noh
I like you.	*Mi piaci.* mee pee-AH-chee
I love you.	*Ti amo.* tee ah-moh
I'm lonely.	*Mi sento solo/a.* me sen-toh soh-loh/ah
You're …	*Sei …* sey
beautiful.	*bellissimo/a.* bel-LEES-see-moh/ah
fascinating.	*affascinante.* af-fah-she-NAHN-teh
trouble.	*un disastro.* oon dee-ZAH-stroh
dangerous.	*un pericolo.* oon peh-REE-koh-loh
sweet as honey.	*dolce come il miele.* dol-cheh koh-meh eel mee-YEH-leh
Kiss me.	*Baciami.* BAH-chah-mee
Stay with me.	*Stai con me.* stahy kohn meh
You're nothing but trouble.	*Porti solo guai!* por-tee soh-loh gwai
What a mama's boy!	*Che Mammone!** kay mam-MOH-neh
What a princess!	*Che principessa!* kay preen-chee-PES-sah

* *This is the term used to describe an unmarried, adult male living at home and highly dependent on his mama. No equivalent word seems to exist for adult females.*

Excuses and Apologies (*Le Scuse*)

I'm sorry.	*Mi dispiace.* mee dees-pee-AH-cheh
I can explain.	*Posso spiegare.* pohs-soh spee-yeh-GAH-reh
I tried calling.	*Ho provato a telefonare.* oh pro-VAH-toh ah teh-leh-foh-NAH-reh
I lost your number.	*Ho perso il tuo numero di telefono.* oh per-soh eel too-oh NOO-meh-roh dee teh-LEH-foh-noh
I meant to call you.	*Volevo telefonarti.* voh-LEH-voh teh-leh-foh-NAR-tee
I've been really busy.	*Sono stato/a molto impegnato/a.* soh-noh stah-toh/ah mol-toh eem-peh-NYAH-toh/ah
I've been away.	*Sono stato/a via.* soh-noh stah-toh/ah via
Please forgive me.	*Perdonami.* per-DOH-nah-mee
I had a bad hair day.	*Ho avuto una brutta giornata.* oh ah-VOO-toh oo-nah broot-tah jor-NAH-tah
It's not a good time.	*Non è il momento giusto.* nohn AY eel moh-MEN-toh joos-toh
I have a headache.	*Ho mal di testa.* oh mal dee tes-tah

Italy's LGBT Culture

LGBT rights have come a long way and Italian attitudes have shifted toward a much greater acceptance of *all* people regardless of their sexual identity. Gay clubs are popular and displaying affection—already a cultural norm—is widely accepted, especially in larger cities. For more about Italian gay culture, visit www.arcigay.it.

bisexual	*bissesuale* bee-ses-soo-AH-leh
gay	*gaio* guy-oh
lesbian	*lesbica* LEZ-bee-kah
LGBT	*LGBTI* elle-jee-bee-tee-ee
partner	*compagno/a* kohm-PAHN-yoh/yah
platonic love (just friends)	*amore platonico* amor-eh plah-TOH-nee-koh

Family Planning

Birth control (*il controllo delle nascite*) is available in pharmacies and supermarkets. There are also condom vending machines often found outside a pharmacy (*farmacia*). Birth control pills are available through a prescription. (Note: In the following, the infinitive verb is offered in parentheses.)

I'm looking for …	*Cerco … (cercare)* cher-koh
I (don't) have …	*(Non) ho … (avere)* nohn oh

I brought ...	*Ho portato ...* oh por-TAH-toh
I use ...	*Uso (usare) ...* oo-zoh
abstinence.	*l'astinenza.* l'as-tee-NEN-zah
birth control.	*il controllo delle nascite.* eel kohn-TROL-loh deh-leh NAH-shee-teh
a condom.	*il preservativo, il condom.* eel preh-ser-vah-TEE-voh, eel condom
contraception.	*la contraccezione.* lah kon-trah-cheh-zee-OH-neh
a contraceptive.	*contraccettivo* oon kon-trah-cheh-TEE-voh
a diaphragm.	*il diaframma.* eel dee-ah-FRAHM-mah
a morning-after pill.	*la pillola del giorno dopo.* lah PEE-loh-lah del jor-noh doh-poh
a pill.	*la pillola, la pasticca.* lah PEE-loh-lah, lah pas-TEE-chah
a prescription.	*la ricetta medica.* lah ree-CHEH-tah MEH-dee-kah
a vasectomy.	*la vasectomia.* lah vah-sek-toh-MEE-yah

Dissing in Italian

You're ...	*Sei ...* say
a liar.	*un bugiardo/a.* oon boo-JAR-doh/ah
a lowlife.	*un delinquente.* oon deh-leen-KWEN-teh

continues

a witch.	*una strega.* oo-nah streh-gah
an idiot.	*un'idiota.* oon-ee-dee-OH-tah
a no-good trickster.	*un maledetto furbone.* oon mah-leh-DET-toh foor-BOH-neh
Calm down.	*Calmati.* (This phrase often has the opposite effect.) KAL-mah-tee
Chill!	*Tranquillo/a!* tran-KWEE-loh/ah
Take a chill pill.	*Non esaggerare.* (Don't exaggerate.) nohn eh-sah-jeh-RAH-reh
Go to hell!	*Va' all'inferno!* vah ah-leen-FER-noh

Texting Your Sweetheart (*Dolcezza*) in Italian

Here are a few of the most commonly used abbreviations used to text in Italian. A brief explanation will make them even more fun. For example, to say "you are" using the verb *essere*, use *sei*, which also happens to be the same word as the number 6. The sign for multiplication (x) is called *per* in Italian. The plus sign (+) is called *più* and is used to express "a lot."

You're the best	6la+	*Sei la migliore*
Where are you?	d6	*Dove sei?*
I love you	ta	*Ti amo*
I hate you	to	*Ti odio*
a bunch of kisses	xxx	*Tanti baci*
kisses and hugs	ba&ab	*Baci e abbracci*

Love	am	*amore*
Love forever	amxse	*Amore per sempre*
I miss you a lot	mm+	*Mi manchi molto*

The Florist (*Il Fioraio*)

carnation	*il garofano* eel gah-ROH-fah-noh
chrysanthemum	*il crisantemo* eel kree-SAN-teh-moh
daffodil	*la giunchiglia* lah joon-CHEEL-yah
daisy	*la margherita* lah mar-gheh-REE-tah
dandelion	*il dente di leone* eel den-teh dee leh-OH-neh
lily	*il giglio* eel JEEL-yoh
orchid	*l'orchidea* l'or-kee-DEYA
pansy	*la viola del pensiero* lah vee-OH-lah del pen-see-YEH-roh
poppy	*il papavero* eel pah-PAH-veh-roh
rose	*la rosa* lah roh-zah
sunflower	*il girasole* eel jee-rah-SOH-leh
violet	*la violetta* lah vee-yoh-LET-tah

Chapter 10

Staying Healthy

Like a car's engine, your body (*corpo*) requires regular maintenance. This chapter gives you the language you'll need to stay healthy and how to describe when you're not feeling your regular self. You'll also learn some Italian hand gestures.

Your Body (*Il Corpo*)

ankle	*la caviglia* la kah-VEE-lyah
appendix	*l'appendice* l'ahp-PEN-dee-cheh
arm	*il braccio* eel BRAH-choh
back	*la schiena* lah skee-YEH-nah
blood	*il sangue* eel sahn-gweh
body	*il corpo* eel kor-poh
bone	*l'osso* l'ohs-soh
brain	*il cervello* eel cher-VEHL-loh
breast	*il seno* eel seh-noh
buttock	*il sedere* eel seh-DEH-reh
chest	*il petto* eel peht-toh
chin	*il mento* eel men-toh
ear	*l'orecchio* l'oh-REK-kee-oh
eye	*l'occhio* l'oh-kee-yoh
face	*il viso, la faccia* eel vee-zoh, lah fah-chah
finger	*il ditto* eel dee-toh
foot	*il piede* eel pee-EH-deh
gland	*la ghiandola* lah ghee-AHN-doh-lah
hand	*la mano* lah mah-noh

head	*la testa* lah teh-stah
heart	*il cuore* eel kwoh-reh
joint	*l'articolazione* l'ar-tee-koh-lah-zee-OH-neh
knee	*il ginocchio* eel jee-NOHK-kee-loh
leg	*la gamba* lah gahm-bah
ligament	*il legamento** eel leh-gah-MEN-toh
mouth	*la bocca* lah bohk-kah
muscle	*il muscolo* eel MOO-skoh-loh
nails	*le unghie* leh oon-gyeh
neck	*il collo* eel kohl-loh
nose	*il naso* eel nah-zoh
shoulder	*la spalla* lah spahl-lah
skin	*la pelle* lah pehl-leh
stomach	*lo stomaco* loh STOH-mah-koh
throat	*la gola* lah goh-lah
toe	*il dito* eel dee-toh
tongue	*la lingua* lah leen-gwah
tooth	*il dente* eel den-teh
wrist	*il polso* eel pol-soh

* This word is also related to the Italian verb legare *(to tie).*

What Ails You? (*Che C'è?*)

What's the problem?	*Qual è il problema?* kwahl AY eel prohb-LEH-mah
Are you having trouble breathing?	*Ha problemi con la respirazione?* ah proh-BLEH-mee kohn lah res-pee-rah-zee-OH-neh
How do you feel?	*Come si sente?* (formal) koh-meh see sen-teh
	Come ti senti? (informal) koh-meh tee sen-tee
How old are you?	*Quanti anni ha?* KWAHN-tee AHN-nee ah
How long have you been suffering?	*Da quanto tempo soffre?* dah kwahn-toh tem-poh sohf-freh
Are you taking any medications?	*Prende delle medicine?* pren-deh del-leh meh-dee-CHEE-neh
Do you have any allergies?	*Ha delle allergie?* ah del-leh ahl-ler-GEE-eh
Do you suffer from … ?	*Soffre di … ?* sohf-free dee
Have you had … ?	*Ha avuto … ?* ah ah-VOO-toh
What hurts you?	*Che cosa Le fa male?* keh koh-zah leh fah MAH-leh

Headaches and Pain (*Mal di Testa e Dolori*)

I feel bad.	*Mi sento male.* mee sen-toh MAH-leh
I don't feel well.	*Non mi sento bene.* nohn mee sen-toh beh-neh
I'm exhausted.	*Sono esausto/a.* soh-noh eh-ZOW-stoh/ah

It hurts here.	*Mi fa male qui.* mee fah MAH-leh kwee
My (head) hurts.	*Mi fa male (la testa).** mee fah mah-leh (lah tes-tah)
I have/I suffer from …	*Ho/Soffro di …* oh/sohf-froh dee
a backache.	*mal di schiena.* mahl dee skee-YEH-nah
a bad heart.	*mal di cuore.* mahl dee kwoh-reh
a cough.	*la tosse.* lah tos-seh
a fever.	*la febbre.* lah feb-breh
a headache.	*mal di testa.* mahl dee tes-tah
nausea.	*la nausea.* lah NOW-zee-ah
a sore throat.	*mal di gola.* mahl dee goh-lah
a stomachache.	*mal di stomaco.* mahl dee STOH-mah-koh

* *Replace the word in parentheses with another word to describe your specific problem.*

abscess	*un ascesso* oon ah-SHEHS-soh
allergy	*un'allergia* oon-ahl-ler-JEE-ah
blister	*la vescica* lah veh-SHEE-kah
blood	*il sangue* eel sahn-gweh
broken bone	*un osso rotto* oon ohs-soh roht-toh
bruise	*un livido* oon LEE-vee-doh
bump	*una botta* oo-nah boht-tah

continues

burn	*una scottatura* oo-nah skoht-tah-TOO-rah
chills	*i brividi* ee BREE-vee-dee
constipation	*la stitichezza* lah stee-tee-KEH-tsah
cough	*la tosse* lah tohs-seh
cramps	*i crampi* ee kram-pee
diarrhea	*la diarrea* lah dee-ahr-REH-ah
dizziness	*le vertigini* leh ver-TEE-jee-nee
exhaustion	*l'esaurimento* l'eh-zow-ree-MEN-toh
fever	*la febbre* lah feb-breh
fracture	*una frattura* oo-nah frat-TOO-rah
headache	*il mal di testa* eel mahl dee teh-stah
indigestion	*l'indigestione* l'een-dee-jes-tee-OH-neh
insomnia	*l'insonnia* l'een-SOHN-nee-ah
lump (on the head)	*un bernoccolo* oon ber-NOHK-koh-loh
migraine	*l'emicrania* l'eh-mee-KRAH-nee-ah
nausea	*la nausea* lah NOW-zee-ah
pain	*un dolore* oon doh-LOH-reh
rash	*un'irritazione* oon-eer-ree-tah-zee-OH-neh
sprain	*una distorsione* oo-nah dee-stor-see-OH-neh
stomachache	*il mal di stomaco* eel mahl dee STOH-mah-koh

swelling	*un gonfiore* oon GOHN-fyoh-reh
toothache	*un mal di denti* oon mahl dee den-tee
wound	*una ferita* oo-nah feh-REE-tah

Disease (*Le Malattie*)

angina	*l'angina* l'an-GEE-nah
appendicitis	*l'appendicite* l'ap-pen-dee-CHEE-teh
asthma	*l'asma* l'ahz-mah
bronchitis	*la bronchite* lah bron-KEE-teh
cancer	*il cancro* eel kan-kroh
cold	*il raffreddore* eel rahf-fred-DOR-reh
diabetes	*il diabete* eel dee-yah-BEH-teh
dysentery	*la dissenteria* lah dees-sen-TEH-ree-yah
flu	*l'influenza* l'een-floo-EN-zah
German measles (rubella)	*la rosolia* lah roh-SOL-yah
gonorrhea	*la gonorrhea* lah goh-nor-REH-yah
gout	*la gotta* lah goht-tah
heart attack	*l'infarto* l'een-FAR-toh
hemophilia	*l'emofilia* l'eh-moh-FEEL-yah

continues

hepatitis	*l'epatite* l'eh-pah-TEE-teh
measles	*il morbillo* eel mor-BEEL-loh
mumps	*gli orecchioni* ylee oh-reh-kee-OH-nee
pneumonia	*la polmonite* lah pol-moh-NEE-teh
polio	*la poliomielite* lah poh-lee-oh-meel-YEE-teh
stroke	*il ictus* eel eek-tus
sunstroke	*il colpo di sole* eel kol-poh dee soh-leh
tetanus	*il tetano* eel TEH-tah-noh
tuberculosis	*la tubercolosi* lah too-ber-koh-LOH-zee
whooping cough	*la pertosse* lah per-TOHS-seh

Medical Emergencies

Help!	*Aiuto!* AY-yoo-toh
Call …	*Chiamate …* kee-ah-MAH-teh
an ambulance!	*un'ambulanza!* oon-ahm-boo-LAHN-zah
the paramedics!	*il pronto soccorso!* eel pron-toh sohk-KOR-soh
a doctor!	*un medico!* oon MEH-dee-koh
I'm allergic to … .	*Sono allergico/a a … .* soh-noh ahl-LER-jee-koh/ah ah
I can't breathe.	*Non posso respirare.* nohn pohs-soh reh-spee-RAH-reh
I have a wound.	*Ho una ferita.* oh oo-nah feh-REE-tah

I'm diabetic.	*Sono diabetico/a.* soh-noh dee-ah-BEH-tee-koh/ah
It hurts.	*Fa male.* fah mah-leh
There's a lot of blood.	*C'è molto sangue.* ch'AY mohl-toh sahn-gweh
Where's the hospital?	*Dov'è l'ospedale?* doh-VAY l'oh-speh-DAH-leh

At the Pharmacy (*Alla Farmacia*)

Do you have anything for … ?	*Avete qualcosa per … ?* ah-VEH-teh kwal-koh-zah per
Do you know where I can find an (all-night) pharmacy?	*Sa dove posso trovare una farmacia (notturna)?* sah doh-veh pohs-soh troh-VAH-reh oo-nah far-mah-CHEE-ah (noht-TOR-noh)
I need … .	*Ho bisogno di … .* oh bee-ZOH-gnoh dee
Is a prescription necessary?	*Mi serve una ricetta medica?* mee ser-veh oo-nah ree-CHET-tah MEH-dee-kah
ace bandage	*la fascia elastica* lah fah-shah eh-LAS-tee-kah
antibiotics	*gli antibiotici* ylee ahn-tee-bee-OH-tee-chee
antiseptic	*l'antisettico* l'ahn-tee-seht-TEE-koh
aspirin	*l'aspirina* l'as-pee-REE-nah
baby bottle	*il biberon* eel bee-beh-ROHN
Band-Aids	*i cerotti* ee cheh-ROHT-tee

continues

bandages	*le benda* leh ben-dah
body lotion	*la crema per il corpo* lah kreh-mah per eel kor-poh
brush	*la spazzola* lah SPAH-tsoh-lah
castor oil	*l'olio di ricino* l'ohl-yoh dee ree-CHEE-noh
comb	*il pettine* eel PET-tee-neh
conditioner	*il balsamo* eel BAHL-sa-moh
condoms	*i preservativi* ee preh-zer-vah-TEE-vee
contraception	*la contraccezione* lah kon-trah-cheh-tsee-OH-neh
cotton balls	*i batuffoli di cotone* ee bah-TOOF-foh-lee dee koh-TOH-neh
cotton swabs	*i cottonfioc* ee koh-TOHN-fee-yohk
cough syrup	*lo sciroppo per la tosse* loh shee-ROHP-poh per lah tohs-seh
deodorant	*il deodorante* eel deh-OH-doh-rahn-teh
diapers	*i pannolini* ee pahn-noh-LEE-nee
drug	*la medicina, il farmaco* lah meh-dee-CHEE-nah, eel FAR-mah-koh
eye drops	*il collirio* eel cohl-LEE-ree-oh
floss	*il filo interdentale* eel fee-loh in-ter-den-TAH-leh
gauze	*la garze* lah gar-zeh
heating pad	*l'impacco caldo* l'eem-PAH-koh kahl-doh

ice pack	*la borsa del ghiaccio* lah bor-sah del ghee-AH-choh
laxative	*il lassativo* eel lahs-sah-TEE-voh
mirror	*lo specchio* loh SPEH-kee-yoh
nail file	*la limetta* lah lee-MET-tah
nose spray	*le gocce per il naso* leh goh-cheh per eel nah-zoh
pacifier	*il ciuccio* eel choo-choh
pills	*le pastiglie* leh pas-TEEL-yeh
prescription	*la ricetta medica* lah ree-CHET-tah MEH-dee-kah
razor	*il rasoio* eel rah-ZOY-oh
safety pin	*la spilla di sicurezza* lah speel-lah dee see-koo-REH-stah
sanitary napkins	*gli assorbenti* ylee ahs-sor-BEN-tee
scissors	*le forbici* leh FOR-bee-chee
shampoo	*lo shampoo* loh sham-poh
shaving cream	*la crema da barba* lah kreh-mah dah bar-bah
sleeping pill	*il sonnifero* eel sohn-NEE-feh-roh
soap	*il sapone* eel sah-POH-neh
syringe	*la siringa* lah see-REEN-gah
talcum powder	*il talco* eel tal-koh
tampons	*i tamponi* ee tam-POH-nee

continues

thermometer	*il termometro*
	eel ter-moh-MEH-troh
tissues	*i fazzoletti*
	ee fah-tsol-LET-tee
toothbrush	*lo spazzolino da denti*
	loh spah-tsoh-LEE-noh dee den-tee
toothpaste	*il dentifricio*
	eel den-tee-FREE-choh
tweezers	*le pinzette*
	leh peen-ZEH-teh
vitamins	*le vitamine*
	leh vee-tah-MEE-neh

At the Dentist (*Dal Dentista*)

amalgam	*l'amalgama*
	l'ah-MAL-gah-mah
braces	*l'apparecchio per i denti*
	l'ap-pah-REH-kee-oh per ee den-tee
bridge	*il ponte*
	eel pon-teh
cavity	*la carie*
	lah KAH-ree-yeh
crown	*la corona*
	lah koh-ROH-nah
dentist	*il/la dentista* (m./f.)
	eel/lah den-TEE-stah
denture	*la dentiera*
	lah den-tee-EH-rah
extraction	*l'estrazione*
	l'eh-strah-ZEE-oh-neh
floss	*il filo interdentale*
	eel fee-loh in-ter-den-TAH-leh
gums	*le gengive*
	leh JEN-gee-veh
jaw	*la mascella*
	lah mah-SHEL-lah

nerve	*il nervo* eel ner-voh
oral hygiene	*l'igiene orale* l'ee-jee-YEH-neh oh-RAH-leh
painkiller	*un analgesico* oon ah-nahl-JEH-see-koh
plaque	*la placca dentale* lah plah-kah den-TAH-leh
tartar removal	*l'ablazione tartaro* l'ah-blah-zee-OH-neh tar-tah-ROH
throat	*la gola* lah goh-lah
tongue	*la lingua* lah leen-gwah
tooth	*il dente* eel den-teh
toothache	*il mal di denti* eel mahl dee den-tee
treatment	*il trattamento* eel trah-tah-MEN-toh
wisdom tooth	*il dente del giudizio* eel den-teh del joo-DEE-z'yoh
x-ray	*la radiografia* lah rah-dee-oh-grah-FEE-ah
Open/Close your mouth.	*Apra/Chiuda la bocca.* ah-prah/kyoo-dah lah bohk-kah
Rinse.	*Si sciacqui.* see shah-kwee
Does this hurt?	*Fa male?* fah mah-leh
When was your last appointment?	*Quando è stata la Sua ultima visita?* quan-doh ay stah-tah lah soo-ah OOL-tee-mah VEE-zee-tah
I'd like to schedule a follow-up appointment.	*Vorrei programmare una visita di controllo.* vohr-RAY prog-ram-MAH-reh oo-nah vee-ZEE-tah dee kohn-TROL-loh

continues

At the Optician (*Dall'Ottico*)

astigmatism	*l'astigmatismo* l'ah-steeg-mah-TEEZ-moh
contact lens	*le lenti a contatto* lah len-tee ah kohn-TAH-toh
eyes	*gli occhi* ylee oh-kee
far-sighted	*presbite* PRES-bee-teh
frame	*la montatura* lah mon-tah-TOO-rah
glasses	*gli occhiali* ylee oh-kee-AH-lee
lens	*le lenti* leh len-tee
near-sighted	*miope* mee-OH-peh
prescription	*la ricetta medica* lah ree-CHET-tah MEH-dee-kah
sunglasses	*gli occhiali da sole* ylee oh-kee-AH-lee dah soh-leh

Talking With Your Hands (*Gesticulazioni*)

There are a few hand gestures Italians use that have universal meaning. The history of gestures goes back to when Italy was a collection of city-states and monarchies, each owned by a different faction or family. Everyone spoke dialects—there was no central language.

As a result, people developed visuals to express themselves and it's hard not to know what someone's saying when they use them. The middle finger seems to have universal meaning. That said, be wary of your hands: What might seem like an innocent gesture (such as the thumbs-up signal) might have an entirely different meaning in a foreign country. Best to keep your hands in your pockets and placed in your lap unless you know exactly what you're saying without words.

Your fingertips are brought together with your thumb, and then as you gently point upward, move your wrist.	Give me a break!
Your hands are held up in front with fingers brought together and slightly flicked.	What the heck?
Your index finger is pointed to your cheek.	Mmmmmmm! Yummy! (used for food and for a very attractive person)
Cross your fingers in the form of an X.	I swear! Your secret is safe with me.
Pull your eyelid down with your index finger.	I've got my eyes open! I'm watching!
Bring your fingers together and point them toward your open mouth.	I'm starving!
Rub your belly in circles.	I'm full.
Stick your thumb out toward your open mouth.	I'm thirsty!
Wave behind your shoulder.	A long, long time ago

continues

Bite your hand while scrunching your face.	Don't make me get upset. You're in big trouble.
Tap the side of your temple.	You're crazy.
Smack your forehead with an open palm.	Argh! I forgot! I'm an imbecile!
Fan your fingers beneath your chin outward and flick your chin.	I really don't care.
Place your hands together as if in prayer and put them next to your tilted ear. Close your eyes.	I'm ready for bed.

Chapter 11

Business & Communications

Whether you're traveling for business or pleasure, a few skills can take you a long way, including making phone calls, writing emails, and being able to read and understand a contract or balance statement. This chapter includes these topics as well as computer lingo, technology terms, and some sports words.

The Telephone (*Il Telefono*)

Like most places, Italy has come a long way since the days when you used tokens (*gettoni*) specifically designed for the ubiquitous telephone booths that used to dot every piazza and town square. These days, most people rely on their *cellulare* (cell phone).

Find out ahead of time any local numbers (*numeri di telefono*) you might need. Italian area codes (*prefissi*) can be a little tricky; if the number (*numero*) begins with a zero, it's sometimes dropped when dialing from abroad. For a conference call, Italians say *una teleconferenza* (oo-nah teh-leh-kohn-feh-REN-zah).

international call*	*una telefonata internazionale* oo-nah teh-leh-foh-NAH-tah een-ter-nah-zee-yoh-NAH-leh
local call	*una telefonata urbana* oo-nah teh-leh-foh-NAH-tah oor-BAH-nah
long-distance call	*una telefonata interurbana* oo-nah teh-leh-foh-NAH-tah een-ter-oor-BAH-nah
operator/receptionist	*centralinista telefonico* chen-tra-lee-NEES-tah teh-leh-FOH-nee-koh

* *Within Europe*

bill	*la fattura* lah faht-TOO-rah
conversation/discussion*	*la conversazione* lah kohn-ver-sah-tsee-YOH-neh
home network	*la rete d'origine* lah REH-teh d'oh-REE-jee-neh
network	*la rete* ("the net") lah REH-teh
outside network (visited network)	*la rete ospitante* ("host network") lah REH-teh ohs-pee-TAHN-teh

* *The word* discussione *refers to an "argument," while the word* argomento *actually refers to the notion of "subject" (like in academia).*

data	*i dati* ee DAH-tee
roaming service	*il servizio di dati in roaming* eel ser-VEE-zee-yoh roaming
geographic (location) data	*i dati geografici* ee DAH-tee jay-oh-GRAH-fee-chee
Internet service provider	*il fornitore di internet* eel for-nee-TOH-reh dee in-TEHR-net
purchases	*gli acquisti* ylee ah-KWEES-tee
ringtones	*le suonerie* leh swoh-neh-REE-yeh
automatic debit	*l'addebito diretto* l'ad-DEH-bee-toh dee-RET-toh
call rates	*il costo delle chiamate* eel kos-stoh del-leh kee-yah-MAH-teh
price	*il prezzo* eel preh-tsoh
services	*i servizi* ee ser-VEE-zee
speaker	*l'altoparlante* l'ahl-toh-par-LAHN-teh
sale	*la vendita* lah VEN-dee-tah
technology	*la tecnologia* lah tek-noh-loh-JEE-ah
I have ...	*Ho ...* oh
a question.	*una domanda.* oo-nah doh-MAHN-dah
a request.	*una richiesta.* oo-nah ree-KYES-tah
I need ...	*Mi serve ...* mee ser-veh

continues

assistance.	*assistenza.* ass-see-TEN-zah
Internet access.	*l'accesso a internet.* l'ah-ah-CHES-soh ah een-TEHR-net
Where can I plug in my phone?	*Dove posso caricare il mio telefono?* doh-veh pos-soh kah-ree-KAH-reh eel m'yoh teh-LEH-foh-noh
Where can I purchase an adapter?	*Dove posso comprare un adattatore?* doh-veh pohs-soh kohm-PRAH-reh oon ah-dat-tah-TOH-reh
Where can I find an outlet?	*Dove posso trovare una presa?* doh-veh pohs-soh troh-VAH-reh oo-nah PREH-zah
Where can I find a free wireless network?	*Dove posso trovare una rete wireless gratis?* doh-veh pohs-soh troh-VAH-reh oo-nah reh-teh wireless gratis
electrical plug	*la spina* lah spee-nah
outlet	*la presa* lah pre-zah

Set up an international calling plan with your local carrier before you arrive in Italy and ensure your plan includes texting, talking, and data. Remember that every call you make in Italy will be considered an international call. When using a local number, add "+39" before it, which is Italy's country code.

With whom do I speak?	*Con chi parlo?* kohn kee par-loh
I'd like to …	*Vorrei fare …* vohr-RAY fah-reh
make a phone call.	*una telefonata.* oo-nah teh-leh-foh-NAH-tah

speak with a manager.	*parlare con il responsabile.* par-LAH-reh kohn eel res-pohn-SAH-bee-leh
Do you sell telephone cards?	*Vendete schede telefoniche?* ven-deh-teh skeh-deh teh-leh-FOH-nee-keh
Do you have pay-as-you-go cell phones?	*Avete i telefonini ricaricabili?* ah-VEH-teh ee teh-leh-foh-NEE-nee ree-kah-ree-KAH-bee-lee
I'd like to top up my phone.	*Vorrei fare una ricarica.* vohr-RAY fah-reh oo-nah ree-KAH-ree-kah
I'd like a subscription.	*Vorrei un abbonamento.* vohr-RAY oon ab-boh-nah-MEN-toh
I'd like a fixed plan.	*Vorrei un piano tariffario.* vohr-RAY oon pee-YAH-noh tah-reef-FAH-r'yoh
I've run out of data.	*Ho finite i Giga.* oh fee-NEE-toh ee GEE-gah

Talking on the Phone

Hello!*	*Pronto!* prohn-toh
Let's stay in touch.	*Ci sentiamo.* chee sen-tee-YAH-moh
Let's stay in touch via Whatsapp.	*Ci sentiamo via Whatsapp.* (Replace Whatsapp with your preference.) chee chee sen-tee-YAH-moh vee-yah whatsapp
Is (Robert) there?	*C'è (Roberto)?* ch'AY (...)
It's (Gabriella).	*Sono (Gabriella).* soh-noh (...)
Can I speak with ...	*Posso parlare con ...* pohs-soh par-LAH-reh kohn

continues

| I'd like to speak with ... | *Vorrei parlare con ...*
vohr-RAY PAR-lah-reh kohn |
| I'll call back later. | *Richiamo più tardi.*
ree-kee-YAH-moh p'YOO tar-dee |

* *Used only on the telephone and literally meaning "Ready!"*

Speaking With an Operator (*Parlere con un Operatore*)

I have a problem.	*Ho un problema.* oh oon proh-BLEH-mah
The line was disconnected.	*È caduta la linea.* ay kah-DOO-tah lah LEE-neh-ah
The line is always busy.	*La linea è sempre occupata.* lah LEE-neh-ah ay sem-preh ohk-koo-PAH-tah
Sorry, I dialed the wrong number.	*Mi scusi, ho sbagliato numero.* mee skoo-zee oh sbal-YAH-toh noo-meh-roh
Is there someone who speaks English?	*C'è qualcuno che parla inglese?* ch'AY kwahl-KOO-noh kay par-lah een-GLEH-zeh

What number did you dial?	*Che numero ha fatto?* kay NOO-meh-roh ah FAHT-toh
No one is answering.	*Non risponde nessuno.* nohn ree-SPON-deh nes-SOO-noh
That number is out of service.	*Quel numero è fuori servizio.* kwel NOO-meh-roh ay fwoh-ree ser-VEE-zee-yoh
Hold please. The line is busy.	*La linea è occupata.* lah LEE-neh-ah ay ohk-koo-PAH-tah

It's busy.	*La linea è occupata.* lah LEE-neh-ah AY ohk-koo-PAH-tah
There's no signal/ reception.	*Non c'è campo.* nohn ch'AY kam-poh
800 number	*un numero verde* oon NOO-meh-roh ver-deh
area code	*il prefisso* eel pre-FEES-soh
call	*la telefonata* lah teh-leh-foh-NAH-tah
call rates	*il costo delle chiamate* eel kos-stoh del-leh kee-yah-MAH-teh
cellular phone	*il telefono mobile* eel teh-LEH-foh-noh MOH-bee-leh
fax	*il fax* eel fax
fax machine	*il facsimile* eel facsimile
fax number	*il numero di fax* eel NOO-meh-roh dee fax
message	*il messaggio* eel mes-SAH-joh
operator	*l'operatore* l'oh-peh-rah-TOH-reh
public phone	*il telefono pubblico* eel teh-LEH-foh-noh POOB-lee-koh
voice mail	*la segreteria telefonica* lah seg-reh-teh-R'YAH teh-leh-FOH-nee-kah
to call back	*richiamare* ree-k'yah-MAH-reh
to dial	*comporre il numero* kohm-POR-reh eel NOO-meh-roh
to hold	*attendere* aht-TEN-deh-reh

continues

to insert	*introdurre* een-tro-DOOR-reh
to leave a message	*lasciare un messaggio* lah-SHAH-reh oon mes-SAH-joh
to make a call	*fare una telefonata* fah-reh oo-nah teh-leh-foh-NAH-tah
to receive	*ricevere una chiamata* ree-CHEH-veh-reh oo-nah kee-yah-MAH-tah
to ring	*suonare/squillare* swoh-NAH-reh/squeel-LAH-reh
to send a fax	*inviare un fax* een-vee-YAH-reh un fax
to send or receive texts	*inviare o ricevere un SMS* een-vee-YAH-reh oh ree-CHEH-veh-reh oon esse-emme-esse
to speak	*parlare* par-LAH-reh
to telephone	*telefonare* teh-leh-foh-NAH-reh

Business Trip Packing List

adapter	*l'adattatore* l'ah-dat-tah-TOH-reh
belt	*la cintura* lah cheen-TOO-rah
book	*il libro* eel leeb-roh
cash	*i contanti* ee kohn-TAHN-tee
cellphone charger	*il caricabatterie* eel kah-ree-kah-bat-teh-R'YEH
comb	*il pettine* eel PEHT-tee-neh
credit cards	*la carte di credito* lah kar-teh dee KREH-dee-toh

makeup	*il trucco* eel TROO-koh
passport	*il passaporto* eel pahs-sah-POR-toh
plane ticket	*il biglietto* eel beel-YET-toh
razor	*il rasoio* eel rah-ZOY'oh
sweater	*la maglione/il golf/il pullover* lah mahl-YOH-neh/eel golf/eel pullover
sweatshirt	*la felpa* lah fel-pah
tie	*la cravatta* lah krah-VAHT-tah
toothbrush	*lo spazzolino di denti* loh spah-zoh-LEE-noh dee den-tee
toothpaste	*il dentifricio* eel den-tee-FREE-choh
underwear	*le mutande* leh moo-TAHN-deh

Post Office (*L'Ufficio Postale*)

I'd like to send this ...	*Vorrei spedire questo ...* vohr-RAY speh-DEE-reh kweh- stoh
by airmail.	*per posta aerea.* per poh-stah ah-RAY-yah
by express mail.	*per posta Raccomandata Urgente.* per poh-stah rahk-koh- mahn-DAH-tah oor-JEN- teh
by registered mail.	*per posta raccomandata.* per poh-stah rahk-koh- mahn-DAH-tah

continues

by special delivery.	*per corriere speciale.* per kor-ree-YEH-reh speh-CHAH-leh
by C.O.D.	*con pagamento alla consegna.* kohn pah-gah-MEN-toh ahl-lah kohn-SEH-nyah
When will (it) arrive?	*Quando arriverà?* kwahn-doh ahr-ree-veh-RAH
How many stamps are required to send this letter to … ?	*Quanti francobolli ci vogliono per inviare questa lettera a … ?* kwahn-tee fran-koh-BOHL-lee chee VOH-lyoh-noh per een-vee-YAH-reh kweh-stah LET-teh-rah ah
I'd like to insure this package.	*Vorrei assicurare questo pacco.* vohr-RAY ahs-see-koo-RAH-reh kweh-stoh PAK-koh

addressee/recipient	*il recipiente* eel reh-chee-P'YEN-teh
box	*la scatola* lah SKAH-toh-lah
envelope	*la busta* lah BOOS-tah
extra postage	*la soprattassa postale* lah soh-prah-TAHS-sah pos-TAH-leh
letter	*la lettera* lah LET-teh-rah
mail	*la posta* lah POHS-tah
mail carrier	*il postino* eel pos-TEE-noh
mailbox	*la cassetta postale* lah kahs-SET-tah pos-TAH-leh
money order	*il vaglia* eel VAHL-yah
package	*il pacco* eel PAK-koh

packing paper	*la carta da pacchi* lah kar-tah dah PAH-kee
post office	*l'ufficio postale* L'OO-fee-choh pos-TAH-leh
postcard	*la cartolina* lah kar-tah-LEE-nah
receipt	*la ricevuta* lah ree-cheh-VOO-tah
sender	*il mittente* eel meet-TEN-teh
service window	*lo sportello* loh spor-TEL-loh
stamps	*i francobolli* ee frah-koh-BOHL-lee
telegram	*il telegramma* eel teh-leh-GRAHM-mah

You might not be able to write an entire letter in Italian, but a few Italian terms can always spice up any correspondence.

Dear, (informal)	*Caro/a,* cah-roh/ah
Dear, (formal)	*Egregio/a,* eh-GREH-joh/ah
A big kiss,	*Un bacione,* oon bah-CHOH-neh
A hug,	*Un abbraccio,* oon ab-BRAH-choh
Affectionately,	*Affettuosamente,* af-fet-twoh-zah-MEN-teh
Cordially, (formal)	*Cordialmente,* kor-d'yal-MEN-teh
Sincerely, (formal)	*Sinceramente,* seen-cheh-rah-MEN-teh
Until later,	*A più tardi,* ah p'YOO tar-dee
Yours, (formal)	*Il Suo/la Sua* (m./f.), eel SOO-oh/lah SOO-ah

Yours, (informal)

Il tuo/la tua (m./f.),
eel TOO-oh/la TOO-ah

Money (*il Denaro*)

ATM	*Il Bancomat* eel BAHN-koh-mat
balance	*l'estratto conto* l'es-TRAT-toh kohn-toh
bank	*la banca* lah bahn-kah
bank account	*il conto* eel kohn-toh
bill	*la bolletta* lah bohl-LET-tah
to borrow	*prendere in prestito* PREN-deh-reh een PRES-tee-toh
branch	*la filiale* lah feel-YAH-leh
cash	*i contanti* ee kohn-TAN-tee
cashier	*il cassiere* eel kas-see-YEH-reh
change	*gli spiccioli* ylee SPEE-choh-lee
charge	*una tariffa, un addebito* oo-nah tah-REEF-fah, oon ahd-DEH-bee-toh
check	*l'assegno* l'as-SEN-yoh
checkbook	*il libretto* eel lee-BRET-toh
checking account	*il conto corrente* eel KOHN-toh koh-REN-teh
coins	*le monete* leh moh-NEH-teh

credit	*il credito* eel KREH-dee-toh
currency (foreign)	*la valuta* lah vah-LOO-tah
customer	*il cliente* eel klee-YEN-teh
debt	*il debito* eel DEH-bee-toh
deposit	*il deposito* eel deh-POH-zee-toh
down payment	*l'anticipo* l'ahn-TEE-chee-poh
exchange	*il cambio* eel KAHM-b'yoh
exchange rate	*il tasso di scambio* eel TAS-soh dee SKAHM-b'yoh
final payment	*il saldo* eel sahl-doh
finance	*il finanza* lah fee-NAHN-zah
guarantee	*la garanzia* lah gah-rahn-ZEE-yah
holder	*il titolare* eel tee-toh-LAH-reh
interest	*l'interesse bancario* l'een-teh-RES-seh
investment	*l'investimento* l'een-ves-tee-MEN-toh
loan	*il prestito* eel PRES-too-toh
money	*i soldi/il denaro* ee sol-dee/eel deh-NAH-roh
monthly statement	*l'estratto conto* l'es-TRAH-toh kon-toh
mortgage	*il mutuo* eel MOO-tuoh
payment	*il pagamento* eel pah-gah-MEN-toh
rate	*la rata* lah rah-tah

continues

receipt	*la ricevuta* lah ree-cheh-VOO-tah
sale	*la vendita degli assegni* lah VEN-dee-tah deh-ylee ahs-SEN-yee
signature	*la firma* lah feer-mah
statement	*il conto* eel kohn-toh
stock	*le azioni* leh ah-zee-YOH-neh
sum	*la somma* lah SOHM-mah
teller	*l'impiegato di banca* l'eem-p'yeh-GAH-toh/ah dee BAHN-kah
total	*il totale* eel toh-TAH-leh
window	*lo sportello* loh spor-TEL-loh

Computer and Technology (*Il Computer e La Tecnologia*)

adapter	*l'adattatore* l'ah-daht-tah-TOH-reh
address	*l'indirizzo* l'een-dee-REE-zoh
at (@)	*la chiocciola** lah kee-YOH-choh-lah
battery	*la batteria, la pila* lah bat-teh-R'YAH, lah pee-lah
calculator	*la calcolatrice* lah kal-koh-lah-TRI-che
computer	*il computer* eel computer
dialog box	*la finestra di dialogo* lah fee-NES-trah dee dee-YAH-loh-goh

email	*la posta elettronica* lah pos-tah eh-let-TROH-nee-kah
folder	*la cartella* lah kar-TEL-lah
keyboard	*la tastiera* lah tas-tee-YEH-rah
laptop computer	*il computer portatile* eel computer por-TAH-tee-leh
mouse	*il mouse* eel mee-yaus
online	*in linea* een LEEN-y'ea
page	*la pagina* lah PAH-jee-nah
password	*la password* lah password
printer	*la stampante* lah stam-PAHN-teh
screen	*lo schermo* loh SKER-moh
search engine	*il motore di ricerca* eel moh-TOH-reh dee ree-CHER-kah
website	*il sito internet, il sito* eel see-toh internet, eel see-toh

* *Pronounced* kee-YOH-choh-lah, *this word also means "snail."*

to back up	*salvare i dati* sahl-VAH-reh ee dah-tee
to browse	*navigare* nah-vee-GAH-reh
to chat online	*ciattare* chat-TAH-reh
to click	*cliccare* klee-KAH-reh
to connect	*connettersi* kohn-NET-ter-see

continues

to crash	*andare in bomba* ahn-DAH-reh een BOHM-bah
to debug	*fare il debugging* fah-reh eel debugging
to download	*scaricare* skah-ree-KAH-reh
to format	*formattare* for-maht-TAH-reh
to google	*googolare* goo-goh-LAH-reh
to scan	*fare una scansione* fah-reh oo-nah scan-see-OH-neh
to search	*fare una ricerca/cercare* fah-reh oo-nah ree-CHER-kah/ cer-KAH-reh
to silence (a phone)	*togliere la suoneria* TOL-yeh-reh lah swoh-neh-R'yah
to switch off	*spegnere* spen-YEH-reh
to switch on	*accendere* ah-CHEN-deh-reh
to turn down the volume	*abbassare il volume* ah-bahs-SAH-reh eel volume
to turn up the volume	*alzare il volume* ahl-ZAH-reh eel volume
to zip	*zippare* zeep-PAH-reh
to zoom	*zoomare* zoo-MAH-reh

Italian Texting Abbreviations

anyways	*comunque*	cmq
for	*per*	x

I am/they are	*sono*	sn
I love you	*Ti voglio bene*	tvb
not	*non*	nn
something	*qualcosa*	qlcs
Thanks!	*Grazie!*	Grz!
wait	*aspetta*	asp
Where are you from? (informal)	*Di dove sei?*	di dv 6?
Who cares/ Whatever (slang)	*Chi se ne frega*	Chissene
why/because	*perché*	xke

English Abbreviations Used by Italians

Laugh out loud	LOL
For your information	FYI
Kisses and hugs	XOXO

Emergencies (*L'emergenze*)

In case of emergency, keep these numbers handy:

- General SOS: 113

- *Carabinieri* (police): 112

- Automobile Club d'Italia (car accidents and breakdowns): 116

Help!	*Aiuto!* ay-YOO-toh
Call an ambulance!	*Chiamate un'ambulanza!* kee-ah-mah-teh oon-am-boo-LAN-zah
Call the police!	*Chiamate la polizia!* kee-ah-MAH-teh lah poh-lee-ZEE-ah

continues

Call the emergency medical service!	*Chiamate il pronto soccorso!* kee-ah-MAH-teh eel pron-toh sohk-KOR-soh
Call the fire department!	*Chiamate i pompieri!* kee-ah-MAH-teh ee pom-pee-YEH-ree
I lost my passport.	*Ho perso il mio passaporto.* oh per-soh eel mee-oh pahss-sah-POR-toh
My bag was stolen.	*Mi hanno rubato la borsa.* mee ahn-noh roo-BAH-toh lah bor-sah
Thief!	*Ladro!* lah-droh
There's been an accident.	*C'è stato un incidente.* ch'AY stah-toh oon een-chee-DEN-teh
I've been assaulted.	*Sono stato assalito/a.* soh-noh stah-toh ahs-sah-LEE-toh/ah
Where's the embassy/ consulate?	*Dov'è l'ambasciata/ il consolato?* doh-vay L'AHM-bah-shah-tah/ kohn-SUL-a-toh

The Business of Sports

baseball	*il baseball* eel baseball
basketball	*la pallacanestro* lah pahl-lah-kah-NES-troh
court/field	*il campo* eel KAM-poh
cycling	*il ciclismo* eel chee-KLEEZ-moh
football	*il football americano* eel football ah-meh-ree-KAH-noh
game/match	*la partita* lah par-TEE-tah

golf	*il golf* eel golf
hockey (field/ice)	*lo hockey (prato/ghiaccio)* loh hockey (prah-toh/ghee-AH-choh)
jogging	*il futing* eel futing
racing	*la corsa* lah kor-sah
rowing	*il canottaggio* eel kah-noht-TAH-joh
skiing	*lo sci* loh shee
soccer	*il calcio* eel KAHL-choh
swimming	*il nuoto* eel NWOH-toh
table tennis	*il ping pong* eel ping pong
team	*la squadra* lah SQUAH-drah
tennis	*il tennis* eel tennis
volleyball	*la pallavolo* lah pahl-lah-VOH-loh

Italians take their sports very seriously! If you're in Italy for business, definitely try to catch a game with your business associates.

Verbs at a Glance

Effective use of verbs greatly enhances your communication skills. The following tables offer an overview of Italian verb conjugations—regular and irregular—some of which have been presented throughout the book.

Italian has several forms of the past. Included here are the *passato prossimo* (present perfect), the *imperfetto* (imperfect), and the *passato remoto* (past absolute). *Passato prossimo* and *imperfetto* are primarily used in speech, while *passato remoto* is used to denote an event that's relegated to the distant past, such as in history books or children's fables.

To form the past perfect, future perfect, or conditional perfect, the auxiliary verb does the work and changes accordingly. The past perfect would use the imperfect form of the auxiliary verb, the future perfect would use the future form, and the conditional perfect would use the conditional form.

While it can be intimidating at first, you'll see how this map can help you along your journey for many years to come. *Buon viaggio!*

Regular Verbs

Keep in mind that there's no imperative in the first person.

Key: Present: *Presente*; Present Perfect: *Passato Prossimo*; Imperative: *Imperativo*; Imperfect: *Imperfetto*; Future: *Futuro*; Conditional: *Condizionale*; Subjunctive: *Congiuntivo*; Past Absolute: *Passato Remoto*.

Parlare (to speak)

Present	Present Perfect	Imperative	Imperfect
parlo	ho parlato		parlavo
parli	hai parlato	parla	parlavi
parla	ha parlato	parli	parlava
parliamo	abbiamo parlato	parliamo	parlavamo
parlate	avete parlato	parlate	parlavate
parlano	hanno parlato	parlino	parlavano

Future	Conditional	Subjunctive	Past Absolute
parlerò	parlerei	parli	parlai
parlerai	parleresti	parli	parlasti
parlerà	parlerebbe	parli	parlò
parleremo	parleremmo	parliamo	parlammo
parlerete	parlereste	parliate	parlaste
parleranno	parlerebbero	parlino	parlarono

Scrivere (to write)

Present	Present Perfect	Imperative	Imperfect
scrivo	ho scritto		scrivevo
scrivi	hai scritto	scrivi	scrivevi
scrive	ha scritto	scriva	scriveva
scriviamo	abbiamo scritto	scriviamo	scrivevamo
scrivete	avete scritto	scrivete	scrivevate
scrivono	hanno scritto	scrivano	scrivevano

Future	Conditional	Subjunctive	Past Absolute
scriverò	scriverei	scriva	scrissi
scriverai	scriveresti	scriva	scrivesti
scriverà	scriverebbe	scriva	scrisse
scriveremo	scrive-remmo	scriviamo	scrivemmo
scriverete	scrivereste	scriviate	scriveste
scriveranno	scrivereb-bero	scrivano	scrissero

Partire (to start)

Present	Present Perfect	Imperative	Imperfect
parto	sono partito/a		partivo
parti	sei partito/a	parti	partivi
parte	è partito/a	parta	partiva
partiamo	siamo partiti/e	partiamo	partivamo

continues

Present	Present Perfect	Imperative	Imperfect
partite	siete partiti/e	partite	partivate
partono	sono partiti/e	partano	partivano

Future	Conditional	Subjunctive	Past Absolute
partirò	partirei	parta	partii
partiraì	partiresti	parta	partisti
partirà	partirebbe	parta	partì
partiremo	partiremmo	partiamo	partimmo
partirete	partireste	partiate	partiste
partiranno	partirebbero	partano	partirono

Capire (to understand)

Present	Present Perfect	Imperative	Imperfect
capisco	ho capito		capivo
capisci	hai capito	capisci	capivi
capisce	ha capito	capisca	capiva
capiamo	abbiamo capito	capiamo	capivamo
capite	avete capito	capite	capivate
capiscono	hanno capito	capiscano	capivano

Future	Conditional	Subjunctive	Past Absolute
capirò	capirei	capisca	capii
capirai	capiresti	capisca	capisti
capirà	capirebbe	capisca	capì
capiremo	capiremmo	capiamo	capimmo

Future	Conditional	Subjunctive	Past Absolute
capirete	capireste	capiate	capiste
capiranno	capirebbero	capiscano	capirono

Essere (To Be) and Avere (To Have)

Essere (to be)

The irregular verbs *essere* and *avere* are used on their own and additionally serve as auxiliary (helping) verbs in compound tenses, such as *passato prossimo* (present perfect) and others.

Present	Present Perfect	Imperative	Imperfect
sono	sono stato/a		ero
sei	sei stato/a	sii	eri
è	è stato/a	sia	era
siamo	siamo stati/e	siamo	eravamo
siete	siete stati/e	siate	eravate
sono	sono stati/e	siano	erano

Future	Conditional	Subjunctive	Past Absolute
sarò	sarei	sia	fui
sarai	saresti	sia	fosti
sarà	sarebbe	sia	fu
saremo	saremmo	siamo	fummo
sarete	sareste	siate	foste
saranno	sarebbero	siano	furono

Avere (to have)

Present	Present Perfect	Imperative	Imperfect
ho	ho avuto		avevo
hai	hai avuto	abbi	avevi
ha	ha avuto	abbia	aveva
abbiamo	abbiamo avuto	abbiamo	avevamo
avete	avete avuto	abbiate	avevate
hanno	hanno avuto	abbiano	avevano

Future	Conditional	Subjunctive	Past Absolute
avrò	avrei	abbia	ebbi
avrai	avresti	abbia	avesti
avrà	avrebbe	abbia	ebbe
avremo	avremmo	abbiamo	avemmo
avrete	avreste	abbiate	aveste
avranno	avrebbero	abbiano	ebbero

Irregular Verbs

Italian possesses many irregular verbs. An irregular verb is just a verb that changes from established verb patterns.

Andare (to go)

Present	Present Perfect	Imperative	Imperfect
vado	sono andato/a		andavo
vai	sei andato/a	va	andavi
va	è andato/a	vada	andava

Present	Present Perfect	Imperative	Imperfect
andiamo	siamo andati/e	andiamo	andavamo
andate	siete andati/e	andate	andavate
vanno	sono andati/e	vadano	andavano

Future	Conditional	Subjunctive	Past Absolute
andrò	andrei	vada	andai
andrai	andresti	vada	andasti
andrà	andrebbe	vada	andò
andremo	andremmo	andiamo	andammo
andrete	andreste	andiate	andaste
andranno	andrebbero	vadano	andarono

Dire (to say)

Present	Present Perfect	Imperative	Imperfect
dico	ho detto		dicevo
dici	hai detto	di'	dicevi
dice	ha detto	dica	diceva
diciamo	abbiamo detto	diciamo	dicevamo
dite	avete detto	dite	dicevate
dicono	hanno detto	dicano	dicevano

Future	Conditional	Subjunctive	Past Absolute
dirò	direi	dica	dissi
dirai	diresti	dica	dicesti

continues

Future	Conditional	Subjunctive	Past Absolute
dirà	direbbe	dica	disse
diremo	diremmo	diciamo	dicemmo
direte	direste	diciate	diceste
diranno	direbbero	dicano	dissero

Dovere (to have to/must)

Present	Present Perfect	Imperative	Imperfect
devo	ho dovuto		dovevo
devi	hai dovuto		dovevi
deve	ha dovuto		doveva
dobbiamo	abbiamo dovuto		dovevamo
dovete	avete dovuto		dovevate
devono	hanno dovuto		dovevano

Future	Conditional	Subjunctive	Past Absolute
dovrò	dovrei	debba (deva)	dovei/ dovetti
dovrai	dovresti	debba (deva)	dovesti
dovrà	dovrebbe	debba (deva)	dové/dovette
dovremo	dovremmo	dobbiamo	dovemmo
dovrete	dovreste	dobbiate	doveste
dovranno	dovrebbero	debbano (devano)	doverono/ dovettero

Fare (to do/make)

Present	Present Perfect	Imperative	Imperfect
faccio	ho fatto		facevo
fai	hai fatto	fa'/fai	facevi
fa	ha fatto	faccia	faceva
facciamo	abbiamo fatto	facciamo	facevamo
fate	avete	fate	facevate
fanno	hanno	facciano	facevano

Future	Conditional	Subjunctive	Past Absolute
farò	farei	faccia	feci
farai	faresti	faccia	facesti
farà	farebbe	faccia	fece
faremo	faremmo	facciamo	facemmo
farete	fareste	facciate	faceste
faranno	farebbero	facciano	fecero

Morire (to die)

Present	Present Perfect	Imperative	Imperfect
muoio	sono morto/a		morivo
muori	sei morto/a	muori	morivi
muore	è morto/a	muoia	moriva
moriamo	siamo morti/e	moriamo	morivamo
morite	siete morti/e	morite	morivate
muoiono	sono morti/e	muoiano	morivano

continues

Future	Conditional	Subjunctive	Past Absolute
morirò	morirei	muoia	morii
morirai	moriresti	muoia	moristi
morirà	morirebbe	muoia	morì
moriremo	moriremmo	moriamo	morimmo
morirete	morireste	moriate	moriste
moriranno	morirebbero	muoiano	morirono

Nascere (to be born)

Present	Present Perfect	Imperative	Imperfect
nasco	sono nato/a		nascevo
nasci	sei nato/a	nasci	nascevi
nasce	è nato/a	nasca	nasceva
nasciamo	siamo nati/e	nasciamo	nascevamo
nascete	siete nati/e	nascete	nascevate
nascono	sono nati/e	nascano	nascevano

Future	Conditional	Subjunctive	Past Absolute
nascerò	nascerei	nasca	nacqui
nascerai	nasceresti	nasca	nascesti
nascerà	nascerebbe	nasca	nacque
nasceremo	nasceremmo	nasciamo	nascemmo
nascerete	nascereste	nasciate	nasceste
nasceranno	nascerebbero	nascano	nacquero

Potere (to be able)

Present	Present Perfect	Imperative	Imperfect
posso	ho potuto		potevo
puoi	hai potuto		potevi
può	ha potuto		poteva
possiamo	abbiamo potuto		potevamo
potete	avete potuto		potevate
possono	hanno potuto		potevano

Future	Conditional	Subjunctive	Past Absolute
potrò	potrei	possa	potei
potrai	potresti	possa	potesti
potrà	potrebbe	possa	poté
potremo	potremmo	possiamo	potemmo
potrete	potreste	possiate	poteste
potranno	potrebbero	possano	poterono

Rimanere (to remain, to stay)

Present	Present Perfect	Imperative	Imperfect
rimango	sono rimasto/a		rimanevo
rimani	sei rimasto/a	rimani	rimanevi
rimane	è rimasto/a	rimanga	rimaneva

continues

Present	Present Perfect	Imperative	Imperfect
rimaniamo	siamo rimasti/e	rimaniamo	rimanevamo
rimanete	siete rimasti/e	rimanete	rimanevate
rimangono	sono rimasti/e	rimangano	rimanevano

Future	Conditional	Subjunctive	Past Absolute
rimarrò	rimarrei	rimanga	rimasi
rimarrai	rimarresti	rimanga	rimanesti
rimarrà	rimarrebbe	rimanga	rimase
rimarremo	rimarremmo	rimaniamo	rimanemmo
rimarrete	rimarreste	rimaniate	rimaneste
rimarranno	rimarrebbero	rimangano	rimasero

Salire (to go up)

Present	Present Perfect	Imperative	Imperfect
salgo	sono salito/a		salivo
sali	sei salito/a	sali	salivi
sale	è salito/a	salga	saliva
saliamo	siamo saliti/e	saliamo	salivamo
salite	siete saliti/e	salite	salivate
salgono	sono saliti/e	salgano	salivano

Future	Conditional	Subjunctive	Past Absolute
salirò	salirei	salga	salii
salirai	saliresti	salga	salisti
salirà	salirebbe	salga	salì
saliremo	saliremmo	saliamo	salimmo
salirete	salireste	saliate	saliste
saliranno	salirebbero	salgano	salirono

Sapere (to know)

Present	Present Perfect	Imperative	Imperfect
so	ho saputo		sapevo
sai	hai saputo	sappi	sapevi
sa	ha saputo	sappia	sapeva
sappiamo	abbiamo saputo	sappiamo	sapevamo
sapete	avete saputo	sappiate	sapevate
sanno	hanno saputo	sappiano	sapevano

Future	Conditional	Subjunctive	Past Absolute
saprò	saprei	sappia	seppi
saprai	sapresti	sappia	sapesti
saprà	saprebbe	sappia	seppe
sapremo	sapremmo	sappiamo	sapemmo
saprete	sapreste	sappiate	sapeste
sapranno	saprebbero	sappiano	seppero

Venire (to come)

Present	Present Perfect	Imperative	Imperfect
vengo	sono venuto/a		venivo
vieni	sei venuto/a	vieni	venivi
viene	è venuto/a	venga	veniva
veniamo	siamo venuti/e	veniamo	venivamo
venite	siete venuti/e	venite	venivate
vengono	sono venuti/e	vengano	venivano

Future	Conditional	Subjunctive	Past Absolute
verrò	verrei	venga	venni
verrai	verresti	venga	venisti
verrà	verrebbe	venga	venne
verremo	verremmo	veniamo	venimmo
verrete	verreste	veniate	veniste
verranno	verrebbero	vengano	vennero

Volere (to want)

Present	Present Perfect	Imperative	Imperfect
voglio	ho voluto		volevo
vuoi	hai voluto	vuoi	volevi
vuole	ha voluto	voglia	voleva
vogliamo	abbiamo voluto	vogliamo	volevamo
volete	avete voluto	vogliate	volevate
vogliono	hanno voluto	vogliano	volevano

Future	Conditional	Subjunctive	Past Absolute
vorrò	vorrei	voglia	volli
vorrai	vorresti	voglia	volesti
vorrà	vorrebbe	voglia	volle
vorremo	vorremmo	vogliamo	volemmo
vorrete	vorreste	vogliate	voleste
vorranno	vorrebbero	vogliano	vollero

Reflexive Verbs (*Verbi Reflessivi*)

All reflexive verbs use *essere* in compound tenses, such as the *passato prossimo* (present perfect), and can be recognized by the *si* at the end. Reflexive verbs are conjugated according to regular rules and must include the following reflexive pronouns.

mi (mee)	myself
ti (tee)	yourself
si (see)	himself, herself, yourself
ci (chee)	ourselves
vi (vee)	yourselves
si (see)	themselves

For example:

> *(Chiamarsi) Come si chiama?*
> (kyah-MAR-see) koh-meh see kee-YAH-mah

What's your name?

Mi chiamo	I call myself
Ti chiami	You call yourself

continues

Si chiama	He calls himself/She calls herself
Ci chiamiamo	We call ourselves
Vi chiamate	You call yourselves
Si chiamano	They call themselves

Commonly used reflexive verbs include:

alzarsi	to get up
annoiarsi	to become bored
arrabbiarsi	to become angry
chiamarsi	to name
conoscersi	to know each other
divertirsi	to enjoy
fermarsi	to stop
laurearsi	to graduate
lavarsi	to wash oneself
mettersi	to put on
radersi	to shave
sentirsi	to feel
sposarsi	to get married
svegliarsi	to wake up

Irregular Past Participles

This chart includes a quick review of the irregular past participles used in compound tenses, such as the *passato prossimo* (present perfect). Unless otherwise indicated, past participles are used in conjunction with the helping verb *avere*. Verbs with an asterisk (*) require *essere* as their helping verb.

Past Infinitive	Past Participle
accendere (to light, to turn on)	*acceso*
aprire (to open)	*aperto*
assumere (to hire)	*assunto*
bere (to drink)	*bevuto*
chiedere (to ask)	*chiesto*
chiudere (to close)	*chiuso*
conduct (to conduct)	*condotto*
correggere (to correct)	*corretto*
correre (to run)	*corso*
cuocere (to cook)	*cotto*
decidere (to decide)	*deciso*
dipingere (to paint)	*dipinto*
dire (to say)	*detto*
discuttere (to discuss)	*discusso*
dividere (to divide)	*diviso*
esprimere (to express)	*espresso*
essere (to be)	*stato**
fare (to do/make)	*fatto*
leggere (to read)	*letto*
mettere (to put)	*messo*
morire (to die)	*morto**
muovere (to move)	*mosso*
nascere (to be born)	*nato**
offendere (to offend)	*offeso*
offrire (to offer)	*offerto*
permettere (to permit)	*permesso*
piangere (to cry)	*pianto*
piacere (to please)	*piaciuto**
prendere (to take)	*preso*
promettere (to promise)	*permesso*
ridurre (to reduce)	*ridotto*

continues

Past Infinitive	Past Participle
rimanere (to remain)	*rimasto**
rispondere (to respond)	*risposto*
rompere (to break)	*rotto*
scegliere (to choose)	*scelto*
scendere (to descend)	*sceso*
scrivere (to write)	*scritto*
soffrire (to suffer)	*sofferto*
spendere (to spend)	*speso*
stare (to be, to stay)	*stato**
succedere (to happen)	*successo*
tradurre (to translate)	*tradotto*
vedere (to see)	*visto/veduto*
venire (to come)	*venuto**
vincere (to win)	*vinto*
vivere (to live)	*vissuto*

Commonly Used Expressions in Everyday Conversation

Auguri! ow-GOO-ree	Congrats!
Basta! bah-stah	Enough!
Beh. beh	Whatever.
In bocca al lupo! een boh-kah ahl loo-poh	Break a leg!
Che ne pensi? kay nay pen-see	What do you think about it?
Che roba! kay roh-bah	What stuff! (I don't believe it!)
Che schifo! kay SKEE-foh	How disgusting! (slang)
Come? koh-meh	Huh?
Come mai? koh-meh my	How on Earth?
Come va? koh-meh vah	How's it going?
D'accordo. d'ak-KOR-doh	Agreed/Okay/Sure.
Dai! dye	Come on! You're kidding.
Davvero? dav-VEH-roh	Really?
Di mamma cè n'è una sola. dee mahm-mah ch'AY ney oo-nah soh-lah	Of mothers, there's only one.
Dio mio. d'yoh m'yoh	My God.
Facciamo alla Romana fah-CHAH-moh ahl-lah roh-MAH-nah	Let's go Roman. (to go Dutch)
Figurati! fee-GOO-rah-tee	Don't give it anothe thought.
Mi piace fare le ore piccole. mee pee-AH-cheh fah-reh leh or'ay PEEK-koh-leh	I like to do the wee hours. (to burn the midnight oil)

Non fare lo spiritoso! nohn fah-reh loh spee-ree-TOH-zoh	Don't be a wise guy!
Fa un freddo cane. fah oon FRED-doh kah-neh	It's dog cold. (really cold)
Lascia perdere. lah-shah PER-deh-reh	Forget it.
Ma che! mah keh	What the heck!
Ma va! mah vah	Come on!
Magari! mah-GAH-ree	Wouldn't that be nice!
Manco per sogno! mahn-koh per SOHN-yoh	In your dreams!
Meno male! meh-noh mah-leh	Luckily!
Non c'è di che. nohn ch'AY dee kay	It's nothing. Don't think about it.
Penso di sì/no. pen-soh dee see/noh	I think so/not.
Per carità! per kah-ree-TAH	For goodness sake!
Di la verità. dee lah veh-ree-TAH	Tell the truth.
Santo cielo! sahn-toh CHIEL-loh	Holy heaven! My goodness!
Scemo/a! sheh-moh/ah	Fool!
Senza dubbio. sen-zah DOOB-b'yoh	Without a doubt.
Stai zitto/a! sty zee-toh/ah	Shut up!
Sul serio? sool SEH-r'yoh	Really?
Ti voglio bene. tee VOHL-yoh beh-neh	I love you. (I wish you well.)
Va bene/male. vah beh-neh/mah-leh	It's going well/badly.

continues

Vale la pena. vah-leh lah PEH-nah	It's worth it.
Non vedo l'ora! nohn veh-doh l'oh-rah	I can't wait!

Give your Tongue a Twist

Gli scioglilingua (tongue twisters) are a great way to practice your Italian. Try saying any of these popular "tongue melters" or, better yet, ask an Italian friend to give you a demonstration:

Trentatré trentini entrarono in Trento, tutti e trentatré trotterellando.

Li vuoi quei kiwi? E se non vuoi quei kiwi che kiwi vuoi?

Apelle, figlio di Apollo, fece una palla di pelle di pollo. Tutti i pesci vennero a galla per vedere la palla di pelle di pollo fatta da Apelle, figlio di Apollo.

A quest'ora il questore in questura non c'è.

Sopra la panca la capra campa, sotto la panca la capra crepa.

Tre tigri contro tre tigri.

English–Italian Dictionary

All feminine nouns (f.), irregular masculine nouns (m.), and plural (pl.) nouns are indicated. Where you see (m./f.), the word can be used for both genders. Irregular past participles are in parentheses.

to be able (can) *potere*

about (approximately) *circa*

about (consists of) *di*

above, on *sopra*

accent *l'accento*

accident *l'incidente* (m.)

across *attraverso*

activity *l'attività* (f.)

address *l'indirizzo*

admission charge *il prezzo d'entrata*

adult *l'adulto*

advance, in *in anticipo*

adventure *l'avventura* (f.)

after *dopo*

afternoon *il pomeriggio*

again *ancora, di nuovo*

against *contro*

age *l'età* (f.)

agency *l'agenzia* (f.)

agreement *l'accordo*

air *l'aria* (f.)

air-conditioning *l'aria condizionata* (f.)

airplane *l'aereo*

airport *l'aeroporto*

alarm clock *la sveglia* (f.)

alcohol *alcol*

alive *vivo*

allergic *allergico*

allergy *l'allergia* (f.)

alley *il vicolo*

alone *solo*

although *benché, sebbene*

always *sempre*

ambulance *l'ambulanza* (f.)

and *e, ed (before vowels)*

angry *arrabbiato*

animal *l'animale* (m.)

answer *la risposta* (f.)

antiques *l'antiquariato*

apartment *l'appartamento*

aperitif *l'aperitivo*

to apologize *scusarsi*

appetizer *l'antipasto*

aquarium *l'acquario*

area *l'area* (f.)

area code *il prefisso*

arm *il braccio, le braccia* (pl.)

around *intorno a*

arrival *l'arrivo*

art *l'arte* (f.)

artist *l'artista* (m./f.)

ashtray *il portacenere* (m.)

to ask *chiedere (chiesto)*

aspirin *l'aspirina* (f.)

assistance *l'assistenza* (f.)

ATM *il Bancomat*

attention! *attenzione!*

aunt *la zia* (f.)

automobile *la macchina* (f.), *l'automobile* (f.), *l'auto* (f.)

autumn *l'autunno* (m.)

available *disponibile*

avalanche *la valanga* (f.)

to avoid *evitare*

away *via*

baby *il bambino/la bambina*

baby bottle *il biberon* (m.)

bachelor *lo scapolo*

back, behind *indietro*

backpack *lo zaino*

bad *male*

bag (purse) *la borsa* (f.)

baker *il fornaio*

balcony *il balcone* (m.)

bank *la banca* (f.)

bar *il bar* (m.)

barber *il barbiere* (m.)

bartender *il/la barista* (m./f.)

basement *la cantina* (f.)

basketball *la pallacanestro, il basket*

bathroom *il bagno*

battery *la batteria* (f.), *la pila* (f.)

bay *la baia* (f.)

to be *essere* (stato), *stare* (stato)

beach *la spiaggia* (f.)

beard *la barba* (f.)

beauty *la bellezza* (f.)

because *perché*

bed *il letto*

beef *il manzo*

beer *la birra* (f.)

before *prima*

to begin *iniziare, cominciare*

behind *dietro*

bell *la campana* (f.)

beneath *sotto*

bunk bed *la cuccetta* (f.)

beside, next to *accanto a*

better *meglio*

between *tra*

beverage *la bibita* (f.)

big, large *grande*

bill *il conto*

bird *l'uccello*

birth *la nascita* (f.)

birthday *il compleanno*

bishop *il vescovo*

bitter *amaro*

blanket *la coperta* (f.)

blood *il sangue* (m.)

blouse *la camicetta* (f.)

Bluetooth *Bluetooth*

boarding *l'imbarco*

boat *la barca* (f.)

body *il corpo*

book *il libro*

bookstore *la libreria* (f.)

boot *lo stivale* (m.)

border *la frontiera* (f.)

boring *noioso/noiosa*

boss *il padrone/la padrona* (f.)

both *entrambi, tutt'e due*

bottle *la bottiglia* (f.)

bottom *il fondo*

boulevard *il viale* (m.)

bowl *la ciotola* (f.), *la scodella* (f.)

box *la scatola* (f.)

boy *il ragazzo*

brand *la marca* (f.)

bread *il pane* (m.)

breakdown *il guasto*

breakfast *la prima colazione* (f.)

bridge *il ponte* (m.)

broken *rotto*

brother *il fratello*

brother-in-law *il cognato*

brown *castano, marrone*

bruise *la contusione* (f.), *il livido*

building *l'edificio, il palazzo*

bus *l'autobus* (m.), *la corriera* (f.), *il pullman* (m.)

busy *impegnato, occupato*

butcher shop *la macelleria* (f.)

button *il bottone* (m.)

to buy *comprare*

by *da, in*

cabin *la cabina* (f.)

cable *il cavo*

cable car *la funivia* (f.)

cafeteria *la mensa* (f.)

to call *chiamare*

camera *la macchina fotografica* (f.)

can opener *l'apriscatole*

candle *la candela* (f.)

car *(See automobile.)*

car rental *l'autonoleggio*

carafe *la caraffa* (f.)

card *la carta* (f.)

careful *attento*

cash *i contanti* (m. pl.)

cash register *la cassa* (f.)

castle *il castello*

cat *il gatto*

cathedral *la cattedrale* (f.)

Catholic *cattolico*

cave *la grotta* (f.)

ceiling *il soffitto*

center *il centro*

central *centrale*

century *il secolo*

certain *certo*

chair *la sedia* (f.)

to change *cambiare*

channel *il canale* (m.)

chapel *la cappella* (f.)

check *l'assegno*

to check *controllare*

cheese *il formaggio*

to choose *scegliere (scelto)*

Christian *cristiano/cristiana* (f.)

Christmas *Natale*

church *la chiesa* (f.)

circle *il circolo*

citizen *il cittadino/la cittadina* (f.)

citizenship *la cittadinanza* (f.)

city *la città*

to clean *pulire*

clear *chiaro*

clever *furbo* (slang), *intelligente*

clock *l'orologio*

closed *chiuso*

clothing *l'abbigliamento*

coast *la costa* (f.)

coat *il cappotto, il giubbotto*

coffee *il caffè* (m.)

coin *la moneta* (f.)

colander *il colapasta* (m.)

cold *freddo, il raffreddore* (m.)

color *il colore* (m.)

to come *venire*

community *la comunità* (f.)

company *l'azienda* (f.), *la ditta* (f.), *la società* (f.)

concert *il concerto*

condom *il profilattico, il preservativo*

congratulations! *auguri!*

conference *la conferenza* (f.), *il congresso*

conflict *il conflitto*

connection *la coincidenza* (f.)

consulate *il consolato*

contact *il contatto*

contest *il concorso, la gara* (f.)

contraceptive *il contraccettivo*

convenient *comodo, pratico*

conversation *la conversazione* (f.)

to cook *cucinare, cuocere*

cooked *cotto*

copy *la copia* (f.)

cork *il tappo*

corkscrew *il cavatappi* (m.)

corn *il mais* (m.)

cornmeal *la polenta* (f.)

correct *corretto, a posto*

cosmetics shop *la profumeria* (f.)

cost *il costo, il prezzo*

to cost *costare*

costly *costoso*

to count *contare*

counter *il banco, lo sportello*

country *la campagna* (f.), *il paese* (m.)

couple *la coppia* (f.)

course *il corso*

court *la corte* (f.)

cousin *il cugino/la cugina* (f.)

cover charge *il coperto*

cow *la vacca* (f.)

crazy *matto, pazzo*

cream (food) *la crema* (f.), *la panna* (f.)

to create *creare*

credit *il credito*

credit card *la carta di credito* (f.)

crib *la culla* (f.)

cross *la croce* (f.)

crowded *affollato*

cruise *la crociera* (f.)

culture *la cultura* (f.)

cup *la tazza* (f.)

currency *la valuta* (f.), *la moneta* (f.)

current event *l'attualità* (f.)

curtain *la tenda* (f.)

curve *la curva* (f.)

customs *la dogana* (f.)

cute, pretty *carino*

cutting board *il tagliere* (m.)

cycling *il ciclismo*

daddy *papà, babbo*

dairy store *la latteria* (f.)

dam *la diga* (f.)

damaged *danneggiato*

dance *il ballo, la danza* (f.)

danger *il pericolo*

dangerous *pericoloso*

dark *il buio, scuro*

darn! *accidenti!*

date *la data* (f.)

daughter *la figlia* (f.)

daughter-in-law *la nuora* (f.)

day *il giorno, la giornata*

dead *morto*

dear *caro*

death *la morte* (f.)

decision *la decisione* (f.)

degree *il grado* (temperature), *la laurea* (f.) (diploma)

delicious *delizioso*

dentist *il/la dentista* (m./f.)

to depart *partire*

department *il dipartimento*

department store *il grande magazzino*

departure *la partenza* (f.)

desk *la scrivania* (f.)

dessert *il dolce*

destination *la destinazione* (f.)

detergent *il detersivo*

detour *la deviazione* (f.)

diabetes *il diabete* (m.)

diaper *il pannolino*

dictionary *il dizionario*

diet *la dieta* (f.)

different *differente, diverso*

difficult *difficile*

dining room *la sala da pranzo* (f.)

dinner *la cena* (f.)

dinner plate *il piatto*

direct *diretto*

direction *la direzione* (f.), *l'indicazione* (f.)

director *il direttore/la direttrice* (f.)

director (film) *il/la regista* (m./f.)

dirty *sporco*

discount *lo sconto*

distance *la distanza* (f.)

distracted *distratto*

divorced *divorziato/divorziata*

to do *fare (fatto)*

doctor *il dottore/la dottoressa* (f.), *il medico*

document *il documento*

dog *il cane* (m.)

dome *la cupola* (f.), *il duomo*

door *la porta* (f.)

doorbell *il campanello*

down *giù*

drawing *il disegno*

dress *il vestito*

to drive *guidare*

driver's license *la patente* (f.)

drug *la droga* (f.)

drugstore *la drogheria* (f.)

dry *asciutto, secco*

dry-cleaner *la lavanderia a secco, la tintoria* (f.)

during *durante, mentre*

each *ciascuno, ogni, ognuno*

earrings *gli orecchini* (m. pl.)

earth *la terra* (f.)

east *est*

Easter Monday *lunedì dell'Angelo, Pasquetta* (f.)

Easter *Pasqua*

easy *facile*

to eat *mangiare*

to eat breakfast *fare la prima colazione*

to eat dinner *cenare*

to eat lunch *pranzare*

egg *l'uovo, le uova* (pl.)

election *l'elezione* (f.)

electricity *l'elettricità* (f.)

elevator *l'ascensore* (m.)

embassy *l'ambasciata* (f.)

emergency *l'emergenza* (f.)

to emigrate *emigrare*

empty *vuoto*

end *la fine* (f.)

enemy *il nemico/la nemica*

English *inglese*

engraved *inciso*

enough *abbastanza, basta!*

to enter *entrare*

entrance *l'entrata* (f.), *l'ingresso*

envelope *la busta* (f.)

Epiphany (Jan. 6) *la Befana* (f.), *l'Epifania* (f.)

error *l'errore* (m.)

to escape *scappare*

essential *essenziale*

even *persino*

evening *la sera* (f.), *la serata* (f.)

event *l'avvenimento, l'evento*

every *ogni*

everybody *ognuno*

everyone *tutti*

everything, all *tutto*

everywhere *dappertutto*

exactly *esattamente*

excellent *eccellente, ottimo*

exchange *il cambio, lo scambio*

to exchange *scambiare*

excursion *l'escursione* (f.), *la gita* (f.)

excuse me! *permesso!*

exercise *la ginnastica* (f.)

exit *l'uscita* (f.)

expense *la spesa* (f.)

expensive *caro*

experience *l'esperienza* (f.)

to export *esportare*

express *espresso*

eyeglasses *gli occhiali* (m. pl.)

fabric *la stoffa* (f.), *il tessuto*

face *la faccia* (f.), *il viso*

factory *la fabbrica* (f.)

faith *la fede* (f.)

to fall *cadere*

to fall in love *innamorarsi*

family *la famiglia* (f.)

far *lontano*

fare *la tariffa* (f.)

farm *la fattoria* (f.)

farmer *il contadino/la contadina*

fat *grasso*

father *il padre* (m.)

father-in-law *il suocero*

faucet *il rubinetto*

fear *la paura* (f.)

to feel *sentirsi*

feeling *il sentimento, la sensazione* (f.)

ferry *il traghetto*

fever *la febbre* (f.)

fiancé/fiancée *il fidanzato/ la fidanzata*

field *il campo, il prato*

to fill up (a gas tank) *fare il pieno*

film *il film* (m.), *la pellicola* (f.)

finally *finalmente*

finance *la finanza* (f.)

to find *trovare*

finger *il dito, le dita* (pl.)

to finish *finire*

fire *il fuoco*

firefighter *il pompiere* (m.), *il vigile del fuoco*

fireplace *il caminetto*

first *primo*

first aid *pronto soccorso*

fish *il pesce* (m.)

flight *il volo*

floor *il pavimento, il piano*

Florence *Firenze*

flour *la farina* (f.)

flower *il fiore* (m.)

flu *l'influenza* (f.)

fly *la mosca* (f.)

fog *la nebbia* (f.)

food *il cibo*

foot *il piede* (m.)

for *per*

foreigner *lo straniero/la straniera* (f.)

forest *la foresta* (f.)

fork *la forchetta* (f.)

forward *avanti*

fountain *la fontana* (f.)

fragile *fragile*

free *libero*

free of charge *gratis*

fresh *fresco*

fried *fritto*

friend *l'amico/l'amica* (f.)

friendship *l'amicizia* (f.)

from *di, da*

fruit *la frutta* (f.)

full *pieno*

funny *buffo*

fur *la pelliccia* (f.)

furnishings *l'arredamento*

future *il futuro*

game *il gioco, la partita* (f.)

game room *la sala giochi* (f.)

garage *il garage* (m.)

garden *il giardino, l'orto*

garlic *l'aglio*

gas pump *il distributore di benzina*

gas tank *il serbatoio*

gasoline *la benzina* (f.)

gate *il cancello*

gift *il regalo*

girl *la ragazza* (f.)

to give *dare*

glad *contento*

gladly! *volentieri!*

glass (champagne, wine glass) *la coppa* (f.)

glass (drinking) *il bicchiere* (m.)

glass (material) *il vetro*

gloves *i guanti* (m. pl.)

to go *andare*

god *il dio*

goddess *la dea* (f.)

gold *l'oro*

good *buono*

to google *googolare*

government *il governo*

gram *il grammo*

granddaughter *la nipote* (f.)

grandfather *il nonno*

grandmother *la nonna* (f.)

grandson *il nipote* (m.)

grapes *l'uva* (f.)

greengrocer's *il fruttivendolo*

to greet *salutare*

grilled *alla griglia*

groceries *gli alimentari* (m. pl.)

ground *la terra*

ground floor *il pianterreno*

group *il gruppo*

guest *l'ospite* (m./f.)

guide *la guida* (f.)

gym *la palestra* (f.)

hair *il pelo*

hair (on head) *i capelli* (m. pl.)

hair dryer *il fon* (m.)

half *la metà, mezzo*

hall *la sala* (f.)

hand *la mano* (f.), *le mani* (pl.)

handle *la maniglia* (f.)

hanger *la gruccia* (f.), *la stampella* (f.)

to happen *capitare, succedere (successo)*

happy *allegro, felice*

Happy Birthday! *Buon Compleanno!*

Happy Easter! *Buona Pasqua!*

Happy Holidays! *Buone Feste!*

Happy New Year! *Buon Anno!*

harbor *il porto*

hard *duro*

hat *il cappello*

to have *avere*

to have to (must) *dovere*

hazelnut *la nocciola* (f.)

he *lui, egli*

head *la testa* (f.)

headphones *le cuffie* (f. pl.)

health *la salute* (f.)

healthy *sano*

to hear *sentire, udire*

heart attack *l'infarto*

heat *il riscaldamento*

heavy *pesante*

hectogram *l'ettogrammo*

height *l'altezza* (f.)

hello *ciao, buon giorno, pronto!* (telephone)

helmet *il casco, l'elmetto*

help! *aiuto!*

here *ecco, qua, qui*

highway *l'autostrada* (f.)

hill *la collina* (f.)

history *la storia* (f.)

holiday *la festa* (f.)

homemade *della casa, fatto in casa*

honest *onesto*

honey *il miele* (m.)

honeymoon *la luna di miele* (f.)

hope *la speranza* (f.)

hospital *l'ospedale*

hostel *l'ostello*

hot *caldo*

hotel *l'albergo, l'hotel* (m.)

hour *l'ora* (f.)

house *la casa* (f.)

housekeeper *la cameriera* (f.)

housewife *la casalinga* (f.)

how *come*

how much? *quanto?*

human *l'umano*

humble *umile*

humidity *l'umidità* (f.)

humor *l'umore*

hunger *la fame* (f.)

husband *il marito*

I *io*

ice *il ghiaccio*

ice cream *il gelato*

ice cream parlor *la gelateria* (f.)

identification card *la carta d'identità* (f.)

if *se*

ignorant *ignorante*

illness *la malattia* (f.)

image *l'immagine* (f.)

imagination *l'immaginazione* (f.)

imitation *l'imitazione*

immediately *subito*

immigration *l'immigrazione* (f.)

imperfect *imperfetto*

to import *importare*

important *importante*

impossible *impossibile*

in *a, in*

in a hurry *in fretta*

in care of (c/o) *presso* (for letters), *a cura di* (a person)

in front of *davanti a*

in season *della stagione*

incredible *incredibile*

indirect *indiretto*

indoor *dentro, al coperto*

industry *l'industria* (f.)

inexpensive *economico*

infection *l'infezione* (f.)

inferior *inferiore*

to inform *informare*

information *l'informazione* (f.)

information office *l'ufficio informazioni*

ingredient *l'ingrediente* (m.)

inhabitant *l'abitante* (m./f.)

injury *la ferita* (f.)

inn *la pensione* (f.), *la locanda* (f.)

insect *l'insetto*

insect bite *la puntura* (f.)

inside *dentro*

instead *invece*

insulin *l'insulina* (f.)

insurance *l'assicurazione* (f.)

intelligent *intelligente*

interesting *interessante*

intermission *l'intermezzo, l'intervallo*

interpreter *l'interprete*

to introduce *introdurre* (*introdotto*)

invitation *l'invito*

to invite   *invitare*

is   *è*

island   *l'isola* (f.)

Italian   *italiano*

Italy   *l'Italia* (f.)

itinerary   *l'itinerario*

jack (car)   *il cric* (m.)

jacket   *la giacca* (f.)

jail   *il carcere* (m.)

jeans   *i jeans* (m. pl.)

Jesus   *Gesù*

jeweler's   *l'oreficeria* (f.)

jewelry store   *la gioielleria* (f.)

Jewish   *ebreo/ebrea*

journalist   *il/la giornalista* (m./f.)

juice   *il succo*

just   *giusto, proprio*

key   *la chiave* (f.)

kilogram   *il chilogrammo*

kilometer   *il chilometro*

kind   *gentile*

kindness   *la gentilezza* (f.)

king   *il rè*

kiss   *il bacio*

knife   *il coltello*

to know (someone)   *conoscere (conosciuto)*

to know (something)   *sapere*

kosher   *kasher*

lace   *il merletto*

lake   *il lago*

lamb   *l'agnello*

lamp   *la lampada* (f.)

landlord   *il padrone di casa*

lane   *la corsia* (f.)

language   *la lingua* (f.)

large   *grande, grosso*

last   *scorso, ultimo*

late   *tardi*

laundry   *il bucato*

laundry service   *la lavanderia* (f.)

law   *il Diritto, la giurisprudenza* (f.), *la legge* (f.)

lawyer   *l'avvocato*

lazy   *pigro*

leaf   *la foglia* (f.)

to learn   *imparare*

leather   *il cuoio, la pelle* (f.)

to leave (behind)   *lasciare*

to leave (depart)   *partire*

left   *sinistro*

leg   *la gamba* (f.)

length   *la lunghezza* (f.)

less   *meno*

lesson   *la lezione* (f.)

letter   *la lettera* (f.)

license   *la patente* (f.)

license plate   *la targa* (f.)

life   *la vita* (f.)

light   *la luce* (f.)

lightning flash   *il lampo*

line   *la linea* (f.)

lip   *il labbro*

list   *l'elenco*

liter   *il litro*

literature   *la letteratura* (f.)

little   *piccolo, un po'* (a little)

to live   *abitare, vivere (vissuto)*

living room *il salotto, il soggiorno*

local *locale*

to lodge *alloggiare*

long *lungo*

to look *guardare*

to lose *perdere (perso)*

lost and found *l'ufficio oggetti smarriti*

lotion *la lozione* (f.)

love *l'amore* (m.)

lunch *il pranzo*

luxury *lusso*

magazine *la rivista* (f.)

magic *la magia* (f.)

magnificent *magnifico*

mail *la posta* (f.)

to mail *inviare, spedire*

mailbox *la cassetta postale* (f.)

man *l'uomo*

management *l'amministrazione* (f.)

manager *il/la dirigente* (m./f.)

to manufacture *fabbricare*

map *la carta* (f.), *la mappa* (f.)

marble *il marmo*

marina *la marina* (f.), *il lido*

market *il mercato*

married *sposato/sposata*

masculine *maschile*

mass *la messa* (f.)

matches *i fiammiferi* (m. pl.)

maybe *forse*

mayor *il sindaco/la sindaca*

me *mi, a me*

meal *il pasto*

meaning *il significato, il senso*

measure *la misura* (f.)

meat *la carne* (f.)

mechanic *il meccanico*

medicine *la medicina* (f.)

to meet *incontrare*

meeting *il congresso, la riunione* (f.)

menu *la lista* (f.), *il menù*

merchandise *la merce* (f.)

merchant *il/la mercante* (m./f.)

Merry Christmas *Buon Natale*

message *il messaggio*

messenger *il corriere*

metal *il metallo*

midnight *la mezzanotte* (f.)

mile *il miglio, le miglia* (pl.)

milk *il latte* (m.)

mind *la mente* (f.)

minister *il ministro*

minority *la minoranza* (f.)

minute *il minuto*

mirror *lo specchio*

Miss, young lady *la signorina* (f.)

model *il modello*

modern *moderno*

modest *modesto*

moment *l'attimo, il momento*

monastery *il monastero*

money *il denaro, i soldi* (m. pl.)

money exchange office *l'ufficio cambio*

money order *il vaglia postale* (m.)

month *il mese* (m.)

monument *il monumento*

moon *la luna* (f.)

more *più*

more than, in addition to *oltre*

morning *la mattina* (f.)

morsel, nibble *il bocconcino*

mosaic *il mosaico*

mosquito *la zanzara* (f.)

mother *la madre* (f.)

mother-in-law *la suocera* (f.)

motor *il motore* (m.)

motorcycle *la motocicletta* (f.)

mountain *la montagna* (f.)

mouth *la bocca* (f.)

movie *il film*

Mr. *il signore* (m.)

Mrs. *la signora* (f.)

museum *il museo*

music *la musica* (f.)

musician *il/la musicista* (m./f.)

Muslim *mussulmano/ musulmana*

mustard *la senape* (f.)

myth *il mito*

name *il nome* (m.)

name of spouse *il nome del coniuge*

napkin *la salvietta* (f.), *il tovagliolo*

nationality *la nazionalità* (f.)

native language *la madrelingua* (f.)

natural *naturale*

nausea *la nausea* (f.)

near *vicino*

necessary *necessario*

necessity *la necessità* (f.)

necklace *la collana* (f.)

need, I *ho bisogno*

neighbor *il vicino/la vicina*

neighborhood *il quartiere* (m.)

neither *neppure*

neither ... nor *né ... né*

nephew *il nipote*

nervous *nervoso*

never *mai*

new *nuovo*

news *la notizia* (f.)

newspaper *il giornale* (m.), *il quotidiano*

newspaper vendor *il giornalaio*

newsstand *l'edicola* (f.)

next *prossimo*

nice *simpatico/simpatica*

niece *la nipote* (f.)

night *la notte* (f.)

no entrance *vietato l'ingresso*

no one *nessuno*

no parking *divieto di sosta*

noisy *rumoroso*

noon *mezzogiorno*

normal *normale*

north *nord*

not   *non*

notebook   *il quaderno*

nothing   *niente, nulla*

noun   *il nome* (m.)

novel   *il romanzo*

now   *adesso, ora*

number   *il numero*

nurse   *l'infermiera* (f.)

occupied   *occupato*

ocean   *l'oceano*

of   *di*

offer   *l'offerta* (f.)

office   *l'ufficio*

often   *spesso*

oil   *l'olio*

old   *vecchio*

olive   *l'oliva* (f.)

on   *su*

on board   *a bordo*

one-way street   *senso unico*

only   *solamente*

open   *aperto*

opinion   *l'opinione* (f.)

opposite   *il contrario, opposto*

optician   *l'ottico*

or   *o, oppure*

original   *originale*

outdoor   *all'aperto*

outfit   *l'abito*

outside   *fuori*

oven   *il forno*

overcoat   *il cappotto, il soprabito*

overdone   *scotto, troppo cotto*

owner   *il proprietario*

package   *il pacco*

pain   *il dolore* (m.)

paint   *la vernice* (f.)

painter   *il pittore/la pittrice* (f.)

painting   *la pittura* (f.), *il quadro*

pair   *il paio, le paia* (pl.)

pan   *la padella* (f.)

pants   *i pantaloni* (m. pl.)

paper   *la carta* (f.)

paradise   *il paradiso*

parents   *i genitori* (m. pl.)

park   *il parco*

parking lot   *il parcheggio*

passport   *il passaporto*

pastry shop   *la pasticceria* (f.)

path   *il sentiero, la via* (f.)

payment   *il pagamento*

peace   *la pace* (f.)

peanut   *la nocciolina* (f.), *la arachide* (f.)

pen   *la penna* (f.)

penalty   *la pena* (f.)

pencil   *la matita* (f.)

people   *la gente* (f.)

pepper   *il pepe* (m.)

percentage   *il percento, la percentuale* (f.)

perfume   *il profumo*

person   *la persona* (f.)

pharmacy   *la farmacia* (f.)

photocopy   *la fotocopia* (f.)

photograph   *la fotografia* (f.)

phrase   *la frase* (f.)

piece   *il pezzo*

pill   *la pillola* (f.)

pillow   *il cuscino*

pink   *rosa*

place *il locale* (m.), *il luogo*,
il posto

plain *la pianura* (f.)

plan *il programma* (m.)

plant *la pianta* (f.)

plate *il piatto*

please *per favore, per piacere*

pleasing *piacevole*

pocket *la tasca* (f.)

poem, poetry *la poesia* (f.)

poet *il poeta* (m.), *la poetessa*
(f.)

poison *il veleno*

police *la poliziu* (f.)

police headquarters *la
questura* (f.)

police officer *il carabiniere*
(m.), *il poliziotto, il vigile*

political party *il partito*

politics *la politica* (f.)

pollution *l'inquinamento*

pond *lo stagno*

poor *povero*

Pope *il Papa* (m.)

population *la popolazione* (f.)

pork *il maiale* (m.), *il porco*

portion *la porzione* (f.)

portrait *il ritratto*

post office *l'ufficio postale*

postage stamp *il francobollo*

postal carrier *il postino*

postcard *la cartolina* (f.)

pot *la pentola* (f.)

poultry *il pollame* (m.)

poverty *la miseria* (f.), *la
povertà* (f.)

practice *la pratica* (f.)

prayer *la preghiera* (f.)

pregnant *incinta*

prescription *la ricetta* (f.)

present *il presente*

preservatives *i conservanti*
(m. pl.)

price *il prezzo*

priest *il prete* (m.)

print *la stampa* (f.)

printing *la tipografia* (f.)

prison *il carcere* (m.), *la
prigione* (f.)

private property *la
proprietà privata* (f.)

problem *il problema* (m.)

product *il prodotto*

production *la produzione* (f.)

profession *la professione* (f.)

progress *il progresso*

prohibited *vietato, proibito*

project *il progetto*

pronunciation *la pronuncia*
(f.)

Protestant *protestante*

proud *orgoglioso*

psychology *la psicologia* (f.)

public *il pubblico*

publicity *la pubblicità* (f.)

pupil *l'allievo, lo scolaro*

pure *puro*

purple *viola*

purse *la borsa* (f.)

quality *la qualità* (f.)

quantity *la quantità* (f.)

queen *la regina* (f.)

to question *domandare*

quickly, early *presto*

to quit *smettere (smesso)*
rabbi *il rabbino*
race *la corsa* (f.)
radio *la radio* (f.)
rail car *il vagone* (m.)
railroad *la ferrovia* (f.)
rain *la pioggia* (f.)
raincoat *l'impermeabile* (m.)
rare *raro, al sangue*
raw *crudo*
razor *il rasoio*
ready *pronto*
receipt *la ricevuta* (f.), *lo scontrino*
recent *recente*
reception *il ricevimento*
recipe *la ricetta* (f.)
record *il disco*
red *rosso*
refreshment *la bevanda* (f.)
refrigerator *il frigorifero*
refund *il rimborso*
region *la regione* (f.)
relationship *il rapporto*
relative *il/la parente* (m./f.)
religion *la religione* (f.)
remainder *il resto*
Renaissance *il Rinascimento*
rent *l'affitto*
to rent *affittare, noleggiare*
to repair *riparare*
to repeat *ripetere*
reservation *la prenotazione* (f.)
to reserve *prenotare*
reserved *riservato*

reservoir *la riserva d'acqua* (f.)
residence *il domicilio, la residenza* (f.)
resident *l'abitante* (m./f.)
responsible *responsabile*
restaurant *il ristorante* (m.)
result *il risultato*
to return *ritornare, tornare*
rice *il riso*
rich *ricco*
right (direction) *destro/destra*
right (legal) *il diritto*
ring *l'anello*
ripe *maturo*
river *il fiume* (m.)
robbery *la rapina* (f.)
rock *la pietra* (f.), *la roccia* (f.)
romantic *romantico*
roof *il tetto*
room *la camera* (f.), *la stanza* (f.)
root *la radice* (f.)
rope *la corda* (f.)
round-trip (ticket) *il biglietto d'andata e ritorno*
route *il percorso, la via*
row *la fila* (f.)
ruckus *il baccano*
ruins *le rovine* (f. pl.)
rush hour *l'ora di punta* (f.)
sad *triste*
safe *sicuro*
sailboat *la barca a vela* (f.)
saint *il santo/la santa* (f.)
salad *l'insalata* (f.)

sale *i saldi* (m. pl.), *la svendita* (f.)

salesclerk *il commesso/la commessa* (f.)

salt *il sale* (m.)

same *stesso*

sand *la sabbia* (f.)

sandwich *il panino*

sanitary napkin *l'assorbente* (m.)

sauce *la salsa* (f.)

to say *dire (detto)*

scarf *la sciarpa* (f.)

schedule *l'orario, il programma, la tabella* (f.)

school *la scuola* (f.)

science *la scienza* (f.)

scissors *le forbici* (f. pl.)

scooter *il motorino*

screwdriver *il cacciavite* (m.)

sculpture *la scultura* (f.)

sea *il mare* (m.)

seashell *la conchiglia* (f.)

season *la stagione* (f.)

seat *il posto, il sedile*

seatbelt *la cintura di sicurezza* (f.)

second *secondo*

see you later! *arrivederci! ci vediamo!*

to see *vedere (visto)*

to send *inviare, mandare, spedire*

sentence *la frase* (f.)

separated *separato*

serious *grave, serio*

service *il servizio*

set *fisso, fissato*

sex *il sesso*

she *lei, ella*

sheet (bed) *il lenzuolo*

sheet of paper *il foglio*

ship *la nave* (f.)

shirt *la camicia* (f.)

shoe *la scarpa* (f.)

shoe store *la calzoleria* (f.)

shop *la bottega* (f.), *il negozio*

shop window *la vetrina* (f.)

short *basso, corto*

shorts *i pantaloncini* (m)

show *lo spettacolo, la mostra* (f.) *(art)*

shower *la doccia* (f.)

shrimp *il gambero*

Sicily *la Sicilia*

sick *ammalato*

side dish *il contorno*

sidewalk *il marciapiede* (m.)

sign *il cartello, il segno*

signal *il segnale* (m.)

signature *la firma* (f.)

silence *il silenzio*

silk *la seta* (f.)

silver *l'argento*

singer *il/la cantante* (m./f.)

single (relationship) *solo/sola*

single room (hotel) *stanza singola*

sink *il lavandino*

sister *la sorella* (f.)

sister-in-law *la cognata* (f.)

size *la misura* (f.), *la taglia* (f.)

sketch *lo schizzo*

skiing   *lo sci* (m.)

skirt   *la gonna* (f.)

sky   *il cielo*

Skype   *Skype*

sleep   *il sonno*

to sleep   *dormire*

sleeping pill   *il sonnifero*

slide   *la diapositiva* (f.)

slow down   *rallentare*

small   *piccolo*

to smoke   *fumare*

snack   *lo spuntino*

snow   *la neve* (f.)

so-so   *così così*

soap   *il sapone* (m.)

soccer   *il calcio*

soccer player   *il calciatore* (m.)

socks   *le calze* (f. pl.), *i calzini* (m. pl.)

sofa   *il divano*

soft   *soffice*

sold out   *esaurito*

soldier   *il soldato*

some   *alcuni/alcune, qualche*

someone   *qualcuno*

something   *qualcosa*

sometimes   *qualche volta, talvolta*

son   *il figlio*

son-in-law   *il genero*

soon   *subito, presto*

soul   *l'anima* (f.)

soup   *la minestra* (f.), *la zuppa* (f.)

south   *sud*

space   *lo spazio*

sparkling wine   *lo spumante* (m.)

special   *speciale*

spicy   *piccante*

spiritual   *spirituale*

splendid   *splendido*

spoiled   *guasto, rovinato*

sponge   *la spugna* (f.)

spoon   *il cucchiaio*

sport   *lo sport* (m.)

sports ground   *il campo sportivo*

spouse   *lo sposo/la sposa* (f.)

spring   *la sorgente* (f.), *la primavera* (f.) *(season)*

squid   *i calamari* (m. pl.)

stadium   *lo stadio*

stage   *il palcoscenico*

stain   *la macchia* (f.)

stairs   *la scala* (f.), *le scale* (f. pl.)

star   *la stella* (f.)

station   *la stazione* (f.)

stationery store   *la cartoleria* (f.)

statue   *la statua* (f.)

steak   *la bistecca* (f.)

stepfather   *il patrigno*

stepsister   *la sorellastra* (f.)

stewardess   *la hostess* (f.)

still (again)   *ancora*

stockings   *le calze* (f. pl.), *i collant*

stomach   *lo stomaco, la pancia*

stop   *la fermata* (f.)

to stop   *fermare*

storm   *la tempesta* (f.)

story (tale, fable) *il racconto, la favola*

stove burner *il fornello*

straight *diritto*

strange *strano*

straw (drinking) *la cannuccia* (f.)

stream (brook) *il ruscello, il corso d'acqua*

street *la strada* (f.), *la via* (f.)

stress *lo stress*

strong *forte*

student *lo studente/la studentessa* (f.)

studio apartment *il monolocale* (m.)

stuff *la roba* (f.)

stuffed *ripieno*

stupid *stupido*

suburbs *la periferia* (f.)

subway *la metropolitana* (f.)

sugar *lo zucchero*

suit *l'abito, il vestito*

suitcase *la valigia* (f.)

summer *l'estate* (f.)

sun *il sole* (m.)

sunrise *l'alba* (f.)

sunset *il tramonto*

supermarket *il supermercato*

swamp *la palude* (f.)

sweater *la maglia* (f.)

sweet *dolce*

swimming pool *la piscina* (f.)

symphony *la sinfonia* (f.)

synagogue *la sinagoga* (f.)

synthetic *sintetica*

table *il tavolo* (restaurant), *la tavola*

tablecloth *la tovaglia* (f.)

tablet *la compressa* (f.)

tailor *il sarto*

tall *alto*

tape *l'adesivo, il nastro*

taste *il gusto, il sapore* (m.)

taste, a *un assaggio*

tax *la tassa* (f.)

taxi *il tassì*

taxi meter *il tassametro*

tea *il tè* (m.)

teacher *l'insegnante* (m./f.)

teaspoon *il cucchiaino*

telephone *il telefono*

telephone call *la telefonata* (f.)

telephone card *la carta telefonica* (f.)

to telephone *telefonare*

to tell *dire (detto), raccontare*

terrace *il terrazzo*

thank you! *grazie!*

that *quello/quella*

theater *il teatro*

then *allora, poi*

there *ci, lì/là*

there is *c'è*

thermometer *il termometro*

they *loro*

thief *il ladro*

thin *magro*

thing *la cosa* (f.)

thirst *la sete* (f.)

this *questo*

this evening *stasera*

this morning　*stamattina*

thunder　*il tuono*

ticket　*il biglietto*

ticket counter　*la biglietteria* (f.)

tide　*la marea* (f.)

tie　*la cravatta* (f.)

tight　*stretto*

tile　*la piastrella* (f.)

time　*l'ora* (f.), *il tempo*

tip　*la mancia* (f.)

tire　*il pneumatico*

tired　*stanco*

tissue　*il fazzoletto*

to　*a, in*

tobacco shop　*la tabaccheria* (f.)

today　*oggi*

together　*insieme*

toilet　*il gabinetto, la toilette* (f.)

toilet paper　*la carta igienica* (f.)

toll　*il pedaggio*

toll-free number　*il numero verde*

tomato　*il pomodoro*

tomorrow　*domani*

tonight　*stanotte*

too　*troppo*

tooth　*il dente* (m.)

toothbrush　*lo spazzolino da denti*

toothpaste　*il dentifricio*

total　*totale*

tour　*il giro*

tourism　*il turismo*

tourist　*il/la turista* (m./f.)

toward　*verso*

town square　*la piazza* (f.)

toy　*il giocattolo*

track　*il binario*

traffic　*il traffico*

traffic light　*il semaforo*

train　*il treno*

translation　*la traduzione* (f.)

to transport　*trasportare*

trash　*i rifiuti* (m. pl.), *la spazzatura* (f.)

trash can　*il bidone della spazzatura*

to travel　*viaggiare*

tree　*l'albero*

trip　*il viaggio*

trouble　*il guaio*

truck　*il camion* (m.)

true　*vero*

trust　*la fiducia* (f.)

truth　*la verità* (f.)

to try　*provare*

tub　*la vasca* (f.)

tunnel　*la galleria* (f.), *il sotterraneo*

turn　*il turno*

to turn　*girare*

to turn off　*spegnere (spento)*

type, kind　*la specie* (f.), *il tipo*

ugly　*brutto*

umbrella　*l'ombrello*

uncle　*lo zio*

uncomfortable　*scomodo*

understood!　*capito!*

underwear　*la biancheria intima* (f.)

unemployed *disoccupato*

United States *gli Stati Uniti* (m. pl.)

unmarried *celibe* (m.), *nubile* (f.)

until *fino a*

urgent *urgente*

to use *usare*

vacation *la vacanza* (f.)

vaccination *la vaccinazione* (f.)

validated *convalidato*

variety *la varietà* (f.)

vase *il vaso*

VAT/sales tax *I.V.A.* (*Imposta Valore Aggiunto*)

vegetarian *vegetariano*

vehicle *il veicolo*

verb *il verbo*

very *molto*

victim *la vittima* (f.)

view *la vista* (f.)

villa *la villa* (f.)

village *il villaggio*

vinegar *l'aceto*

violence *la violenza* (f.)

visible *visibile*

visit *la visita* (f.)

to visit *visitare*

vitamin *la vitamina* (f.)

vocabulary *il vocabolario*

to wait *aspettare*

waiter *il cameriere*

waiting room *la sala d'attesa* (f.)

waitress *la cameriera* (f.)

to walk *camminare, passeggiare*

wall *il muro, la parete* (f.)

wallet *il portafoglio*

to wake up *svegliarsi*

to want *volere*

war *la guerra* (f.)

warm *caldo*

warning *l'avviso*

to wash *lavare*

watch *l'orologio*

water *l'acqua* (f.)

wave *l'onda* (f.)

weak *debole*

to wear *indossare, portare*

weather *il tempo*

week *la settimana* (f.)

weekend *il fine settimana*

to weigh *pesare*

weight *il peso*

welcome! greetings! *benvenuto!*

well (feeling) *bene*

well *il pozzo*

west *ovest*

wet *bagnato*

what *che, che cosa*

wheel *la ruota* (f.)

when *quando*

where *dove*

wherever *ovunque*

which *quale*

while *mentre*

who *chi*

wholesale *all'ingrosso*

why *perché*

wife *la moglie* (f.)

wind *il vento*

window *la finestra* (f.)
(house/building), *il finestrino*
(car/train/plane)

windshield *il parabrezza*
(m.)

wine *il vino*

wine bar *l'enoteca* (f.)

winery *l'azienda vinicola* (f.)

winter *l'inverno*

wish *il desiderio, la voglia* (f.)

with *con*

within *fra*

without *senza*

woman *la donna* (f.), *la
femmina* (f.), *la signora* (f.)

wood *il legno*

woods *il bosco, la selva* (f.)

wool *la lana* (f.)

work *il lavoro*

worker *l'impiegato, l'operaio*

world *il mondo*

worried *preoccupato*

worse *peggio*

to write *scrivere (scritto)*

writer *lo scrittore/la scrittrice*
(f.)

to be wrong *sbagliare*

year *l'anno*

yes *sì*

yesterday *ieri*

you *Lei* (polite), *tu*
(familiar), *voi* (plural)

you're welcome! *prego!*

young *giovane*

zero *zero*

zipper *la cerniera* (f.)

zoo *lo zoo*

Italian–English
Dictionary

a, ad (before vowels) at, in, to, by

a bordo on board

abbastanza enough

l'abbazia (f.) abbey

l'abbigliamento clothing

abbronzarsi to get tanned

l'abitante (m./f.) resident, inhabitant

abitare to live

l'abito outfit, suit

accanto a besides, next to

accendere (acceso) to light, to turn on

l'accento accent

l'accesso access

accidenti! darn!

accompagnare to accompany

accordo agreement

l'aceto vinegar

l'acqua (f.) water

acqua non potabile unpotable water

l'acquario aquarium

adesso now

l'adulto adult

l'aereo airplane

l'aeroporto airport

l'affare (m.) business, deal

affittare to rent (a house or apartment)

affittasi for rent

l'affitto rent

l'agenzia (f.) agency

aiuto! help!

al coperto indoors

al forno baked

al sangue rare

l'alba (f.) sunrise

l'albergo hotel

l'albero tree

alcol alchohol (m.)

alcuni/alcune some

gli alimentari (m. pl.) groceries

all'aperto outdoors, open air

allegro happy

l'allergia (f.) allergy

allora then

almeno at least

altezza (f.) height

alto tall

altro other

alzare to raise, lift

alzarsi to get up

amare to love

amaro bitter

l'ambasciata (f.) embassy

l'ambulanza (f.) ambulance

l'amicizia (f.) friendship

l'amico/l'amica (f.) friend

ammalato sick, ill

l'amministrazione (f.) management, administration

l'amore (m.) love

anche also

ancora still, again, yet

andare to go

andata e ritorno round-trip (ticket)

l'anello ring

l'anima (f.) spirit

l'animale (m.) animal

l'anno year

l'annuncio announcement

antico ancient, antique

l'antipasto appetizer

antipatico unpleasant, disagreeable

anzi on the contrary, but rather

anziano elderly

l'aperitivo aperitif

aperto open, outside

aprire (aperto) to open

l'area (f.) area

l'aria (f.) aria, air, appearance

l'aria condizionata (f.) air-conditioning

arrabbiato angry

l'arredamento furnishings

arrivare to arrive

arrivederci! see you later!

l'arrivo arrival

arrosto roasted

l'arte (f.) art

l'artista (m./f.) artist

l'ascensore (m.) elevator

asciutto dry

ascoltare to listen to

l'asilo kindergarten, day-care center

aspettare to wait for

assaggiare to taste

l'assegno check

l'assicurazione (f.) insurance

l'assistenza (medica) (f.) assistance (medical), insurance (health)

l'Assunzione (f.) Feast of the Assumption

l'atleta (m./f.) athlete

attendere prego! please hold!

attenzione! attention! warning!

l'attimo moment

l'attività (f.) activity

attivo active

l'atto document, record

l'attore actor

attraverso across

l'attrice (f.) actress

auguri! best wishes!

l'autobus (m.) bus

l'automobile (f.) car

l'autonoleggio car rental

l'autostop (m.) hitchhiking

l'autostrada (f.) highway

l'autunno (m.) autumn

avanti forward

avere to have

avvenire to happen

l'avventura (f.) adventure

avvertire to warn

avvicinarsi to approach, to get near

l'avvocato lawyer

l'azienda (f.) firm, company

azzurro light blue

il babbo dad

baciare to kiss

il bacio kiss

bagnato wet

il bagno bath

la baia (f.)   bay

il balcone (m.)   balcony

il ballo   dance

il bambino   baby, child

la banca (f.)   bank

la bancarella (f.)   stall, booth

il banco   counter

il Bancomat   ATM

il bar (m.)   bar, café

la barba (f.)   beard

il barbiere (m.)   barber

la barca (f.)   boat

il/la barista (m./f.)   bartender

la barzelletta (f.)   joke

basso   short, low

basta!   enough!

la Befana (f.)   Epiphany (January 6)

la bellezza (f.)   beauty

benché   although

bene   well

benvenuto!   welcome!

la benzina (f.)   gasoline

bere (bevuto)   to drink

la bestia (f.)   beast

la bevanda (f.)   refreshment

la biancheria intima (f.)   underwear

la Bibbia (f.)   Bible

il biberon (m.)   baby bottle

la bibita (f.)   refreshment, beverage

il bicchiere (m.)   glass

la biglietteria (f.)   ticket counter

il biglietto   ticket

il binario   track, platform

il bocconcino   morsel, nibble

bordo, a   aboard

la borsa (f.)   bag, purse

il bosco   woods

la bottega (f.)   shop

il braccio   arm

bravo   good, able

breve   brief, short

la brioche (f.)   brioche, croissant

il brodo   broth

bruciato   burnt

brutto   ugly

il bucato   laundry

buffo   funny

il buio   dark

Buon Anno!   Happy New Year!

Buon Compleanno!   Happy Birthday!

Buon giorno!   good day!/ hello!

Buon Natale!   Merry Christmas!

Buona Feste!   Happy Holidays!

Buona Pasqua!   Happy Easter!

buono   good

la bustina (f.)   bag

c'è   there is

il caffè (m.)   coffee, café

i calamari (m. pl.)   squid

il calcio   soccer, kick

caldo   heat, hot

le calze (f. pl.)   stockings

i calzini (m. pl.) socks

il calzolaio shoe repair shop

la calzoleria (f.) shoe store

i calzoncini (m. pl.) shorts

il cambio exchange

la camera (f.) room

la cameriera (f.) waitress, maid

il cameriere waiter

la camicetta (f.) blouse

la camicia (f.) dress shirt

il caminetto fireplace

il camino chimney

il camion (m.) truck

camminare to walk

la campagna (f.) country, countryside

il campanello doorbell

il campeggio camping

il campionato match, championship

il campo sportivo sports field

il cancello gate

la candela (f.) candle

il candidato candidate

il cane (m.) dog

il/la cantante (m./f.) singer

i capelli (m. pl.) hair (on head)

capito! understood!

la cappella (f.) chapel

il cappello hat

il cappotto overcoat, coat

il carabiniere (m.) police officer

la caramella (f.) candy

il carcere (m.) jail

carino cute, pretty

la carne (f.) meat

caro dear, expensive

la carta (f.) paper

la carta di credito (f.) credit card

la carta d'identità identification card

la carta igienica (f.) toilet paper

la carta stradale (f.) map

il cartello sign

la cartoleria (f.) stationery store

la cartolina (f.) postcard

la casa (f.) house, home

il casco helmet

la cassa (f.) cash register

castano brown

il castello castle

la cattedrale (f.) cathedral

cattivo bad, evil, naughty

cattolico Catholic

il cavallo horse

il cavatappi (m.) corkscrew

il cavo cable

celibe unmarried, single (m.)

la cena (f.) dinner

cenare to dine

il centro center, downtown

cercare to search, look for

il certificato certificate

certo certain, sure, of course

che what?, who?, which? that

che cosa what?

chi who?, whom?, the one who

chiamare to call

chiamarsi to call oneself (to be named)

chiaro clear, light

la chiave (f.) key

chiedere (chiesto) to ask

la chiesa (f.) church

il chilogrammo kilogram

il chilometro kilometer

chiudere (chiuso) to close

chiuso closed

la chiusura festiva (f.) holiday closures

ci there

ciascuno each, each one

il cibo food

il cielo sky, heaven

la ciliegia (f.) cherry

il cinema (m.) cinema/movie theater

la cintura (f.) belt

la cintura di sicurezza (f.) seatbelt

ciò that which

circa about, approximately

la città (f.) city

la cittadinanza (f.) citizenship

il cittadino/la cittadina (f.) citizen

classico classical

il/la cliente (m./f.) client, customer

la cognata (f.) sister-in-law

il cognato brother-in-law

il cognome (m.) surname

la coincidenza (f.) connection, coincidence

la colazione (f.) breakfast

la collana (f.) necklace

i collant (m. pl.) stockings

il/la collega (m./f.) colleague

la collina (f.) hill

il colore (m.) color

il coltello knife

il comandamento commandment

come how, like, as

cominciare to begin, to start

il commesso/la commessa (f.) salesclerk

comodo convenient, comfortable

il compleanno birthday

il complimento compliment

il comportamento behavior

comprare to buy

la comprensione (f.) understanding

la compressa (f.) tablet, pill

comunicare to communicate

la comunità (f.) community

comunque however, no matter how

con with

il concerto concert

la conchiglia (f.) seashell

condividere (condiviso) to share

il conflitto conflict

il conforto comfort, convenience

congratulazioni! congratulations!

il congresso meeting, conference

conoscere (conosciuto) to know someone

consecutivo consecutive

la conseguenza (f.) consequence

i conservanti (m. pl.) preservatives

il contadino/la contadina (f.) farmer, peasant

i contanti (m. pl.) cash

il contatto contact

contento glad, satisfied

continuare to continue

il conto check, bill, account

il contorno side dish

il contraccettivo contraceptive

il contrario opposite

contro against

il controllo check, control

convalidare to validate

convalidato validated

il convento convent

la coperta (f.) blanket, cover

il coperto cover charge

la copia (f.) copy

la coppa (f.) cup

la coppia (f.) couple

il coro chorus, choir

il corpo body

corretto correct

il corriere messenger, courier

la corriera (f.) intercity bus

la corsa (f.) race

la corsia (f.) lane

il corso course

cortese courteous

la cosa (f.) thing

così so, thus

così così so-so

la costa (f.) coast

il costo cost, price

costare to cost

costoso costly, expensive

cotto cooked

credere to believe

il credito credit

cristiano Christian

croccante crunchy

la croce (f.) cross

la crociera (f.) cruise

crudo raw, uncooked

la cuccetta (f.) bunk

il cucchiaio spoon

cucinare to cook

il cugino/la cugina (f.) cousin

cui whom, that, which

la cultura (f.) culture

culturale cultural

cuocere (cotto) to cook

il cuoio leather

la cupola (f.) dome

curare to care for, to look after

la curva (f.) curve

il cuscino pillow

da from, by

danneggiato damaged

dappertutto everywhere

dare to give

la data (f.) date

davanti a in front of

davvero really

la dea (f.) goddess

decidere (deciso) to decide

definire to define

la definizione (f.) definition

il delfino dolphin

della casa homemade

della stagione in season

il denaro money

il dente (m.) tooth

il dentifricio toothpaste

il/la dentista (m./f.) dentist

dentro inside

il desiderio wish, desire

la destinazione (f.) destination

destro right

il detersivo detergent

la deviazione (f.) detour

di of, about, from

di solito usually

il dialogo dialogue

il diamante (m.) diamond

la diapositiva (f.) slide

dichiarare to declare

la didattica (f.) pedagogy, teaching

la dieta (f.) diet

dietro a behind

difendere (difeso) to defend

il difetto defect

la differenza (f.) difference

difficile difficult

la diga (f.) dam

la digestione (f.) digestion

diminuire to decrease

dinamico energetic

il Dio God

dipendere (dipeso) to depend

dipingere (dipinto) to paint

dire (detto) to say, to tell

diretto direct

la direzione (f.) direction (management)

dirigere (diretto) to manage, to direct

diritto straight

il diritto law

il discorso speech, discussion, argument

la discussione (f.) discussion, argument

disegnare to draw

il disegno drawing, design

la disgrazia (f.) misfortune

disoccupato unemployed

dispiacere (dispiaciuto) to be sorry

disponibile available

la distanza (f.) distance

il distributore di benzina gas pump

distruggere (distrutto) to destroy

la ditta (f.) firm, business

il divano sofa

diverso different

divertirsi to enjoy oneself

divieto di sosta no parking

divorziato/a divorced

il dizionario dictionary

la doccia (f.) shower

il documento document

la dogana (f.) customs

dolce sweet

il dolce dessert

il dollaro dollar

il dolore (m.) pain

domandare to question

domani tomorrow

la domestica (f.) housekeeper

il domicilio residence

la donna (f.) woman

dopo after, afterward

doppio double

dormire to sleep

dove where

dovere to have to, to must

la droga (f.) drug

il duomo cathedral, dome

dunque thus, then

durante during

duro hard, tough

e, ed (before vowels) and

è is

ebbene well then, so

ebreo Jewish

eccetera etcetera

eccetto except

ecco here is, there is

economico inexpensive

l'edicola (f.) newsstand

l'edificio building

l'elenco list, directory

l'elettricità (f.) electricity

l'emergenza (f.) emergency

l'enoteca (f.) wine bar

entrambi both

entrare to enter

l'entrata (f.) entrance

l'Epifania (f.) Epiphany (Jan. 6)

esaurito sold out, depleted

esportare to export

essenziale essential

essere (stato) to be

est east

l'estate (f.) summer

l'estero abroad

l'età (f.) age

l'etichetta (f.) tag, label

l'etto hectogram

l'Europa (f.) Europe

evitare to avoid

fa ago

la fabbrica (f.) factory

fabbricare to manufacture

la faccenda (f.) thing, matter, chore

la faccia (f.) face

facile easy

la facoltà (f.) school falculty (university)

il fagiolo bean

la fame (f.) hunger

la famiglia (f.) family

famoso famous

fare (fatto) to do, to make

la farina (f.) flour

la farmacia (f.) pharmacy

la fatica (f.) effort

il fatto fact

la fattoria (f.) farm

il fazzoletto tissue

la febbre (f.) fever

la fede (f.) faith

felice happy

la femmina (f.) female

la ferita (f.) injury

la fermata (f.) stop

Ferragosto Assumption Day (August 15)

la ferrovia (f.) railroad

la festa (f.) party, holiday

festeggiare to celebrate

i fiammiferi (m. pl.) matches

il fianco side

la fidanzata (f.) fiancée

il fidanzato fiancé

fiero proud

la fiera (f.) fair

la figlia (f.) daughter

il figlio son

la fila (f.) line, row

il filetto filet

il film film

finalmente finally

la finanza (f.) finance

finanziare to finance

la fine (f.) end

il fine settimana weekend

la finestra (f.) window

il finestrino window (car, train, plane)

fino a until, as far as

la firma (f.) signature

il fiume (m.) river

il fuoco fire

la foglia (f.) leaf

il foglio sheet of paper

il fondo bottom

la fontana (f.) fountain

le forbici (f. pl.) scissors

la forchetta (f.) fork

la foresta (f.) forest

la forma (f.) form

il formaggio cheese

il fornaio baker

il forno oven

forse maybe

forte strong

la fortuna (f.) fortune

la fotocopia (f.) photocopy

la fotografia (f.) photograph

fra within, in, between, among

fragile fragile

il francobollo postage stamp

la frase (f.) phrase, sentence

il fratello brother

freddo cold

fresco fresh

la fretta (f.) haste, hurry

fritto fried

la frutta (f.) fruit

il fruttivendolo greengrocer's

fumare   to smoke
il funerale (m.)   funeral
la funivia (f.)   cable car, funicular
il fuoco   fire
fuori   outside
furbo   clever, sly (slang)
il gabinetto   toilet
la galleria (f.)   tunnel, gallery (art)
la gamba (f.)   leg
il gambero   shrimp
il garage (m.)   garage
garantire   to guarantee
il gatto   cat
il gelato   ice cream
il genero   son-in-law
i genitori (m. pl.)   parents
la gente (f.)   people
gentile   kind, polite
la gentilezza (f.)   kindness
Gesù   Jesus
il ghiaccio   ice
già   already
la giacca (f.)   jacket
giallo   yellow
il giardino   garden
il ginecologo   gynecologist
giocare   to play
il giocattolo   toy
il gioco   game
la gioia (f.)   joy
la gioielleria (f.)   jewelry store
il giornalaio   newspaper vendor
il giornale (m.)   newspaper

la giornata (f.)   day, daytime
il giorno   day
giovane   young
il giro   tour
giù   down
il giubbotto   coat
la giurisprudenza (f.)   law
giusto   just, right, correct
la gonna (f.)   skirt
il governo   government
il grammo   gram
grande   big, large
la grappa (f.)   grappa
grasso   fat
gratis   free of charge
grave   serious, grave
la grazia (f.)   grace
grazie!   thank you!
la griglia (f.)   grill
grosso   large
la grotta (f.)   cave
la gruccia (f.)   hanger
i guanti (m. pl.)   gloves
il guaio   trouble
guardare   to look at, to watch
il guardaroba (m.)   closet, cloakroom
guasto   damaged, broken
il guasto   breakdown
la guerra (f.)   war
la guida (f.)   guide
guidare   to drive
gustare   to taste
il gusto   taste
la hostess (f.)   stewardess
l'hotel (m.)   hotel

I.V.A. (Imposta Valore Aggiunto)   VAT/sales tax

l'identità (f.)   identity

ieri   yesterday

l'imbarco   boarding

l'immagine (f.)   image

l'immigrazione (f.)   immigration

imparare   to learn

l'impermeabile   raincoat

l'impiegato   worker, employee, official

importante   important

importare   to import, to matter

l'impressione (f.)   impression

in   in, to, at

in fretta   in a hurry

incartare   to wrap

l'incidente (m.)   accident

incinta   pregnant

inciso   engraved

incontrare   to meet

l'incrocio   crossing

l'indicazione (f.)   direction, indication

indietro   back, behind

l'indipendenza (f.)   independence

indiretto   indirect

l'indirizzo   address

indossare   to wear

infatti   in fact

inferiore   inferior, lower

l'infermiera (f.)   nurse

l'inferno   hell

l'informazione (f.)   information

l'Inghilterra (f.)   England

inglese   English

ingrassare   to gain weight

l'ingrediente (m.)   ingredient

l'ingresso   entrance

iniziare   to begin

l'inizio   beginning

innamorarsi   to fall in love with

inoltre   also

l'inquinamento   pollution

l'insalata (f.)   salad

l'insegnante (m./f.)   teacher

insegnare   to teach

l'insetto   insect

insieme   together

insolito   unusual

interessante   interesting

l'intermezzo   intermission

interno   internal, inside

interpretare   to interpret

l'interprete   interpreter

l'interurbana (f.)   long-distance call

intorno a   around

introdurre (introdotto)   to introduce

inutile   useless

invece   instead

l'inverno   winter

inviare   to mail, to send

invitare   to invite

l'invito   invitation

io   I

irregolare irregular
l'iscritto student, member
l'isola (f.) island
l'istruzione (f.) instruction
l'itinerario itinerary
i jeans (m. pl.) jeans
kasher kosher
là there
il ladro thief
il lago lake
la lampada (f.) light
la lampadina (f.) light bulb
il lampo lightning
il lampone (m.) raspberry
la lana (f.) wool
largo wide
lasciare to let, to leave behind
il lato side
la latteria (f.) dairy store
la lavanderia (f.) laundry service
la lavanderia a secco dry-cleaner
il lavandino sink
lavare to wash
lavorare to work
il lavoro work
la legge (f.) law
leggere (letto) to read
leggero light
il legno wood
lei she, her
Lei you (polite)
il lenzuolo sheet
la lettera (f.) letter
il letto bed

lì there
libero free
la libreria (f.) bookstore
il libro book
la linea (f.) line
la lingua (f.) language, tongue
la lista (f.) list
il litro liter
lontano far
loro they
la lozione (f.) lotion
la luce (f.) light
lui he, him
la luna (f.) moon
la luna di miele (f.) honeymoon
lunedì dell'Angelo Easter Monday
la lunghezza (f.) length
lungo long
il luogo place
lusso luxury
ma but
la macchia (f.) stain
la macchina (f.) automobile, car, machine
la macchina fotografica (f.) camera
la macelleria (f.) butcher shop
la madre (f.) mother
la madrelingua (f.) native language
il magazzino department store, warehouse
la maggioranza (f.) majority

la maglia (f.) sweater, pullover

magro thin

mai never, ever

il maiale (m.) pork, pig

il mais (m.) corn

malato unhealthy, sick

la malattia (f.) illness

la mancia (f.) tip

mandare to send

mangiare to eat

la maniera (f.) manner, way

la maniglia (f.) handle

la mano (f.) hand

il manzo beef

la marca (f.) brand, type

il marciapiede (m.) sidewalk

il mare (m.) sea

la marea (f.) tide

il marito husband

il marmo marble

marrone brown

la maschera (f.) mask

la mattina (f.) morning

matto crazy

maturo ripe, mature

il meccanico mechanic

la medicina (f.) medicine

il medico doctor

il Medioevo Middle Ages

meglio better

meno less

la mensa (f.) cafeteria

mensile monthly

la menta (f.) mint

la mente (f.) mind

mentre while

il/la mercante (m./f.) merchant

il mercatino farmers market

il mercato market

la merce (f.) merchandise

il mese (m.) month

la messa (f.) mass

il messaggio message

la metà (f.) half

il metallo metal

la metropolitana (f.) subway

mettere (messo) to put, to place

la mezzanotte (f.) midnight

mezzo half

il mezzo means (resources)

mezzogiorno noon

mi me, to me

il miele (m.) honey

il miglio mile

il/la migliore the best

la minestra (f.) soup

il ministro minister

la minoranza (f.) minority

minore smaller, less

il minuto minute

la miseria (f.) poverty

la misura (f.) measure, size

il/la mittente (m./f.) sender

il mobile (m.) piece of furniture

moderno modern

il modo manner, method, way

il modulo form

la moglie (f.) wife

molo pier, dock

molto a lot, much, very

il momento moment

il mondo world

la moneta (f.) coin

monolocale (m.) single room, studio

la montagna (f.) mountain

il monumento monument

morbido soft, smooth

morire (morto) to die

la morte (f.) death

la mosca (f.) fly (insect)

la mostra (f.) show (art)

il motore (m.) motor

il motorino scooter

la multa (f.) fine, ticket

il muro wall

il museo museum

mussulmano Muslim

il mutuo loan, mortgage

la nascita (f.) birth

il nastro tape

la natura (f.) nature

naturale natural

la nave (f.) ship

la nazionalità (f.) nationality

la nazione (f.) nation

ne some of, about it

né … né neither … nor

neanche not even

la nebbia (f.) fog

la necessità (f.) need, necessity

necessario necessary

il negozio shop

nemmeno not even

nessuno no one, nobody

la neve (f.) snow

niente nothing

il nipote grandson, nephew

la nipote (f.) granddaughter, niece

la nocciola (f.) hazelnut

la nocciolina (f.) peanuts, nuts

la noce (f.) walnut

noi we

noioso boring

noleggiare to rent (a vehicle or transportation)

il nome (m.) noun, name

il nome da nubile maiden name

il nome del coniuge spouse's name

il nome di famiglia last name, surname

non not

la nonna (f.) grandmother

il nonno grandfather

nord north

la notizia (f.) news, novelty

la notte (f.) night

la novità (f.) news

nubile unmarried

nulla nothing

il numero number

il numero verde toll-free number

la nuora (f.) daughter-in-law

nuotare to swim

nuovo new

o or

l'occasione (f.) occasion, bargain

gli occhiali (m. pl.) eyeglasses

l'occhio eye

occupato busy, occupied

l'oceano ocean

l'odore (m.) aroma, odor

l'offerta (f.) offer

gli oggetti smarriti (m. pl.) lost property

l'oggetto object

oggi today

ogni each, every

Ognissanti All Saint's Day (Nov. 1)

ognuno everybody

l'olio oil

l'oliva (f.) olive

oltre more than, in addition to

l'ombrello umbrella

l'onda (f.) wave

onesto honest

l'operaio worker

oppure or

l'ora (f.) hour, now

l'ora di punta (f.) rush hour

l'orario schedule

l'ordine (m.) order

l'oreficeria (f.) jeweler's, goldsmith's

orgoglioso proud

l'oro gold

l'orologio watch, clock

l'orto garden

l'ospedale (m.) hospital

l'ospite (m./f.) guest

l'ostello hostel

ottico optician

ottimo excellent, best

l'ottone brass

ovest west

ovunque wherever

il pacco package, parcel

la pace (f.) peace

il padre (m.) father

il padrino godfather

il padrone/la padrona (f.) boss, landlord, owner

il paese (m.) country, town

pagare to pay

il palazzo building, palace

il palco box (theater)

il palcoscenico stage

la palestra (f.) gym

la palla (f.) ball

la pallacanestro (f.) basketball

la palude (f.) swamp, marsh

il pane (m.) bread

la panetteria (f.) bakery

il panino sandwich

la panna (f.) cream (edible)

il pannolino diaper

il pano piano

il panorama (m.) panorama, view

i pantaloni (m. pl.) pants

il **Papa** (m.) Pope
il **papà** (m.) daddy, pop
il **parcheggio** parking lot
il **parco** park
il/la **parente** (m./f.) relative
parere (parso) to seem, to appear
la **partenza** (f.) departure
partire to depart, to leave
la **partita** (f.) game, match
Pasqua Easter
il **passaporto** passport
passare to pass
il **passato** past
la **passeggiata** (f.) stroll, walk
la **passione** (f.) passion
il **passo** step
la **pasticceria** (f.) pastry shop
il **pasto** meal
la **patente** (f.) driver's license
la **patria** (f.) homeland
il **patrigno** stepfather
la **paura** (f.) fear
il **pavimento** floor
peccato! what a shame!
il **pedaggio** toll
il **pelo** hair
la **pelle** (f.) skin, leather
la **pelletteria** (f.) furrier shop
la **pelliccia** (f.) fur
la **pellicola** (f.) film
la **pena** (f.) penalty
la **penisola** (f.) peninsula

la **penna** (f.) pen
pensare to think
la **pensione** (f.) inn, pension
il **pepe** (m.) pepper
per for, in order to
per favore please
per piacere please
il **percento** percentage
perché why, because
il **percorso** route
perdere (perso) to lose
il **pericolo** danger
pericoloso dangerous
la **periferia** (f.) suburbs
permesso! excuse me!
permettere (permesso) to permit
però but, however
la **persona** (f.) person
pesante heavy
il **pesce** (m.) fish
la **pescheria** (f.) fish store
il **peso** weight
il **piacere** (m.) pleasure
piacevole pleasing
piangere (pianto) to cry
il **pianterreno** ground floor
piano softly
la **pianta** (f.) plant
la **pianura** (f.) plain
il **piatto** plate
la **piazza** (f.) town square
piccante spicy
il **picco** peak
piccolo small
il **piede** (m.) foot

pieno full

la pietra (f.) stone

la pila (f.) battery

la pillola (f.) pill

la pioggia (f.) rain

piovere to rain

la piscina (f.) swimming pool

la pista (f.) track, trail, slope

la pittura (f.) painting

più more

piuttosto rather

il pneumatico tire

un po' a little

poco not very much

poi then, afterward

poiché since

la politica (f.) politics

la polizia (f.) police

il poliziotto police officer

la polpetta (f.) meatball

il pomeriggio afternoon

il pomodoro tomato

il pompiere (m.) firefighter

il ponte (m.) bridge

il porco pig, pork

la porta (f.) door

il portabagagli (m.) porter

il portacenere (m.) ashtray

il portafoglio wallet

portare to bring, to carry

il porto harbor, port

la porzione (f.) portion

la posta (f.) mail, post office

il postino postal carrier

il posto seat, place

potere to be able to

pranzare to dine, to eat lunch

il pranzo lunch

pratico convenient, practical, expert

il prato lawn, field

il prefisso area code

pregare to pray, to beg, to ask

la preghiera (f.) prayer

prego! you're welcome!

prendere (preso) to take

prenotare to make a reservation

la prenotazione (f.) reservation

preoccupato worried

presentare to present

il presente (m.) present

presso in care of (c/o)

prestare to lend

presto quickly, early

il prete (m.) priest

il prezzo price

il prezzo d'entrata admission charge

prima before

la primavera (f.) spring

primo first, before

il problema (m.) problem

il profilattico condom

la profumeria (f.) cosmetics shop

il profumo perfume

il programma (m.) plan, program

promettere (promesso) to promise

pronto ready, hello (telephone)

pronto soccorso emergency room, first aid

la pronuncia (f.) pronunciation

pronunciare to pronounce

il proprietario owner

la proprietà privata (f.) private property

proprio just, really

prossimo next

provare to try, to experience

il pubblico public

pulire to clean

il pullman (m.) bus

purché provided that

pure also

qua here

il quadro painting, picture

qualche some

qualche volta sometimes

qualcosa something

qualcuno someone

quale which

qualsiasi any

qualunque any

quando when

quanto? how much?

il quartiere (m.) neighborhood

quasi almost

quattordici fourteen

quello/quella that

la questione (f.) matter

questo this one

la questura (f.) police headquarters

qui here

quindi therefore

quotidiano daily

il quotidiano daily paper

il rabbino rabbi

il raffreddore (m.) cold

la ragazza (f.) girl

il ragazzo boy

rallentare slow down

il rapido express train

la rapina (f.) robbery

il rapporto relationship

recente recent

il regalo gift, present

la regione (f.) region

il/la regista (m./f.) movie director

la religione (f.) religion

la residenza (f.) residence

restare to remain, to stay

il resto remainder, rest

ricco rich

la ricetta (f.) recipe, prescription

il ricevimento reception

la ricevuta (f.) receipt

la richiesta (f.) request

ricordare to remember

ridere (riso) to laugh

riempire to fill out (a form)

i rifiuti (m. pl.) trash

riflettere (riflesso) to reflect

il rifugio refuge

rilassante   relaxing

rimanere (rimasto)   to remain

il rimborso   refund

il Rinascimento   the Renaissance

ringraziare   to thank

riparare   to repair

ripetere   to repeat

riscaldare   to warm, to heat

la riserva d'acqua (f.)   reservoir

la riserva naturale (f.)   nature preserve

riservato   reserved

la risposta (f.)   answer, response

il ristorante (m.)   restaurant

il ritardo   delay

il ritmo   rhythm

ritornare   to return

il ritratto   portrait

la rivista (f.)   magazine

la roba (f.)   stuff, things

la roccia (f.)   rock

il romanzo   novel, fiction, romance

rotto   broken

le rovine (f. pl.)   ruins

rubare   to steal

il rubinetto   faucet

rumoroso   noisy

la rupe (f.)   cliff

il ruscello   stream

la sabbia (f.)   sand

il sacco a pelo   sleeping bag

la sala (f.)   room, hall

la sala d'attesa (f.)   waiting room

la sala da pranzo (f.)   dining room

la sala giochi (f.)   game room

il saldo   sale, discount

il sale (m.)   salt

salire   to climb, to mount

il salotto   living room, lounge

la salsa (f.)   sauce

la salute (f.)   health

il sangue (m.)   blood

il santo/la santa (f.)   saint

il sapone (m.)   soap

il sapore (m.)   taste

il sarto   tailor

sbagliare   to be mistaken

sbarcare   to land, to disembark

la scala (f.)   stairs

scambiare   to exchange

lo scambio   exchange

lo scapolo   bachelor

la scarpa (f.)   shoe

la scatola (f.)   box

scegliere (scelto)   to choose

scemo   silly, idiotic

la scena (f.)   scene

scendere   to descend, to get off

scherzare   to joke

lo schizzo   sketch

lo sci (m.)   skiing

lo sci di fondo   cross-country skiing

la sciarpa (f.)   scarf

scomodo uncomfortable

lo sconto discount

lo scontrino receipt

la scrivania (f.) desk

scrivere (scritto) to write

la scultura (f.) sculpture

la scuola (f.) school

scuro dark

scusarsi to apologize

se if

sé oneself (himself, herself)

sebbene although

secco dry

sedersi to sit down

la sedia (f.) chair

il segnale (m.) signal, sign

segnare to mark, to note

il segno sign

seguente following

seguire to follow

la selva (f.) woods, forest

il semaforo traffic light

sembrare to seem

semplice simple

sempre always

senso unico one-way street

il sentiero path, trail

il sentimento feeling, sentiment

sentire to hear, to smell, to taste

senza without

la sera (f.) evening

il serbatoio gas tank

sereno calm, good weather

serio serious

il servizio service

il sesso sex

la sete (f.) thirst

la settimana (f.) week

si oneself, each other, one, they

sì yes

la signora (f.) Mrs., Ms., lady

il signore (m.) Mr., Sir, man

la signorina (f.) Miss, young lady

simpatico nice, kind

il/la sindaco/a mayor

la sinfonia (f.) symphony

singolo single

sinistro left

il sintomo symptom

Skype Skype

smettere (smesso) to quit

la società (f.) company

soffice soft

solamente only

i soldi (m. pl.) money

il sole (m.) sun

solito usual

solo alone

il sonno sleep

sono I am, they are

sopra above, on

la sorella (f.) sister

la sorellastra (f.) stepsister, half-sister

la sorgente (f.) spring

la sosta (f.) stop, pause

sotto beneath

il sottotitolo subtitle

spaventare to scare, to frighten

la spazzatura (f.) trash

la spazzola (f.) brush

lo spazzolino da denti toothbrush

lo specchio mirror

la specie (f.) type, kind

spedire to send

la spesa (f.) expense, shopping

spesso often

lo spettacolo show

la spiaggia (f.) beach

sporco dirty

lo sportello counter, window

sposare to marry

sposato/a married

lo spumante (m.) sparkling wine

lo spuntino snack

lo stadio stadium

la stagione (f.) season

stamattina this morning

stanco tired

stanotte tonight

la stanza (f.) room

stare (stato) to be, to remain, to stay

stasera this evening

gli Stati Uniti (m. pl.) United States

la stazione (f.) station

stesso same

lo stivale (m.) boot

la stoffa (f.) fabric, cloth

la strada (f.) street

lo straniero foreigner, foreign

stretto tight

su, sul, sulla on top of, on, up

subito soon, immediately

succedere (successo) to happen

il succo juice

sud south

la suocera mother-in-law

il suocero father-in-law

il supermercato supermarket

la sveglia (f.) alarm clock

la svendita (f.) sale

la tabaccheria (f.) tobacco shop

la tabella (f.) schedule, timetable

la taglia (f.) size

tale such, like, similar

tanto so much, so many, a lot

tardi late

la tariffa (f.) fare, charge

la tassa (f.) tax

il tassì (m.) taxi

la tavola (f.) dinner table

il tavolo table (restaurant)

la tazza (f.) cup

te you (familiar)

il tè (m.) tea

il teatro theater

telefonare to telephone

la telefonata (f.) phone call

il tempo weather, time

tenere to hold, to keep

tenero tender, soft, sweet

la terra (f.) earth, dirt

il terrazzo terrace

la tessera (f.) card (membership/pass), ticket

la testa (f.) head

il tetto roof

il tipo type, kind

tirare to pull

toccare to touch

la toilette (f.) toilet

il topo mouse

tornare to return

la torta (f.) cake

il torto wrong, fault

il tovagliolo napkin

tra between

tradurre (tradotto) to translate

la traduzione (f.) translation

il traffico traffic

il traghetto ferry

il tramonto sunset

il treno train

triste sad

trovare to find

tu you (familiar)

il tuono thunder

il turismo tourism

il/la turista (m./f.) tourist

tutt'e due both

tuttavia however, yet

tutti everyone

tutto everything, all

ubriacarsi to get drunk

l'uccello bird

l'ufficio cambio money exchange office

l'ufficio informazioni information office

l'ufficio oggetti smarriti lost and found (office)

l'ufficio postale post office

ultimo last

l'umidità (f.) humidity

un a, an, one

una a, an, one

uno one, a, an

l'uomo man

l'uovo egg

usare to use

uscire to exit

l'uscita (f.) exit

l'uva (f.) grapes

la vacanza (f.) vacation

il vaglia postale (m.) money order

il vagone (m.) rail car

la valigia (f.) bag, valise, suitcase

la valuta (f.) currency, money

la vasca (f.) tub

vecchio old

vedere (visto) to see

vegano vegan

vegetariano vegetarian

il veicolo vehicle

il veleno poison

vendere to sell

la vendità (f.) sale

venire to come

veramente really

verde green

la verdura (f.)   vegetables

la verità (f.)   truth

verso   toward, near, about

il vescovo   bishop

vestire   to dress

il vestito   dress, suit

la vetrina (f.)   shop window

il vetro   glass

la vettura (f.)   carriage, railroad car

la via (f.)   street, way

via   away

viaggiare   to travel

il viaggio   trip

il viale (m.)   boulevard, avenue

vicino   near

il vicolo   alley, lane

vietato   prohibited

vietato di sosta   no parking

vietato l'ingresso   no entrance

il vigile   inspector, traffic officer

il vigile del fuoco   firefighter

vincere (vinto)   to win

il vino   wine

la vista (f.)   view

la vita (f.)   life

il vitello   veal

il vocabolario   vocabulary

la voce (f.)   voice

la voglia (f.)   wish, desire

voi   you (plural)

volare   to fly

volentieri!   gladly!

volere   to want

il volo   flight

vuoto   empty

lo yoga (m.)   yoga

lo yogurt (m.)   yogurt

lo zaino   backpack

la zanzara (f.)   mosquito

la zia (f.)   aunt

lo zio   uncle

lo zucchero   sugar

la zuppa (f.)   soup

Index

A

accent marks, 3–4
  acute accent, 4
  apostrophes, 4
  grave accent, 3
acute accent, 4
adjectives, 13
airport, 71–73
  expressing yourself, 73
  vocabulary, 71–72
alphabet, 6–7
animals, 34–36
apostrophes, 4
appearance, 40
articles, 11–13
  definite, 11–12
  indefinite, 11
asking for directions, 73–74
asking for directions (by foot), 74–76

B

basics, 19–44
  animals, 34–36
  climate, 25–26
  colors, 27
  customs and manners, 36–44
    appearance, 40
    business, 41
    consumption habits, 41
    conversation, 42
    dialects, 44
    Florence, 44
    formal versus not, 39
    gifts, 40
    gum, 42
    inclusion, 40
    Italian history, 38–39
    kisses, 40
    "name day," 41–42
    pizza, 44
    population, 38
    Rome, 38
    San Marino, 43

Slow Food
movement, 43
social media, 42
vacation month, 41
Venice, 43
volcanoes, 44
World Heritage
Sites, 42
dates, 25
days of the week, 23
holidays, 25
months, 24
numbers, 28–31
politeness, 20–21
questions, 33–34
seasons, 24
temperature
conversion, 28
time, 32–33
weather, 26–27
bathroom, 102
bedroom, 106–107
beverages, 137–138
body, 184–185
business, 41
business and
communications,
199–217
computer and
technology, 212–214
emergencies, 215–216
money, 210–212
packing list, 206–207
post office, 207–209

telephone, 200–206
speaking with an
operator, 204–206
using a phone,
203–204
texting abbreviations,
215–216
bus travel, 77–78

C

cars. *See also* driving
breakdowns, 95–96
rental, 84–85
servicing of, 91–92
summoning help,
96–97
vocabulary and
expressions, 85–89
climate, 25–26
cognates, 17–18
definition, 17
false cognates, 18
colors, 27
commonly used
expressions, 237–240
communications.
See business and
communications
computers, technology
and, 212–214
consonants, 8–9
consumption habits, 41

conversation, 42

cosmetics store, 161–165

customs and manners, 36–44
  appearance, 40
  business, 41
  consumption habits, 41
  conversation, 42
  dialects, 44
  Florence, 44
  formal versus not, 39
  gifts, 40
  gum, 42
  inclusion, 40
  Italian history, 38–39
  kisses, 40
  "name day," 41–42
  pizza, 44
  population, 38
  Rome, 38
  San Marino, 43
  Slow Food movement, 43
  social media, 42
  vacation month, 41
  Venice, 43
  volcanoes, 44
  World Heritage Sites, 42

D

dairy products, 131–132

dates, 25

days of the week, 23

definite article, 11–12

dentist, 194–196

dialects, 2, 44

dining. *See* food and eating

dining out. *See* restaurants

diseases, 189–190

dissing, 179–180

drinking and driving, 99

driving, 83–100
  avoiding trouble, 99–101
    drinking and driving, 99
    sign interpretation, 99–100
    surveillance cameras, 98
    texting while driving, 99
  breakdowns and other issues, 95–96
  car rental, 84–85
  car talk, 85–89
  links and numbers, 97
  motorcycles and Vespas, 94–95
  parking, 90–91
  on the road, 89–90

roadways, 84
servicing your car,
91–92
signage, 92–94
summoning help,
96–97
tools, 100
travel verbiage, 98
travel verbs and
expressions, 81
dry-cleaning, 156–157

E

electronics store,
165–169
emergencies, 190–191,
215–216
emphasis, 5–6
English–Italian
dictionary, 241–262
essentials, 21–44
animals, 34–36
climate, 25–26
colors, 27
customs and manners,
36–44
appearance, 40
business, 41
consumption
habits, 41
conversation, 42
dialects, 44
Florence, 44

formal versus not,
39
gifts, 40
gum, 42
inclusion, 40
Italian history,
38–39
kisses, 40
"name day," 41–42
pizza, 44
population, 38
Rome, 38
San Marino, 43
social media, 42
vacation month, 41
Venice, 43
volcanoes, 44
World Heritage
Sites, 42
dates, 25
days of the week, 23
holidays, 25
months, 24
numbers, 28–31
politeness, 20–21
questions, 33–34
seasons, 24
temperature
conversion, 28
time, 32–33
weather, 26–27
everyday expressions,
237–240
exchanges (common),
46–47

F

fabric store, 158–159

family, 48–51
   feminine, 49–50
   masculine, 50–51

family planning, 178–179

fashion store, 155–156

feminine nouns, 11

fish, 132–133

florist, 181

food and eating, 125–150
   beverages, 137–138
   food stores, 126–132
      dairy products, 131–132
      fish, 132–133
      fruits and vegetables, 127–129
      herbs and spices, 129–130
      meat, 131–132
      nuts, 130
      sweets, 133
   kitchen utensils and appliances, 134–137
   packaging and carrying, 139–140
   restaurants, 140–150
      complaints, 145–146
      cooking preferences, 144–145
      first course, 146–147
      menu, 146–149
      ordering a meal, 143
      second course, 147–148
      side dishes, 148–149
      special needs, 144
      types, 140–142
      wine, 138

friends and family, 45–68
   family, 48–51
      feminine, 49–50
      masculine, 50–51
   greetings and common exchanges, 46–47
   honorifics and titles, 58–60
   informal expressions, 47–48
   military terms, 60–61
   occupations and professions, 51–57
   titles (general), 59–60
   verbs, 63–70

friendship and romance, 171–181

dissing, 179–180
excuses and apologies, 177
family planning, 178–179
florist, 181
friendship and dating, 172–173
getting closer, 174–175
LGBT culture, 177–178
sweet talk, 175–176
texting, 180–181
verbs, 173–174
fruits and vegetables, 127–129

G

gender (grammar), 10
gifts, 40
grammar, 9–16. *See also* essentials
adjectives, 13
definite article, 11–12
feminine nouns, 11
gender, 10
indefinite articles, 11
masculine nouns, 11
noun markers, 10
nouns, 10–12
plurals, 10–11
possession, 14–15
prepositions, 13–14

regular verbs, conjugation of, 17
subject pronouns, 15
verb families, 16
verbs, 16
you, 15
grave accent, 3
greetings and common exchanges, 46–47

H

hand gestures, 196–198
hardware store, 118–120
headaches and other pains, 186–189
health, 183–198
body, 184–185
dentist, 194–196
diseases, 189–190
hand gestures, 196–198
headaches and other pains, 186–189
medical emergencies, 190–191
pharmacy, 191–195
questions, 186–187
herbs and spices, 129–130
holidays, 25
home, 101–107
bathroom, 102

bedroom, 106–107
kitchen, 105–106
living room, 104–105
verbs, 103, 116–117,
120–123
honorifics and titles,
58–60
hotel, 110–118
around hotel,
110–112
preferences, 113–114
problems and
solutions, 114–115
reservations, 110
services and
amenities, 112–114

I–J

inclusion, 40
indefinite articles, 11
informal expressions,
47–48
irregular past
participles, 234–236
irregular verbs,
224–233
Italian–English
dictionary, 263–286
Italian history, 38–39
Italian regions, 70

jewelry store, 160–161

K–L

kisses, 40
kitchen, 105–106
kitchen utensils and
appliances, 134–137

LGBT culture, 178
living room, 104–105
love. *See* friendship and
romance

M

manners. *See* customs
and manners
masculine nouns, 11
meat, 131–132
medical emergencies,
190–191
military terms, 60–61
modes of
transportation, 76–79
bus, 77–78
cardinal directions, 78
taxi, 79
train, 77–78
money, 152, 210–212
months, 24
motorcycles and
Vespas, 94–95

N–O

"name day," 41–42
nouns, 10–12
  feminine, 12
  markers, 10
  masculine, 11
numbers, 28–31
nuts, 130

occupations and
 professions, 51–57
optician, 196

P–Q

pain, types of, 186–189
pharmacy, 191–195
pizza, 44
plurals, 10–11
politeness, 20–21
population, 38
possession, 14–15
post office, 207–209
prepositions, 13–14
professions,
 occupations and, 51–57
pronunciation, 1–18
  accent marks, 3–4
    acute accent, 4
    apostrophes, 4
    grave accent, 3

alphabet, 6–7
cognates, 17–18
  definition, 17
  false cognates, 18
consonants, 8–9
dialects, 2
emphasis, 5–6
enunciation, 2–3
grammar, 9–16
  adjectives, 13
  definite article,
   11–12
  feminine nouns, 11
  gender, 10
  indefinite articles,
   11
  masculine nouns,
   11
  noun markers, 10
  nouns, 10–12
  plurals, 10–11
  possession, 14–15
  prepositions, 13–14
  regular verbs,
   conjugation of, 17
  subject pronouns,
   15
  verb families, 16
  verbs, 16
  you, 15
vowels, 8

questions
 basic, 33–34

health, 186–187
transportation, 73–76

R

reflexive verbs, 233–234
regular verbs, 17–18,
220–223
restaurants, 140–150
complaints, 145–146
cooking preferences,
144–145
menu, 146–149
first course,
146–147
second course,
147–148
side dishes,
148–149
ordering a meal, 143
rules, 149–150
special needs, 144
types, 140–142
road signs,
interpretation of,
99–100
romance. *See* friendship
and romance
Rome, 38

S

"Saint's day," 41–42
San Marino, 43

seasons, 24
shoe store, 153
shopping, 151–170
exchanging money,
152
tips, 153
types of stores,
152–153
cosmetics, 161–165
electronics,
165–169
fabrics, 158–159
fashion, 155–156
jewelry, 159–161
shoes, 154
stationery, 169–170
tailoring and dry-
cleaning, 156–157
wardrobe
accessories,
157–158
Slow Food movement,
43
social media, 42
sports, 216–217
stationery store,
169–170
stores
cosmetics, 161–165
electronics, 165–169
fabric, 158–159
fashion, 155–156
florist, 181
food, 125–150

dairy products, 131–132

fish, 132–133

flowers, 181

fruits and vegetables, 127–129

herbs and spices, 129–130

meat, 131–132

nuts, 130

sweets, 133

hardware, 118–120

jewelry, 159–161

shoes, 154

stationery, 169–170

tailoring and dry-cleaning, 156–157

wardrobe accessories, 157–158

subject pronouns, 15

sweets, 133

T–U

tailoring shop, 156–157

taxi, 79

technology, computers and, 212–214

telephone, 200–206

speaking with an operator, 204–206

using a phone, 203–204

temperature conversion, 28

texting

abbreviations, 215–216

while driving, 99

your sweetheart, 180–181

time, 32–33

titles

general, 59–60

honorifics and, 58–60

train travel, 77–78

transportation, 69–81

airport, 71–73

expressing yourself, 73

vocabulary, 71–72

asking for directions, 73–74

asking for directions (by foot), 74–76

making the trip, 79–80

modes, 76–79

bus, 77–78

taxi, 79

train, 77–78

verbs and expressions, 81

travel. *See* transportation

V

Venice, 43
verbs, 63–70, 219–236
  essential, 63–70
  families, 16
  irregular past
    participles, 234–236
  irregular verbs,
    224–233
  reflexive verbs,
    233–234
  regular, conjugation
    of, 17
  regular verbs,
    220–223
Vespas, motorcycles
  and, 94–95
visiting Italy, 101–124
  chores and cleaning
    terms, 115–116
  cleaning terms
    (additional), 119–120
  hardware store,
    118–120
  at home, 101–107
    bathroom, 102
    bedroom, 106–107
    kitchen, 105–106
    living room,
      104–105
    verbs, 103,
      116–117, 120–123
  locations, 107–109
  around hotel,
    108–109
  problems and
    solutions,
    114–115
  reservations, 110
  services and
    amenities,
    112–114
  repairs, 122–123
  verbs, 103, 116–117,
    120–123
vowels, 8

W–X–Y–Z

wardrobe accessories
  store, 157–158
weather, 26–27
wine, 138
World Heritage Sites,
  42

you, 15